Path

by

Sergey Baranov

The author has received permission from individuals and organizations to use the material in this book where the source took the form of conversations and/or pictures. He has also included data that is available to public access. All opinions expressed by the author are his own. Readers may contact the author at his website:

www.shamansworld.org

ISBN-10: 1480040711
ISBN-13: 978-1480040717

Contents

Dedication

My dear daughter, I am dedicating my book to you, so that it will serve you as a guide throughout your life, especially if I happen not to be around to guide you myself. You are not quite two years old right now, beautiful and innocent, walking around the house, smiling at me as I am writing these words. My life wasn't an easy one, but I have no regrets about anything that ever happened to me, be it good or bad, since all of that has brought me to this very moment when I and your mother can watch you enjoying the very first steps in your life, shining with purity and love.

My conscious life began in pain—in a shock that occurred when I was only months older than you are now. That event, which is in this book, was the first moment of memory in my life—many more would follow as years went by. Going through so much and learning lessons the hard way, I now realize that life doesn't have to be difficult to teach us wisdom. Your life was begun from love, and this is what we want you to know and have as the foundation for your life.

I thought about writing a book for a long time, but never knew what to write about. It was only when I moved to Peru in 2009, after years of traveling back and forth, that the desire to write has grown into a mission, and fairly often, felt more like an obsession. We were building our house when your mom was pregnant with you. During that time the need to write became a sort of urgency, which sometime felt even like a threat. I remember walking one day in the mountains, praying to please not break my legs in order to force me into writing. I didn't dare ride my motorcycle until I began writing the book. I promised that I would get to it as soon as I was able. I knew that we needed to finish our house first to give you a warm place waiting for your arrival.

So we built it and moved in on January 2011. All that time I was wondering how to start my book and what to write about, until I realized that if I did write anything, it should be about my life and all that my path has led me through. I felt that truth would be of value to you when you grow up, and to others, who have been on the path and shared similar struggles. These people might see in my story their own challenges, questions, and answers. I thought this book could serve as a mirror reflecting people's lives—each seeing himself or herself at different points. I have always respected and appreciated sincerity and honesty in people—a rare quality nowadays. I continue to feel deep gratitude toward someone who is pouring out their heart without reservation, sharing their feelings and thoughts with others. I believe this is how I learned… .from heart to heart. So I decided to write about my life starting from my early memories, leaving nothing out that seemed to me important. But there is a gap between deciding to do something and actually doing it, and that gets stretched over time.

About three months after we moved to our house, I woke up one night and just started writing. It fell like pressure was finally released.

Thanks to your mother and my dear wife, who has supported me and helped me greatly by taking care of you so I can write as much as I need, days and nights, until it is finished.

I now feel like writing this book was more than just a telling of the facts of my life, but rather a process of self-growth. It has been a little over a year since I started working, but it feels like I have relived through my entire life as I write.

Life can be beautiful if lived right and difficult if not. My wish is to tell you my story just as it is, so you can learn from it and make a reference to it on your own journey. In my story you will learn what my life was about and what it has taught me to believe in, to value, and to cherish.

It is my intention to convey as clearly as I can the virtue of goodness and the vice of evil—as it was revealed to me through my experiences.

I hope that my book will help you to learn to discern between false and real, and between good and evil, so you won't be fooled by anyone as you grow, regardless of their appearance. I hope it will help you to avoid unnecessary suffering and scars, which can take sometimes years to heal.

Finally, this book is about my personal search for the truth and meaning of life—which now I find in you, my sweet little girl.

Acknowledgment

I would like to express my deep gratitude for my dear Peruvian wife Mercedes, who supported me throughout the course of writing my book, taking care of our new born daughter, the house and me, demonstrating the virtues of patience, trust and love.

I would like to thank my parents who believed in my work and waited patiently to see my book in their hands, something that became impossible for my mother who died during the writing.

I would like to give tribute to David Wilkinson who inspired me to translate my book from Russian to English and did the initial editing. My main editor, Rebecca Salome who took the time to turn my book from raw meat into a serving dish. Stephen Parsons who was generous enough to contribute his efforts and time to the book design. Richy, my faithful dog with whom I spent cut time from our daily walks.

And at last but not least, I want to thank the ancient spirit of the sacred cactus Huachuma who inspired me for writing and giving me the clarity I needed to complete this project.

Preface

Dear reader,

Why do you need to read my book? Because it tells it like it is. Fraud, corruption, lies, insanity and evil of a biblical proportion have invaded our world with a force that can only be confronted with the light of the truth, which disperses the darkness like morning sun lights the sky.

My book is not intended to flatter you but rather to shatter you and your world view—which may be sealed with fear imposed on you by all who want your mind numb and asleep. I want to help you to open up the valve that blocks the endless flow of consciousness—which like living water makes all life alive.

I want to inspire you to find your own evil and fight it with all your force for the good of all. We are all in this together: we share one planet, we breathe one air, and we drink one water. We all want peace, prosperity and happiness, and we all need one another to maintain and protect our common values if we want our children to have a future. This fight for humanity is before us now, and each of us can play a part in it.

No single book can address all the evil on Earth, but one good book can be another stepping stone from which you will see farther. My story is not about me as much as it's about possibilities we have as human beings who start from nowhere and find their hearts on the quest for the truth, tirelessly seeking what's real in this world. It is about an awakening of human spirit, which as it grows, cannot be fed on lies.

My path has led me through pain and disappointments that could have broken me many times if I had let it. Instead, I used these challenges as opportunities for overcoming them and coming out stronger.

Among other things, I will address fake spiritual gurus of nowadays who claim false authority over the sincere seekers of truth—who are often ready to submit to the will of psychopaths and perverts who claim to be the saints. I will speak from six years of my own cult experience where I witnessed firsthand the murder of the human spirit and the conscience all in the name of spiritual evolution and enlightenment. I later saw how similar the power structure was in different organizations worldwide—which by definition are also classifiable as cults.

It is of course oxymoronic to think that one must turn to darkness to be enlightened at the end; and it shows how deeply this whole subject of spiritual awakening has been misunderstood. It is reality today that millions of people are still being subjected to and are trapped in various cults the numbers of which are epidemic. There are many different types of cults—religious, scientific, political, militant, and so on. But regardless how diversified they seem, they all need brainwashed minds to serve their agenda—which is not in your best interest as a free human being. The doctrines may sound different, but in essence, they all the same, and this is something I want you to start recognizing for yourself.

The bottom line is that no one can claim authority over your life and your freedom. Claim your succession and live as a sovereign, mature, and responsible human being. Think, speak, and act according to your own conscience and disregard everything and everyone who wants you be or do otherwise. Your liberty and freedom are your birthrights, and striving to live your life unchained is the Natural Law, which a freeborn individual shall follow.

I am here to free your mind by example, not by preaching.

Introduction

This is a book about my personal search for truth and the meaning of life. My path took me through four continents, four cultures, and four languages, went far beyond the walls of religious institutions and far above the boundaries of my "ego." It was a search for answers to intimate questions, in distant places of the world, interacting with people whose ways of life allow them to keep their true connection with Nature—a key to understanding oneself and the world in which one lives. My path began with fear of Death and a thirst for knowledge, and through contemplations and experience I was able to gain an understanding which helped me drop the heavy burden of fear and illusions and begin to live my life with peace in my heart and clarity in my mind. To help you to understand and feel the significance of what occurred in Peru and Mexico, which helped me to heal my past, to understand the present, and to determine my future, I will follow the chain of events in the order in which they occurred.

All names and events described in this book are real.

This is how it all began…

Childhood

I was born on July 3rd of 1976 in Khmelnitsky, Ukraine which at that time was part of the USSR. This is where my first, foggy memories of early childhood have frozen in my mind like snow patterns freezing on the window glass of a winter's morning.

One night, when I was about two and a half, I woke up in my crib feeling pain on my right hand. A metal heating pipe ran between my crib and the wall, which was a common heating system back in those days. The pipe was filled with hot water, and in my sleep, I laid my hand on it and had been badly burnt. I remember crying.

In my next memory, I am standing in the zoo crying. My parents later told me we had gone to Kiev to visit my grandfather. When we passed the lion's cage, my loud childish delight woke the lion up and he roared. I was scared to tears.

I remember that when I was four, I had the mumps, and I watched the 1980 Olympic runners through the window.

Within the next year, two memorable events occurred. First a hurricane, which tore a piece of tin from the theater across the street and sent it flying into our balcony. Then lightning, striking the fluorescent sign that said "Peace to the World," which was installed on our roof and

1

sealed with tar, caused a fire. I remember being held in my father's arms in the middle of the loud crowd that watched our building burning.

I was just over 5 years old when I organized an escape from kindergarten, leading our little group outside. I can only remember standing with the other kids watching the cars. I don't remember being berated by my parents, but they told me later that they talked to me about it at home. They also told me they received their first reprimand from the school regarding my action of inciting others to go out without permission.

Once, after playing football, and getting thirsty, I came home to drink some water. I drank from a bottle on the kitchen table and quickly found out that instead of mineral water it was vinegar. I almost choked and for a while I could barely breathe.

I remember going to a rail yard and waiting for the passing trains. I liked the smell there. While waiting for the trains, we melted lead, which we got out of old car batteries. We melted the lead in metal containers on the fire, and then poured it into different forms and shapes in the sand.

My childhood from age seven has more clear memories. By then we had moved to new place and I had gone to another school. I started to get involved with different kinds of sports: fencing, then swimming and then football. I was 9 when our fencing group went to Krym, to enjoy the Black Sea. I fell asleep on the beach and burnt my shoulders like carbon. I still have sun damage spots to remind me of that time after all these years.

During that time in Krym, I had my first experience with hypnosis, which for some reason did not work on me. I remember sitting in the big room among other people and being so disappointed because I was not influenced by the hypnotist's words. I simply sat there with my hands free while the others were amazed by their hands glued to each other until the hypnotist's command to release them. I remember hearing the applause and thinking something was wrong with me. Coming out of that event same night, I was met by 3 guys, who were older than me. They asked me if I was a Jew—to which I replied yes—after which one of them have sent his fist right into my face. I had the desire to fight with them but didn't know how. On the way back to where I was staying overnight, with a bloody nose, I thought how different things would have been if I had been able to hypnotize them and hold them there while I walked away.

But then, I gave up those sports when martial arts classes came to town. I went to every training session; I never missed in any weather, even if I was sick. Besides martial arts, I liked to go to the river, ride my bicycle, gather herbarium from maple leaves, play with the kittens and puppies, build fires, shoot from self-made bows while playing Indians, climb trees, and explore new construction sites. Once I found a helmet with a hole in it, probably from the Second World War.

I liked to go to the movies. With my parents, I saw "Spartacus." I liked his character back then. And I was fascinated by the movies "One Million Years B.C.", "The Leaders of Atlantis" and "The Legend of the Dinosaur." Some I went to see twice.

For a while I had an interest in photography. I liked to watch how images would appear on the clean white paper in the special water in the darkroom. I liked the red lighting in the room and the specific smell of the water in which pictures were developing. Once, someone gave me a film with heavy metal rock bands, which we developed in the shop and then sold at break time during the school day. This early childhood business didn't last very long because the students from higher grades took it over from me—even though I put up a fight. Later, I started to listen to the music by some of the bands whose pictures I had developed earlier. I felt some freedom with this.

The first significant book in my life was an encyclopedia of the animal world. I was 6 years old and I liked to look at the pictures of different animals. With the same fascination, I studied the globe, locating where I lived on it. When I learned to read, I started reading fables. My favorite was about the Old Man Hotabytch, a genie who lived a thousand years in a bottle before getting released by a student who found the bottle in the river. This magical world was totally absent in observable reality, viewed thru my window. What I saw was a bored crowd waiting for the next bus.

When I turned 9, I began going to a city library. At about 10 years old, I started to read sci-fi books. In our home, my father had books by a Russian sci-fi writer Alexander Belyaev, which he liked to read as well.

My favorite books by him were *Eternal Bread, Lord of the World, The Air Dealer, An Amphibian Man,* and *Ariel.* I was thinking about those books while in the classroom, watching the falling snowflakes through the window. My thoughts were usually interrupted by the ringing of the bell for break. In between the sci-fi books, I read adventure tales such as *Treasure Island* and *Robinson Crusoe,* among others. The following year, I started to read H.G. Wells and was fascinated by *The War of the Worlds, Time Machine, The Invisible Man,* and *The Island of Dr. Moro.* I was reading them at night, falling asleep with the books in my hands.

Reading H.G. Wells at nights was making it difficult to wake up the next morning and go to school, where I was getting bored with Russian history and the fable of Krylov, whose wisdom I was to rediscover much later at 25. Fantastic night readings, flights in the dream world, and a warm bed were much more pleasant than early winter wake ups. But, every morning I overcame my feelings and walked down the dark street and under street lights on the clean, white and crunchy snow. I could still hear the whispering voices from another world, which became silent at the school door.

I didn't like to study; I was bored. I got low grades with long minuses, traces of which could be found on the teacher's desk and probably would go to eternity if the teacher would have had time for it. This upset my parents who had spent all their free time helping me with my homework. I didn't want to upset them and would often change my school diaries, which all students were obligated to carry. The red ink of angry teachers was displayed on every page. I couldn't show this to my parents, so I burned them and bought new ones. Once, I burnt my eyebrows, eyelashes, and hair. But this technique was not enough to prevent consequences. They were called in to talk to my teachers who were all saying the same thing. They all said that I could study if I wanted to and that I was physically present in the classroom but mentally absent. But there were things I liked at school, things that made me feel free. I liked sports, and art, especially drawing in new notebooks.

Once at my mom's job, I drew caricatures of drunken people, which took first place among many other competitors. According to my mom, the people liked the fact that they were simple and easily identifiable with real life images. I remember how easy it was to draw them. Later, in school art classes, I learned a wood burning technique. I spent long days drawing on the wood, and then burning the image with a tool. One of my works was taken to a city wide exhibition. I never knew the fate of it. The most important work for me was drawing the image of a German Shepherd. I worked on it patiently—burning, varnishing and lacquering it. But, shortly afterward, this piece of work disappeared. Twenty years later, I recognized that same image in my dog—to whom I'll dedicate a later chapter.

I loved all the seasons; winter for the coziness and warmth in the house, spring for the sparkles in the melting icicles telling of a coming summer, summer for happiness and freedom and fall - for the sadness. In summer camps I only liked big fires and wandering in the forest. The rest was boring. At the first parent's day I was asking them to take me home, threatening them with escape if they would leave me at the camp. I hated the obligatory trips to the farms to harvest potatoes, but I liked to plant trees.

I remember attending many funerals, which were often held in our yard. We were living in a very long, five-story building which housed a lot of old-age neighbors. I would stand by the coffins with the deceased, watching the faces of the deceased, thinking about where life goes after death. I remember being afraid to go to sleep at night, because falling to sleep reminded me of falling into an abyss and dying. It could have been this that was a reason for my restlessness and fear, which almost led to an illness if my parents hadn't taken me to an old healer in a remote village. From her, my parents learned about my interest in death. While mumbling, she rolled an egg over my body, then broke it into a bowl of water, and after seeing something there, told my parents that I often visited funerals and to forbid me from doing so. My constant attendance had made me think about my own death. Back then I was getting scared by thoughts that one day I would die and never be alive again. Then I began to wonder about the possibility of transcending death.

Suddenly we were moving to Israel; the news was given to me shortly before we were to leave. I was 12 years old then and in the fifth grade. I remember how sad it was to go, regardless of what new and interesting changes this move would bring. I understood that my bright childhood was staying behind, leaving a part of me forever in the past. I made a promise to never forget it, or to forget myself.

Path

Immigration to Israel

The first serious stress in my life was our immigration to Israel in 1989 where life was difficult. We were told that we were going home, but in fact, we had come to a foreign land. Oppressive feelings of inferiority derived from being a Jew in Russia had followed us to Israel, where the same old disdain for us appeared in another form. We now had become "The Russians."

"Russians, go back to Russia!" was screamed at us by the locals. But going back to Russia was not possible since our Soviet passports were taken before leaving. We were told that the way we chose was a one-way.

Difficulty came in many forms: animosity of the locals toward immigrants, our lack of knowledge of the language, and the religious customs which made us look inferior and was insulting to our self-dignity. And with all this there was an absence of money and no possibility of earnings. No one would be hired without the ability to speak the language.

It was hard to go to school. I was the only Russian in the class. Other students were laughing at me, twisting my name, bullying. I had to defend myself often by fighting during the breaks. What kind of studying can be done in this condition? Once, at the end of the year, I came to pick up a paper stating that I had finished a grade, but the security guard didn't want to let me into the graduation party. He said that he had never seen me there before.

Very soon we started to feel the political instability in the country. We were living in a constant state of war with just some breaks in between, which people confused with peace. We became used to terrorist attacks and active waves of war, which were like the changing of seasons. We tried to build our lives in this madness. I didn't see my future there; I believed inside that my future waited in another place.

We were living in the north part of the country, on the hilly terrain. I liked to spend my time wandering on the hills, looking for snakes and scorpions resting under the rocks. I was about 14 when I brought a few black scorpions home and kept them in a container that had once held chocolate butter. I fed them grasshoppers I gathered for them daily. My father didn't like my collection of poisonous friends, so I set them free.

I liked to sit and look far into the horizon, thinking about my life, but of course, I had to go to school. My parents were doing their best to make our lives easier and better, but were limited by not speaking the language and health concerns. My father had already suffered with diabetes in Russia, and it grew worse under the stress of immigration.

To survive somehow, I had to work where I could—delivering pizza, working as a security guard, driving trucks that had no mirrors or power steering, and sometimes even the brakes did not work. Once coming back from Jerusalem, between Tel Aviv and Haifa, on my left I could see the Mediterranean Sea, and on my right, sand and the rocks. My truck had a mechanical problem, and I had to stop and pull off the road. It was in the evening, and when I called my boss to report the problem, he said it was already late and he would send someone my way tomorrow. He told me I would have to sleep the night in the truck. I told him if he did not send someone now, I would abandon the truck on the road and catch a ride with a passing car to go home. Well, he sent people right away, but fired me the next morning.

The fines for going over the speed limit, for parking in forbidden areas for unloading purposes, and for mechanical defects of the trucks were choking drivers, taking almost all their earnings. The owners didn't want to pay them.

At one time I was working in factories where I saw how people had been turned into slaves just to feed their families. But my compassion for them faded away with each new denouncement they made to the management about my dissatisfaction with our working conditions and animal-like treatment of us. There were a lot of good people as well, but our new friendships usually ended with my layoffs.

In between, I was dedicating my time to the martial arts, reading eastern philosophy, and dreaming about the Shaolin monastery. In these monks, masters of kung-fu, I saw more than just mobility and physical endurance. I saw in them another side, more spiritual, based on certain principles, which I wanted to understand.

When I was about 17, a friend of mine gave me a little book with the poetry of the great Persian poet, Omar Khayyam. In his poetry I felt a deep understanding of the mystery of human life. Reflecting upon his writings was like breathing fresh air in the middle of the vacuum of daily life.

The strong sensation of the miraculous, which had been present in me since childhood, was somewhere nearby, kept alive inside and now continuing to grow and strengthen, fed by the Eastern philosophy, poetry and tales. I was searching for knowledge in books, not yet realizing that true knowledge is generated from the inside, and only echoed in written words.

Spending time in libraries, I came across great writers of antiquity—among them was Geoffrey Chaucer, who wrote among the other things *Canterbury Tales*. He wrote it 700 years ago and yet, in these tales, one could easy recognize the present time. Since then, not much has changed in people except perhaps the clothing.

I was feeling sharply that something was wrong with our world and the way it was going wasn't hopeful at all. Degradation in many ways was obvious to me. But expecting changes on the planetary scale was naive. I understood that the only hope was for me to grow up. But "how" was the question. I came to know that even the greatest books on Earth could not lead one to himself. At best, they could direct and inspire just like Sufi music or a magical duduk of G. Gasparyan, in whose music one could hear a longing for something distant and yet familiar to the very soul.

On the Fourth Way

The first book of Carlos Castaneda, which was given to me by a friend when I was 19 years old, felt to me like a new and hopeful breakthrough. From the first pages I recognized the familiar smell of a magical world that had followed me from my childhood. My reading about the mysterious cactus Peyote and Mexican shamans had fanned an inner fire that I had always felt and now was burning. I spent nights looking at the stars, asking for guidance in finding my path. But, searching for don Juan in distant Mexico at that time was about as possible as flying to the moon. It would be five more years before fate would bring me to America, where I was to begin my real search.

I had originally joined an esoteric school, a Fellowship of Friends, which had centers in many countries around of the world. It was a Fourth Way school based on the teaching of G.I. Gourdjieff and P.D. Ouspensky, two Russian philosophers and mystics of the 20th century. I had heard about this school from the same friend who gave me Castaneda's book years before. I was not interested in joining the school until I had read a few works of P. Ouspensky. Especially touching was his little book *The Strange Life of Ivan Osokin*, which literally had fallen into my hands off a bookshelf in a bookstore. Also, in one reading, I finished *In Search of the Miraculous*, feeling in it the sincerity of searching for the path. Now I wanted to see those people and learn more about the "work," as it was called in Fourth Way language. After attending three lectures at one of the teaching centers in Tel Aviv, my friend and I decided to join. We became students of an "enlightened" Teacher, who had achieved a spiritual awakening and, according to G.I Gourdjieff's system, was a "man number 7," the highest possible level a human can achieve. Students considered him to be a god and waited years to meet him.

Time was passing by. The formal meetings were conducted twice a week, and they were led by the "older students." These were students who had been in the school more than 10-15 years. Here were reviewed the ideas of Fourth Way according to G. and O. Besides those formal meetings, we were getting together in the students' homes for further discussions of the work ideas. This was called a "school life."

I was doing my best to attend the most possible meetings with the intention of developing a deeper understanding of the work. After three months of being a student, I moved to Tel Aviv and rented a room in the home of one of the students. All was good until I began to feel a gap between what I myself understood from reading the G. and O. books and the way those ideas were interpreted in the center. At the time, I thought perhaps it could be the long distance between the heart of the school in California, and the center in Tel Aviv. Possibly the teacher's influence was not reaching the center at full volume, which might be the reason for a lack of understanding by students of some ideas. I decided to move to Apollo (a California center and the residence of the Teacher) for a deeper immersion into the "teaching" and "the work." Time was needed to understand what was going on.

My desire to move to California was met with resistance by the older students, who said it would be very hard for me to be there. Also, one of the many rules in the school forbade students to visit Apollo without being a member for minimum of a year. Regardless, as soon as I received my visa, I immediately purchased an airfare ticket and came to the center to say good bye to those students who had earned my respect at the time. To receive a visa to America was significant; for someone who had no job, no money, no property, and no children in Israel, all the things that would guarantee my return, it was nearly impossible. But with a burning desire to follow my heart at the time, I went to the American embassy in Tel Aviv, where I was interviewed by a consulate. I felt that he was in a trance as he asked me a few general questions in just few minutes—after which he gave me a 10-year visa to the states. That was somewhat shocking, but inside I knew I would be given it—because I knew I had to go.

Path

How Personalities Got Erased and Wallets Were Emptied

My arrival at Apollo, in California, was not as welcoming as I had imagined. Instead, I was told I came too early and should have stayed longer in the Tel Aviv center. "But, since you came," they said, "here is your shovel. Our Teacher likes beauty, so you and others like you will be creating it for him." The idea of digging holes in the ground was disappointing, but I remembered reading about the necessity of firm discipline and physical work on the spiritual path. Avoidance of this would show weakness and un-readiness to become a student. I calmed myself down with thoughts that this was a test and my teaching had begun.

Very soon I began to have conflicts with some of the people, and it grew into conflict with the actual administration. I saw here what I had also seen in Israel. But in the school, besides the animal-like treatment of people, I observed a certain kind of emptiness in the students, which they tried to fill with the life of the school—continuous events, meetings, breakfasts, lunches, and dinners—which students had to pay for separately. They also had to pay a monthly membership fee of ten percent of their gross income, or a minimum of $400 a month for those who were "working in life," as they called it, which meant anywhere outside Apollo.

All events were led by the Teacher, and attendance was strongly encouraged. Students were paying $50 for standing room and up to $150 for seating. Those who didn't have the money could work a full day digging holes, moving a heavy pots with palm trees, planting them, or working in the "quarry." This was a place where limestone was cut and prepared for building a non-permitted Greek-style amphitheater. It was still under construction when the Russian Bolshoi Ballet was invited to perform. Tickets to the performance were sold separately and at different prices, depending on the seats. The ballet dancers were the only "life people" (this is how those who were not school members were disdainfully called in the Fellowship of Friends) who could enter the property and have personal contact with the Teacher and even share a table with him after the performance. It was explained to us that this "special relationship" was permitted because of the Teacher's passion for ballet.

Once we were told that the building inspectors from the county were going to pay a visit. All of the workers were assigned to move the heavy pots with growing palms to the amphitheater and place them on every seat. From early morning to late night we moved trees with the intention of disguising the construction. When the inspectors arrived, the management had closed the only road leading to the site and had placed signs that read "road work ahead." After denying access to the inspectors, they took them over the hill to "get a better view of the entire center." From up there, the amphitheater now looked like a grove of trees. Obviously the inspectors found nothing wrong, and went back with an empty file. As they left, we were told to begin returning all the pots to the green house and continue working on the amphitheater. I never saw the actual dollar figures, but I sure do recall the frequent fundraisings and the mention of one million dollars. And I don't know how much the limestone cost, but I do know what we laborers were paid: there were 5-10 people working, each at $400 monthly. So, total salaries paid came to a fraction of the total money raised. Of course, we wondered about that and were told that limestone was very expensive to use to build a space to hold approximately 800 people. Sadly, the truth of what really happened with all that money will never be known.

During the clean-up I shared my thoughts about what happened with a friend, and he said (with some disdain) that cheating "life people" wasn't really a sin, since they all were asleep and their lives were only a dream. He reminded me of the Teacher's words, which he often re-peated, called the Higher Truth. This Higher Truth always implied pref-erence to school, the Teacher, and the Higher Forces—or as he often called them—the Gods. Unfortunately, my friend's take on it wasn't only his personally; this same attitude was shared among the members.

Money was always being raised for something—for a new Poseidon fountain, which cost over $100, 000, a Rembrandt painting that was ru-mored to cost more than one million dollars at auction, and other proj-ects, like a new road, for example, which once built, was quickly destroyed and then rebuilt at the Teacher's will. I remember donating my last money, while I was still in Israel, for that road in Apollo. The sum was raised at that point was over $140,000. When I arrived in Cali-fornia, the road was almost finished. Then one day the Teacher didn't like the angle the road was taking, so he ordered the entire road de-stroyed, and new fundraising was ordered to rebuild. Students were told that this was how the Teacher was teaching us to not identify with things, in other words, to not get attached to things. This explanation was satisfying to some and of course dissatisfying to others—like my-self.

In regards to money issues, it is also important to mention a couple of other highlights. Raffles were held often. The Teacher's ring—which had been bought with students' donations in the first place—might be offered as the Grand Prize, or perhaps his very expensive watch. All students were "encouraged" to purchase tickets. Strangely enough, the only people who ever won anything were members of the Teacher's staff.

Additionally, a student could have the Teacher and his entourage to his house for a meal. The Teacher would come and repeat one of his "teachings" during breakfast, lunch, or dinner. The set-up was that the student paid the Teacher several thousands (depending on which meal it was). This was all filmed and then offered (for a fee) to be seen by other students. It was a way of using students' desire to gain prestige as a way of raising more money for the school. Sad to say some students did indeed take the bait.

To return to the subject of teaching—during all events led by the Teacher, students looked at him like a miracle was unfolding right before their eyes, and yet, when the meetings ended, they walked outside with faces as if they had just come from a funeral. I watched them and thought how distant their somber expressions were from that feeling of ease and joyfulness that one experiences when in the truly higher states of consciousness. They talked so much about it, but never appeared to actually experience it. I thought if knowledge does not liberate the man, if it does not bring a peace into his heart and clarity to his mind, then what is this knowledge good for? Is it possible to strive for spiritual freedom locked in the shackles of a blind belief and fear?

All the Teacher's monologues were recorded on video and were shown later for a fee on the screen for those students who could not afford the live show. The Teacher's attention and presence were considered a blessing, and people were even going into debt for sharing a breakfast, lunch, dinner or attending a meeting with him where he was repeating the same things over and over again. When I asked one of the "older students" why the Teacher repeated himself all the time like a broken record, his answer was: "It is because we are asleep and cannot understand the words of an Awakened one in another way."

It would be good to mention here that the Teacher had his own special "methods" of "awakening" students. In a teaching meeting, he would be talking about something and would suddenly take his shoe off and throw it into the crowd—of course creating a shock—which he would consider a moment of awakening he had created in the students. Or during a formal lunch, where everyone is elegantly dressed, he would put a napkin on his head and sit there with a serious face. This was his idea of creating "moments of presence" in his students. Or maybe he would deliberately spill a glass of water on the tablecloth—for no apparent reason except to shock us.

As I reflect on all of this, I think how ridiculously pathetic both his teaching and methods were—and I am still sad for all those people who were taken in by him.

New students were never told before joining that a membership fee didn't buy you anything except access to the property. For all events including teaching, they would need to pay separately. Also, they were not told that after joining, they would need to reject their past and leave it to oblivion. That included their relationships to their family and friends. "Now you have a new family and new friends," they were told. Life before joining the school was considered like a meaningless and mechanical existence in "sleep leading to perdition." Thus all that had been learned in this state was insignificant and useless. In the words of P. Ouspensky, "No work can be done in sleep." His words, however, were not being quoted in good faith. P. Ouspensky was actually only referring to the need to wake up one's consciousness in order to engage reality. Then one could see what work is required. The school misappropriated his words to imply that this waking up could only happen within the school.

The same concept about who the student was before joining was applied to the student's personality, which was labeled "false." This false personality was supposed to be erased and with it, its moral values, numbing the conscience in the process. Some people were receiving new names directly from the Teacher, others, in imitation, were changing their names on their own. With new names, new thoughts and personalities were being formed. This (sickening to me) concept was supported by one of the stories about a professor who came to see a zen master to talk about zen Buddhism. While the professor was sharing his thoughts and ideas, the zen master was pouring tea into his cup. When the tea started to go over the edge of the cup, the professor asked the master whether he did not see what he was doing. The Master responded that he (the professor) was full like this cup, and unless he could empty it, the Master would not be able to show him real zen.

Like all other parables, the meaning is supposed to be clear and logical. But if you apply this one to our school experience, it means all the knowledge we received before joining the school was invalid, and unless a student "emptied" his cup, throwing out everything, including himself, he would not be able to understand the real Teaching. A methodology like this might possibly have some meaning in the very beginning, to help a new student start to open to new ideas, but keeping it as a permanent framework for thinking (we can't do anything, don't know anything, and always need help), I considered a mistake. I felt this approach was disabling people's ability for critical thinking, denying them the opportunity to compare new ideas with the knowledge and experience of previous years prior to becoming a member. If a man's cup "was already empty" to what could he compare it? The only thing left was to believe the Teaching was the only truth. This zen story could have been useful if presented in good faith, but in our case, it became a weapon against us, gradually turning us into zombies. This was not a true experience of learning.

By now, sadly, it was also becoming obvious to me that the almost-unbelievable friendliness of the older students, which was there in the beginning, was slowly fading away, and with it, my sense that the miraculous was anywhere within reach.

Mutual Antipathy

Just three months after arriving to Apollo, I received an official letter from the president, the number two man in power. It was a request to leave. After reading, I mentally told him to get lost, tore the letter to pieces and threw it into the trash can. ¨I didn't cross the Atlantic Ocean to go back," I thought. My relationship with the administration had become quite tense, and I understood that my days there were now numbered. In my mind I was ready for anything, but the thought of going back to Israel didn't make me happy. Back then I still believed in the Teacher, regardless of his contradictions, fake public smile, and weekly splurges in the most expensive stores in Beverly Hills where he was buying silk clothing, gold rings, and medallions. There were overseas trips made numerous times a year surrounded by his entourage, weekly traveling in his Mercedes to LA, done always from Monday thru Thursday and returning on Fridays, where they visited clothing shops, ate in high-end restaurants, stayed in expensive hotels, and did a lot of other things, which were not in harmony with why I joined this supposedly esoteric school.

With these thoughts, hard physical work had become almost unbearable. When somebody got hurt during hard physical work, instead of receiving medical help, they were told their bodies were just machines and they should think only about their souls.

Thus students were left alone with their pain, and told to continue working. Suffering was encouraged by the Teacher. He used to say that by transforming our suffering we were creating our souls. So the more suffering a person experienced, the better it was for his soul. Those who were going through the loss of a loved one, either through divorce or death, were considered "the most favored by the Gods, who were providing them with the necessary shocks to be transformed into their souls." I felt so strongly that such a wicked and twisted mind set taken as divine wisdom—for which people were paying a lot of money—was totally misleading, orchestrated by a destructive and spiritually bankrupted individual, rather than an "evolved conscious being," as he often called himself.

It looked like there was nothing good here anymore and nothing to relate to with an open heart. But fate had a plan for me, which was just about to unfold.

During one of the meetings, I had seen a woman, who did not often show up, as I learned later, due to her work outside Apollo. We exchanged a few smiles and words. I liked her appearance, her friendliness, and her maturity. I found her phone number and called her with an offer to meet. She agreed, and we met in the rose garden where from morning till night I usually practiced "my zen." It was an easy encounter, and my bad English at the time was not confusing to her. Instead, she liked it. On our first date, I brought my Russian-English dictionary, which she found funny. I was telling her about my life, about how I found the school, about my search for the truth and thirst for knowledge, everything I could find a word for in English. We started to get together more often, and after a while she offered to let move into her house. A few months later, I asked her if she would like to marry me. My question was shocking to her, but she agreed to think about it. We got married, and a new life began. I was studying English, working part time whenever I could—without leaving Apollo. She had been a long-time student before we met, and I sincerely thought, with her help, I could understand the teaching and the teacher better. But as my English was getting better, I was also beginning to understand more and more what was really happening in this organization—which was masquerading skillfully as a Fourth Way School.

At this same time, the accumulation of hard-to-swallow things said by the Teacher was reaching a critical mass. I will mention only a few—to make a point. In 1999, a few months after I had joined the school, I flew to Russia to meet the Teacher for the first time. One day when he was walking around in St. Petersburg, a gardener had fallen down from one of the trees. The Teacher's take on it was that the Gods had done it to create shock in his students, thus providing them with material for "the work." At another time he was told that while walking in the city, few of his students had seen a man get hit by a car. His response was the same. But most shocking for me was when I moved to Apollo. There was a meeting right after 9/11 happened. One student asked him what he thought about 9/11. He answered that it was done by the Gods who worked with our school. Leaving that meeting I was thinking that whoever those Gods were, I didn't have anything in common with them, and neither did I want to. I was absolutely stunned by the notion that something supposedly divine and highly intelligent would become so despicably evil for whatever reason. Then there was a wild fire that surrounded Apollo, which could have hurt many people if they had not been evacuated quickly. Again, he said these were the "loving Gods" providing us with shocks.

This sick mentality went even further with him stating that when students had an accident or committed suicide, it also was the will of the same Gods, who wanted to help their families to transform through their suffering into their Higher Self. That was really hard to swallow.

While I was still living in Israel, in fact, just shortly after joining the cult, there was an older student in our center who had a family, a business, and was quite an intelligent person as I remember. His wife has joined the center too, and after that so did his daughter, a girlfriend of the student from whom I was renting a room. Well, this man, who was in his early 60s, visited Apollo, I think for the first time. Shortly after coming back home, he committed suicide. It was a big shock for everyone, since he was an example of a good student. I don't remember exactly what business he was in but I think it had something to do with books. I don't really know. But I do know that he was a father and a husband and didn't appear to be depressed. Of course, he could have had his reasons for killing himself, but the fact that no one could see any problem, and that he did it so soon after coming back from Apollo, did raise some questions for me. Even I would disregard this incident if it were not for the other incidents of suicide connected in some way to Apollo. I heard about three but there could well be others which were kept silent. This particular suicide felt very negative to me and wrong, and yet it didn't seem to shock or horrify the Teacher or the other students—in fact they appeared to welcome it as a shock from the Gods. For the first time, I felt a little sick at the time, but didn't pay much attention to that feeling—until I moved to Apollo and saw so much more to feel sick about.

Meanwhile, the tension in my marriage had increased as well. The reason for it was my wife's fanatical faith in the Teacher, which I was unintentionally undermining with my growing questions and doubts regarding his authenticity. This was creating a wall between us. The Teacher was considered untouchable, immune from questions regarding his authority and status, and doubts toward him were strongly discouraged. Any conversations about the Teacher which were not in his favor, were considered and called "gossip," and one of the many rules in the school forbade gossiping.

Reading newspapers, watching TV, or searching the internet were also strongly discouraged; thus any negative information in regards to his power abuse was not reaching students, and any criticism from inside were quickly and effectively suppressed. One of the firmest rules in the school was forbidding contacts with former students. The Teacher's actions were always interpreted in the most favorable light for him, followed by such slogans as, "everything that he does is for the good of your evolution." "Us vs. them" was also at the very foundation of their dogma. Those who were not members (6 billion sleeping machines as the Teacher loved to say) were disparagingly called "food for the moon." The idea of the organic life on Earth being a food for the moon had been originally expressed by G. Gurdjieff and was one of those ideas, which could not be verified, thus leaving us with only the option to blindly believe it.

In Fourth Way teaching, there is an idea that by expressing a negative emotion, a man loses energy that otherwise could be used for "work on oneself." In the Fellowship of Friends, this idea was misused (like so many, if not all); any criticism toward the Teacher was considered to be an expression of negative emotion, which was forbidden in the school, and which students tried to avoid at all cost. Most were striving to acquire the status of being a "good student"—someone who was going along with everything, blindly supporting dogma and the order of things that was convenient to the Teacher.

Individuality and conscience (informally) were considered enemies, and everything possible was done to kill these two characteristics in people. In fact, G. Gurdjieff was speaking about exactly opposite concepts regarding the conscience. He said that thanks to an awakened conscience, a man is capable of seeing thru the lies. But in FOF, the personality with which a person came was considered false, and his "new" personality (or school personality) was viewed as his "true" personality. This twisted mentality showed up everywhere you looked. Those who would be considered unfit by any reasonable person, were becoming managers and being appointed to leading positions, making other people's lives more difficult. Those, who in my opinion were going mad, were elevated to a status of "being in essence." I witnessed things like the words of Jesus Christ, "unless you turn from your sins and become like little children, you will never get into the Kingdom of Heaven" being horribly misused. Supposedly "literal interpretation" of these words resulted in pitiful scenes where 50-year-old women wore braided pigtails and ridiculous childlike dresses and went around smiling at everyone they met. When I asked why they did that, I was told that they were "in essence," and that I was in my false personality, which was judging them and expressing negativity. The truth was I had compassion for them. The fact I was watching them being severely damaged by brainwashing was actually causing me pain. It had become clear to me that everything was upside down. FOF had become a "Kingdom of Crooked Mirrors," where one rich man with a band of sold-out servants was dividing and conquering, breaking up families, and ripping people off.

In regards to what can happen when people suppress negative emotions, in my view, the psychological problems, depressions, and suicides in the FOF were due to the constant inner conflict and suppression of the conscience and common sense. This led to mental illnesses and break downs, fear, anxiety and guilt, which were in fact the "true" negative emotions. Individuals began to be afraid of critical thinking, thus, blocking themselves from the truth. And instead of reacting adequately and naturally in all circumstances, we tried always to remain falsely positive. It destroyed our spiritual balance and harmed us even more. In this context, spiritual balance means living according to your conscience.

With regard to developing individuality, I felt that it was simply a matter of forming one's character rather than following all kinds of rules and restrictions which only benefit the cult and not the person.

I could say so much more about the Teacher's teachings—and the result would probably be that he would be diagnosed and quickly sent to a mental institution, but for my reader's sake, I will mention only one example—which I trust will speak for itself.

An unbelievable interpretation by the Teacher was both shocking to some people and fascinating or absurd to others. It was about a petroglyph found in one ancient cave in France, on which an image of a bull was depicted on the wall. The bull had a trail behind him of six pieces of excrement—in which the "enlightened" Teacher saw undeniable proof for his delusional teaching, which in my opinion could be only believed by mental clinic patients. I confess it is nearly impossible to convey to readers the depth of this madness—unfortunately one would have to join the cult to learn anything more about it. But I can say that this utter nonsense could truly be called "bullshit"—both literally and figuratively speaking. Of course, the "suits" had never been to caves for reasons of their own, but nevertheless, they didn't get dissuaded from using other peoples' pictures for their money making schemes. I had expected more from one who claims to be "the brightest light since Jesus Christ in the last 2000 years."

Besides surrogate teaching offered by the Teacher for a lot of money, which had neither logic nor meaning, he also was making predictions. One of his predictions was about the devastating Earthquake supposed to hit California, taking half of the state into the ocean. The remaining land would have a new ocean view that could be seen from Apollo which was about 200 miles away from the ocean before the earthquake. Armed with such a prediction, naive students went to buy new cars, took new loans, went farther in debt and thought there would be no one to pay it back too. But when "the gods were forgiving California," the waves of bankruptcies swept thru the "conscious society."

The second prediction was about nuclear Armageddon, which according to the Teacher's prophecy, was supposed to happen in 2006. He said it would destroy all humanity leaving alive only the students who lived with him in Apollo. His role then would be to rebuild humanity and start a new civilization.

Those who dared to ask questions regarding the Teaching, sincerely trying to understand it, were immediately asked to leave the school. One was my friend from St. Petersburg who, once during the Teacher's visit to Russia on a formal meeting, asked the "conscious being" a question: "Teacher, you often speak of things which are impossible to verify. For example, you speak about the Influence C (in school jargon it meant higher forces—Gods who were directly working with the school). I am not a religious person and I cannot simply continue to believe and believe…for years. These unverifiable ideas which you are giving to us are becoming a denial force which does not allow me to remain in the school and trust you as my Teacher. My question is: what should I do? The Teacher's answer was the following: "wrong question." That particular question was the last of the event; the video of this meeting was taken away by the Teacher's secretary, and my friend was asked to leave the school.

This is how the great Teacher usually answered an inconvenient question. When he got back to Apollo, he announced that a crime had occurred in St. Petersburg and forever forbade anyone asking him questions. After that, at every meeting, he wound up his "street organ" and went on with his nonsense for an hour looking at students who were listening to him attentively. I am reminded of the allegory about a person who purchases something very desirable, such as sweet fruit to eat, and discovers that he has gotten a burning pepper instead, but because he has paid good money for it, continues to eat it anyway—suffering the entire time.

As I mentioned earlier, rejecting one's past, breaking connections with family and friends who were not part of the school, giving all money and time to the school, and putting all hope and trust in the Teacher were required. One couldn't leave the place because there simply wasn't anywhere to go. Our social life was our school life and people were afraid to lose it. Besides, many were too deeply invested in the school, were employed by students, had bought houses and even had built businesses that were now employing students as well. Leaving the school meant losing their jobs and often more. The teacher understood this very well and abused it, forcing people to remain silent about many things. Indoctrinated students were also afraid to lose all chances for spiritual development. According to the Teacher, spiritual development of man was only possible in the school, and if they were to leave, they would lose everything they had achieved so far (if anything). Only a lifetime membership guaranteed an eternal life. A loss of the school and connection with the Teacher were considered to be equal to a spiritual death, and people were ready and willing to go against their conscience to remain students. "Conscience is a group of I's (thoughts and feelings), which if accumulated, will lead a student out of the school" were the Teacher's words. Paradoxically he was right without knowing it. Conscience truly was leading students out of the school. This is why the main aim of the school was to suppress and numb the conscience, then eventually to destroy it by erasing personality and with it, a personal history of the man.

One of the firmest rules in Fellowship of Friends was to cut all contacts with friends or family members who were outside of the school. At the same time, family ties within the school were keeping many in the school. When I received my green card and could leave it all behind me, feelings for my wife were still holding me there. It continued like that for another four years.

My Eyes Had Opened Wide

Not feeling at peace with what I observed in the FOF, I began to look for material on cults and was shocked to find out that there are thousands of them in the U.S. alone. Studying the principles and mechanisms of a cult, I was able to draw parallels between cults and Fellowship of Friends (which in fact did not have any fellowship or friends, since any friendship was ended with terminated membership.) In fact, the FOF system of control was literally identical to the many other cults I have looked in to.

My eyes had opened wide after reading a book by Timothy Leary called *Techniques of Mind Control in Destructive Cults,* which I stumbled upon on the internet. I could not believe how similar it all was with the Fellowship model and doctrine, which we had been told were the teachings of the only real school for awakening on the planet. Well, I thought, if FOF was the only real school on Earth, than how could other people like T. Leary, who was never part of it, know so much about it? Or maybe there was something else at work?

After finishing his book, I had no doubts that our school was a destructive cult and our Teacher was a charismatic charlatan who was skillfully charming people, manipulating them, ruthlessly removing all barriers in his way, then leaving behind broken hearts, hopes and empty wallets.

In his book *Beelzebub Tales*, G. Gurdjieff called an individual like this a "Hasnamuss," explaining that these were the kind of people who were completely lacking conscience and compassion for others. They were egoistically moving forward while stepping on the corpses.

As a general rule, within all cults, there exists a dictatorial microclimate. At the head of any cult, of course, is the guru who is getting support and help in organizing and maintaining cult mentality from his enablers or from his "inner circle" as it was called in the FOF. The inner circle mainly consisted of dedicated servants and donors who were rich students who bought their way into respected status. There also was an outer circle of students, which consisted of newcomers, naive followers, and the general work force to which I belonged. Both circles were brainwashed by the Teacher into believing that building Apollo was actually building an ark that would save all the students who lived in Apollo from a nuclear Armageddon. Thus, I was one of the builders of the bright future under the coming acid rain and nuclear clouds.

The structure of all cults I studied was actually the same as if it had been produced by a copy machine. The only difference was in the form of salvation. Some cults were waiting for aliens to bail them out, others were waiting for the Messiah, and others believed that the guru would take them to Heaven or some other paradise. The common threads shared by many cults were abuse of power, psychological rape, sexual misconduct by the leaders and slave labor—all were in the name of God who was supposedly testing the faith of his flock.

I don't mean to write a text book on cultism, I mean only to speak about my path and what it developed into. But, for eight years I lived in the US, and six of them were spent in the cult where I was studying this global phenomenon.

For example, my stipend was $400 a month, for a 6-day work week, 10 hours a day—less than $2 per hour—when the minimum hourly wage in California at that time was $7. Even $7 per hour was not enough for the average American to pay for the cost of living, which forces one to go deeper in debt by using credit cards and loans. The consequences of which are always painful to many as the sums of credit debt climb and are usually followed by bankruptcies, foreclosures, broken relationships, etc. We were working for $2 per hour, which was enough to rent a room (which took half of my monthly pay) and eat once a day. I needed to work on Sundays so I could eat more than once a day during the next week. Constant hunger and physical exhaustion were encouraged by the dogma of the cult. They called it a "necessary condition for the work on oneself." This is how Gurdjieff's teaching were twisted to serve the cult agenda.

G. Gurdjieff did say that barriers are very useful for the development of man. If they were not there, we would need to create them intentionally, because only by overcoming them could a man develop real will.

Generally speaking, there is certain logic in G's original idea, but in our case, the idea was used for the plain and simple exploitation of the slave labor of immigrants. The paradox was that working to exhaustion was intended to break the will since the will is what gives man the strength to resist oppression. What supposedly was helping to create the will was, in fact, destroying it. People were getting so exhausted by the work that all they wanted was to be left alone and rest in peace. They had no energy to deal with anything else, and in order to stop the inner conflict, they were avoiding all negative information (the truth) about the Teacher.

Failure to Brainwash

During the first year of my membership in the cult, I already had doubts regarding our Teacher which were growing as time passed. By then, I was truly wondering how the older students, who had spent 20-30 years in the cult, and who were successful lawyers, doctors, psychologists and psychiatrists, were so blind to it. They had been students for many years and still continued to hold firmly to their membership.

I was trying to talk openly about my observations with some of them, but in response, I heard pretty much the same things like, "I was too young and didn't spend enough time working on myself." They were trying to convince me that if I didn't understand something, it was only in me, because a "sleeping machine" cannot have an objective opinion or view. Being "a multiplicity of small I's," I could not judge the indivisible, complete, and higher "Self" of the Teacher, because the "lower can't see the higher." Once again, not in good faith was repeated to me as one of the Fourth-way postulates—which was convenient for them.

A few had quietly confessed that they too did not always understand the Teacher. But, they added that judging the Teacher was always wrong since it was coming from the lowest parts of our machines which did not want to awaken. Usually, my attempts to talk to these people led to new disappointments and a heavy feeling of a dead-end. I started to wonder if I was right in my observations and doubts, thinking maybe they were right and perhaps it was me who did not understand what was going on. How could all these health professionals and social and legal workers be confused about all of it?

Going against a group dynamic in which the minds and hearts of the students were melted into one, while common sense and conscience was replaced by group thinking, was like swimming up river against the current. Not being able to knock on their doors, I was licking my soul scars in loneliness. But at the same time, my self-doubt was disappearing with new observations which were all in my favor. I could clearly see the illogical teaching and immorality of the Teacher. The older students were trying to convince me that his divine level of being was liberating him (but only him) from the morals of the mortals, but I could not agree . If that was the case, then I preferred to remain a sleeping man than become a divine pig.

I won't go into all horrors of the cult, but I will mention two things that happened to make the picture clearer. Many years ago, there was a student in the FOF who was dying from cancer. An attempt to cure it sucked up all the money from her family. When the Teacher heard that a dying student had not paid her membership for the last few months, he ordered a message be given to her that if she did not make her payments current, she would go straight to hell. These were the last words of our Teacher to his loyal, dedicated student, and became known in the letter found by her mom after her death.

In a second case: Once, on behalf of the Teacher, a married couple, who were older students, went to Egypt to gather material on ancient dynasties. They did this to validate the teachings by bringing to it the Egyptian hieroglyphs which were interpreted and presented in the light the Teacher wanted—and for a fee. The Teacher sat on the podium, with a few other students who were so proud sitting there with him. I felt nausea looking at them. Sometimes I had the feeling that I was at a circus watching a show of trained peacocks proudly displaying their colorful feathers for the watching crowd.

It is worthwhile to mention that the Teacher's requests were taken by students as great fortune and were fulfilled without question, always at their own expense. Students were asked to go to other functioning centers to support and maintain the dogma or to open new ones overseas. While fulfilling student duty, some of them were also looking to fulfill other needs, which had only a distant correlation with spirituality.

During that trip to Egypt, while photographing one of the Obelisks, the couple had an accident in which the wife died on the spot and the husband suffered serious injuries and was sent to a hospital where he remained in a coma. Waking up slowly from his coma, he did not find a grieving Teacher by his bed, but, instead, the Teacher's lawyer with a bunch of papers, trying to convince the accident survivor to sign papers transferring his property to the FOF. Luckily, common sense was present in his foggy mind, and he refused to sign anything. Was this an expression of limitless love to a barely surviving student who lost his wife after many years of giving time and money to the cult? If I remember correctly, this was the same couple who had opened a teaching center in India and had spent five years there.

(As a side note, "I love you now and will love you in Eternity" were the Teacher's words, often repeated in the cult.)

A few years later, that same lawyer hung himself from the balcony of his house. He left behind his wife who had cancer, and a few kids, all in financial ruin—which of course were no longer of concern to a lawyer on the end of a rope. An article appeared in a local newspaper regarding his death, saying that he died from natural causes. And when ex-students contacted the newspaper asking why they hid the suicide, they were told that it was a family request. The answer was understood by the former students, and they did not pursued it farther, but I thought that lies are inseparable from a person after death just as they were a companion to him in life. I won't speak badly of the deceased, let God be his judge. But, I will say that I have compassion for all those families who have suffered greatly after discovering their spouses or children were victims of sexual misconduct from the Teacher whose dispicable actions were defended by the same lawyer I mentioned above. My heart goes out to all of you. I will not go into any detail, but the reader can find information about this matter in an article entitled at the following website:

http://www.rickross.com/groups/fof.html

In the FOF, there was a unique idea about lifetimes. According to the

Teacher, a student could only become awakened in his 9th lifetime, but to reach it, he must spend his entire life in the cult and die as a student. Only this could guarantee his reincarnation again as a student. In case the student left the cult before his death, according to the Teacher, he was to lose all he gained (if any), spiritually speaking. The Teacher said that no one else was in his 9th lifetime but him, thus students were to forget about an awakening, at least until their next reincarnation. The Teacher gave out lifetime numbers like rewards. Those loyal servants and enablers who were in the inner circle were given 7th and the 8th; others were lucky if they were mentioned among the 6th. Those who disagreed could get no higher than a 5th lifetime. To be on an early lifetime was considered embarrassing, and people were doing all they could to not to be included in the "early lifetime" scheme.

This 9th lifetime plan allowed the Teacher to live quite rich and lavish lifestyle, guaranteeing him life income. But, he was not alone. Looking at different gurus worldwide in my studies, it has become obvious that the mechanisms and methods are the same. They are all creating an idea, which only they control, and people are lined up to give them money attempting to reach those ideals.

Once, I had an unpleasant conversation with a student who was trying hard to brainwash me into submission. In the process, he lost his cool and said that I was in the very early lifetime and this is why I did not understand the teacher. I responded that I did not understand the Teacher because there was nothing there to understand and that it was probably because I was still "alive," in contrast to others who were already "dead" and turned to zombies.

I shared my doubts with my wife, but she refused to even listen. My attempts to talk to her were creating a heavy tension between us, which sometimes took days to release. But in fact, interpretation of the Fourth Way ideas by the FOF was quite different from those actually presented by G. Gurdjieff and P. Ouspensky in their works. It was explained to us that the reason for this was that the Teacher had surpassed the founders of Four Way and transformed their original ideas to a higher understanding. The truth was that the Teacher was a parasite on the Fourth Way system—using bookmarks for his cult with faces of G. Gurdjieff and P. Ouspensky, which were then secretly placed inside esoteric books in stores around the world. This was a way of recruiting new students, or "fresh blood," an older student had once said. The untouchable status of a "conscious being," which the Teacher considered himself to be, was strongly supported by the older students. This created a heavy pressure on the mind, and unquestioning obedience to him by older students was given as an example to young students.

According to G. Gurdjieff, barriers and difficulties helped the spiritual development of man because they helped to develop qualities needed on the way. I was in agreement with this idea—if those difficulties were coming to a man by his own fate, while overcoming them and remaining human. But, causing suffering and pain intentionally with devastating consequences to a person, in order to help him or her in their spiritual development, was looking to me pathetic and stupid like an intention to help a person with a nasal congestion by breaking his nose.

And, if there was a certain meaning in G.Gurdjieff's idea, in the Fellowship, this idea was abused (like many others) and intended solely for enslaving people. Suffering in Fellowship was elevated to a special status. "God's intention for the good of students" and things like bankruptcies, divorces, terminal illnesses, loss of a loved one, or even a personal death were viewed as positive factors by the the Teacher; he called them, " necessary shocks." According to him, these shocks were helping the students on the spiritual path to awakening. In cases of death, the Teacher said that "the student had completed his role and was now placed by C- influence (gods) in Limbo." According to the Teacher's phantasmagoria, this was an area somewhere near heaven where the student waited until the next reincarnation as a student once again.

As time passed, I stopped attending almost any cult events, explaining the need for working "in life" which meant beyond the property of Apollo. As I mentioned earlier, people who were not students of the Fellowship of Friends were called "life people" and "sleeping machines" who were nothing more than food for the bloody moon while loyal students were to enter Heaven and eternal life with him. Of course, I did not believe in his ridiculous and delusional ideas, but some of those who were dear to me were believers, thus creating heartaches for me much of the time. Even to remember all this madness now, makes me sick. The lingering question was whether I should stay in the cult, play along, and lie to myself and my wife, or to leave, losing the woman who, back then, was dear to my heart, regardless of her blind belief in the Teacher.

I would like to say some final words on the subject of cultism and guruism as a global pandemic. Cultism is an epidemic of our time, and the modern day gurus and self-proclaimed prophets are the carriers of this dangerous virus. It is spread via ignorance and the devotion of the followers and disciples, who are thirsty for knowledge and love, yet limited and confused. In desperation, they confuse true virtues with fraud and an inflated ego wrapped in silky cloth.

But, there are exceptions. For me, one of these exceptions was Shri Nim Caroli Baba, an Indian sage, who was visited by Richard Alpert (Ram Dass). Alpert was working in the department of social psychology in Harvard with his friend Timothy Leary, a lecturer in clinical psychology in the same university. Both were fired for experimenting with psilocybin and LSD within the guidelines of a "psilocybin project." Ram Dass offered a very high dose of LSD to Nim Caroli Baba in order to verify his true identity as spiritual guru (if he lied, his false image would melt away within an hour like butter melts on a frying pan within seconds). Well, Nim Caroli Baba took everything offered to him and remained the same for many hours sitting wrapped in simple sheets, smiling just the same and speaking about love as the most important thing on Earth. Ram Dass was so impressed that he became his student and stopped using LSD. I am pretty sure there are true teachers still alive today, but their simple appearance and hearty smile are invisible to those seekers looking for loud words instead.

Computer Training for the Funeral Home Agent

Seven months after arriving at Apollo, I was deprived of that very small stipend, which I had to work hard for and was not enough to live on. I had to supplement my income with other work like cutting wood, planting trees, and helping richer students with things in the garden. My new unemployed status was upsetting my wife. But soon after, I received a message from one of the students who was working in Yuba City, a nearby town about 40 minutes away. There was a computer training class that provided a job upon completion. I talked to my wife about it saying that intuitively I felt like this was something I had to do, even though the subject was just as interesting to me as a ballet. I say this because to me, ballet is a very restrictive and stylized form of dance expression—as opposed to the freedom of other dance forms, which I truly enjoy. She wasn't happy at first, since this dubious training cost $5,000 and only she had that kind of money. Besides, back then my English was not good enough to understand any training, not to mention a more technical field like this one. I promised to pay her back regardless of success. She trusted me and agreed to pay for it, and I began to study.

This training was led by a black woman who, for some reason, didn't like me from the start. She talked as fast as an automatic weapon, and I didn't understand a thing. Time was passing by, but I wasn't learning much. My questions were frustrating to her. My desire to be there had dropped to nothing, but thoughts about the debt to my wife, and my promise to pay her back, kept me going. Three months later, on the day of graduation, we all received some document stating that we had finished such and such training. My thoughts that the money was wasted were interrupted by the announcement that a job fair would be held the next day in Sacramento where many companies would be offering jobs. Returning home, I shared my disappointment with my wife, telling her that there was no reason for me to go to the job fair, since what I had learned in the training would not be enough to even fill out a blank application with what I knew. She said that it was my choice, but she didn't think that going there would hurt. I agreed and went the next day.

The job fair was held in one of the hotels that was now filled with unbelievably long lines consisting of men in black suits, serious faces and briefcases in their hands. My appearance wasn't exactly a good fit for the black suit scene, but since I came there, I thought I would go through with it. After spending a few hours in the line, I finally entered a big conference room full of many tables among the walls with representatives from different companies. Passing by the tables, I asked some people questions and received brief answers.

Already, I felt like going home but I decided to go thru the torture to the end. Almost finishing the circle, I passed by one table behind which stood a few guys. One of them had a big gold ring on his finger. I asked him what job he was offered, and his response was "pre-arrangement." I didn't know what this word meant so I thanked him and kept walking, but then I heard him ask me what kind of an accent I had? I told him "Russian." He thought for a second, invited me to come to his office saying that Sacramento had a big Russian population, gave me his business card, and told me he would be expecting me on Monday. When I asked my wife what pre-arrangement meant, she said it was a way to organize your funeral, choosing everything from the plot in the cemetery, your coffin, the memorial service, and most of all, making payments for all of it while you were still alive. The prospect of working as a funeral agent at my first formal job in America seemed ironic, a "fatal" joke, but, I thought, in the country where a Terminator could become a Governor, anyone could become anything.

The following Monday, I was led to a little room which had a table, chairs, a writing desk and TV set. Soon the man with the golden ring appeared and started explaining the essence of the work. It was quite simple. I was supposed to find clients and sell them their coffins and the plots where they would be buried one day. Then he started the DVD and left. This was a training video showing how agents going into people's homes, sitting down and repeating a memorized text to them. Afterwards, they were signing papers, making a deal, smiling and leaving. Before I went home that first day, I was given fat, self-made book with the text I was supposed to memorize.

I trained for a week before they decided to take me to a client's home so I could see how things were done in practice. An old lady opened the door. The agent greeted her politely and asked if we could come in to talk. The old lady agreed and we went in. As we sat around the table, the agent turned himself on like a tape, and without pausing for a moment, began repeating memorized text. Some I could understand, but most of it I could not. I was yawning and falling asleep when he finished his tirade, after which the old lady signed some papers for purchasing her coffin, plot and simple service, as well as the way the payment would be made. Right after that, the agent said good bye, wishing her good luck and health. On our way to his car I was thinking about how casually he wished her good health after selling her a coffin. As we sat in the car, he proudly said that everyone needed our product and our job was simply to remind people about their last need. And to build me up, he said that my commission from this deal was $300, for participating, so to speak. On the way to the office we didn't speak a word.

But the thought of my commission was not elevating me. Instead, it was making me feel somewhat sad. I couldn't help remembering how cynically and falsely this agent was forcing his tears while talking to the old woman about how her children would be burdened by the cost of her funeral, which would make the grieving harder and how thoughtful it would be of her to take care of it for them. It reminded me of those salesmen who knocked on people's doors, trying to sell them very expensive vacuum cleaners which they didn't really need. And, the only thought that gave me any peace was that even though this process was cynical, it still had a certain meaning. In America, funerals are very expensive and cost thousands of dollars which is too much to pay at once for an average, hard working person. I've heard some sad stories about people getting into accidents and leaving their loved ones looking for money for the funeral during the immense stress and grief. So, looking at the situation this way, I decided to continue to work there.

Time passed and I became the salesman knocking on people's doors reminding them about something that they usually wanted to forget. Some people crossed themselves not letting me finish my greeting. Others yelled at me and shut the door in my face. Some invited me inside and listened patiently, looking at different coffins in the catalog I brought with me. Some couples were fighting over who would be on top and who would be on the bottom in the case of above-ground double crypts. Some people looked for a place farther from the road and in the shade, probably concerned about the noise of passing cars or being hot while resting underground.

I began to feel like the job was intolerable and that I couldn't do it any longer. The last straw was one event when all the agents were invited to the main funeral building for a meeting and talk with the higher management. I arrived on time and was asked to go up to the second floor to a little conference room, which was full of agents wearing black suits. Like locust, they were eating sandwiches provided by the management. This was disgusting to watch, so I decided wait outside of the room. Wandering around, I passed a room with an open door in which there was a coffin with dead, older woman, lying in wait for the service. As I stood there looking at her, I heard loud voices and laughter from the room full of sandwich-eating agents. I realized we had nothing in common; in that moment I knew I would resign at the end of the month.

Goodbye Coffins

A few days after that, I went to work to finish distributing the fliers, which I had been preparing earlier. These were meant to be left in people's doors in case they weren't home and contained brief information with the address and phone number of the funeral home. It was a very hot Saturday. I came to the office, spent few hours on the phone calling prospective clients, took a bunch of handouts and went out to the area to distribute them. A few hours later, I had only a few of them left in my hand. I finished up with a long street and didn't want to start a new one, so I thought about throwing them in the trash and going home. But, I felt I had to finish what I started, so I took my map and marked the streets where I'd already been and moved to the next one.

I knocked on another door. The door was opened by a black man who asked me what I wanted. I told him that I was from a funeral home and was offering our products and services. He stepped back a little and tried to close the door. Surprising myself, I put my leg a little forward, stopping him from closing his door, while telling him that one day he would be dead and it was better for him to think about it now, while he was being offered a good deal. The situation looked somewhat funny as we both continued to push the door from both sides. He suddenly asked what accent I had. I told him "Russian." He thought a moment and opened his door wide. Now it was my turn to listen. He stepped

43

outside the door, and with excitement, started to explain something to me with his hands. While he was talking, I saw the exact same gold ring on his finger which I had seen once before on the finger of the funeral agent at the job fair. I stood outside listening, while he was drawing pictures in the air about how we could make a lot of money together. Long story short, he asked me if I wanted to become a real estate agent. To me, it was just as strange as being a funeral agent, but sounded a bit more pleasant. I told him that I didn't know anything about it, and he answered that Sacramento had a big Russian community and that I would only be translating in the beginning.

I went back home with new hope. "Finally, I'm done with coffins," I was thinking. My doubts about my success as a realtor were ended when I remembered my earlier realization that in a country where the Terminator can become a Governor, anyone can do anything. I shared this new opportunity with my wife, and she liked the idea. She said that working with houses would be easier for me. Sunday, I rested at home, thinking of my new career to which I would be dedicating about four years. I went on Monday to his office; he showed me my desk which had nothing on it, and said that now I had to find clients. I was puzzled, wondering how I could do that without knowing anyone in the city. Then, seeing the yellow pages on his desk, I ask if I could use it. He gave it to me and I started to look for Russian names in it. When I found some, I called them and explained our services.

People started to respond and come into the office where I translated for them as directed. Later on, I got my real estate license and started working on my own, renting a desk in his office. I liked this job because, relatively speaking, it was an honest job. I was taking people

around, showing them properties, finding them all the necessary information, getting all inspections done and helping them with moving. And I liked the freedom of the schedule—basically being my own boss.

Thanks to this job, I started to have more free time and some money. I was thinking that now I could dedicate myself more to my spiritual search. During this time, I had essentially dropped my "student's duties" and rarely appeared in "school events." That created a lot of tension at home. I thought about leaving the cult, knowing it would most likely mean the end of my relationship as well. But I finally made my choice and told my wife that I decided to leave the cult, but did not want to break up with her.

Path

Stars and Alchemists Pointing the Way

About six months prior to leaving the cult, a friend and I had gone to Santa Rosa, a lovely place located in the forests of northern California, within a two hours north of San Francisco. We went there because I found out that there was an observatory where we could see stars through a big telescope, which was something I had wanted to do all my life. We took a tent, since we thought to spend the night in the forest.

Watching through the telescope, we were stunned by the mystery of such brilliant stars. The person who operated the telescope was passionately answering my questions. It happened that the little, shiny spot we could see thru the telescope was, in fact, our neighbor Andromeda Galaxy, which was twice as big as our galaxy, the Milky Way. The distance from the Earth was over two million light years. I tried to make a calculation, imagining light flying thru space at a speed of 300,000 km (about 190,000 miles) per second, for two million years! I laughed when I heard from the astronomer that Andromeda is actually one of hundreds of billions of galaxies in the Universe—each of them contains billions and maybe trillions of stars. I remember as a child, trying to comprehend infinity by trying to imagine a never ending space. I usually fell asleep in this space travel.

Leaving the observatory, we returned to our camp, built a fire, and discussed what we had seen. Based on what we had seen through telescope, we decided that the idea of being alone in the universe was similar to thinking that the Pacific Ocean had only one kind of fish—or in fact, one single, lonely fish. But, even that comparison was not exactly a full reflection of the scale on which, our planet, solar system and galaxy are just a grain of cosmic dust or nuclear particle in an endless universe. Thinking about all that, I felt like sharing with my friend that I had decided to leave the cult, adding that it most likely would result in the end of my marriage with my wife. That night, I also told him I had a feeling that soon I would be meeting the real teachers whom I had been waiting to meet all along. This was in August of 2005. Exactly one month later, I found shamans in Peru.

I was searching the internet, looking for information about MDMA, which I had used many times, but never knew the history of. Back then, I saw in it the potential for psychiatric healing and a way of studying myself. But, the chemical nature of it, causing a depletion of serotonin, followed by days of depression afterward, was too high of a price to pay. I found out that this chemical was created by Alexander Shulgin, an American chemist and pharmacologist with Russian roots. This genius alchemist was the father of hundreds of psychedelics, with the exception of LSD, which came from Albert Hoffman. Hoffman was a Swiss chemist who learned about lysergic acid on his way home from his laboratory while riding a bicycle. It was a routine trip home, but turned out to be an unforgettable journey. I liked A. Shulgin for the fact that he tried all his new creations on himself before making it available to others. Besides, all the results of his work have been documented in chemical encyclopedias called *PIHKAL: Phenethylamines I Have Known And Loved* and *TIHKAL: Tryptamines I Have Known And Loved.*

It was only later, watching one of his interviews, when I learned the inspiration for his work came from his experience with mescaline extracted from Peyote cactus. This experience inspired him, guided his work, and made him dedicate his life to it. When I became familiar with his biography and the immensity of his scientific work, I was surprised by his words which I had found on his website. "There are many shamans scattered around the world. Search for them."

See Dr. Shulgin online:

http://www.cognitiveliberty.org/shulgin/blg/index.html.

To hear these words from a chemist and scientist, really struck me. Science and spirituality seemed to have gotten separated long ago, and to hear him suggest looking for shamans in the modern world was strange but made me feel hopeful.

But what kind of shaman could I find on the internet? In my mind, they were isolated Indians living somewhere beyond reach, and who had never heard of the internet. Thinking about that, I googled [shamanism] and found numerous different websites on the subject. One of them caught my attention: www.biopark.org

The man behind it was an American who left years ago for Peru and was offering shamanic retreats and pilgrimages working with two sacred teacher healer plants, Ayahuasca and Huachuma. I read his writings on his site, looked at his pictures, and felt that I could trust him. I emailed him and right away he answered back. I asked if he had a phone number, which he gave me. I called him up and we had a long phone conversation. His answers were direct and clear, and I liked the philosophical character of our conversation. It was incredible. Just a few hours ago, the world of the shamans had been somewhere far away, and now, I was talking to one of them in person. I felt good about him, and made the decision that same night to travel to Peru to work with him. I wired all the money for spending five weeks in Peru, starting in the Amazonian rainforest and continuing to the Andes. I knew he was the real deal.

I left for Peru one week after I formally left the cult and spent New Year's Eve in my own vomit in the middle of the jungle. The world of Sacred Grandmother Ayahuasca was beyond all my expectations— beautiful and frightening. The ceremonies were exhausting, despite the strict diet I followed prior to them. Regardless, the magesty of the vine, the symphony of sounds at night in the rainforest, blue sky, and bright white clouds swimming by, have remained forever in my heart.

Path

Meeting the Shamans

 My first visit to Peru lasted five weeks. The first two were dedicated to the master teacher and healer plant, grandmother Ayahuasca, mother of all plants in the rainforest. Following that, I worked with the master teacher and healer plant, grandfather Huachuma, the father of all plants in the Andes.

Huachuma (from one of the Quechua dialects, meaning 'vision') was the original name for the sacred cactus, which later during colonial times, received another name, San Pedro. This new name was a way to safely preserve the original tradition by integrating and using elements of the Catholic religion.

According to the Bible, the apostle Peter held the key to Heaven; thus Huachuma was called by this apostle's name, since Huachuma is considered to be the key to Heaven. Out of respect for the ancient ways, I will be using the original name.

After two weeks of working with Ayahuasca I looked like an old pair of jeans just pulled out of the washing machine—but in fact, inside, I felt newly born. On the second morning after our arrival to the Amazonian retreat, we gathered to meet the native shaman Ayahuascero. He was working with a man named Howard, who had organized the retreat.

I had always thought that a shaman would have a distinct appearance, possibly a beard, maybe a special hat like those I'd seen on gurus in the US, and for sure, a serious facial expression—all the attributes one might imagine a spiritual teacher to have. Having shopped well in the spiritual markets of the West hoping to find real teachers, I had thus far found only salesmen in guru clothing, selling stacks of unnecessary hay in which sometimes could be found a few grains of wisdom. This made an imprint on my mind and colored my expectation.

When don Rober first appeared in front of us, I thought he was a worker passing by, who had stopped to greet gringos. His hair was disheveled, and he was wearing a simple shirt, pants and rubber boots. I later learned shamans wore these boots as protection from poisonous snakes when going deep into the rainforest to gather medicinal plants. His appearance and a simple smile were the first shocks to my imaginary picture of the shamanic world. That evening, we gathered at the same place where we had first met don Rober. He brought a bunch of vines (Banisteriopsis caapi) and Chacruna leafs (Psychotria virdis) so we could all take part in the Ayahuasca brewing process. We took turns with a hammer and smashed the vines into pieces. Then, we passed the bowl with Chacruna leaves around so our hands could touch it, thus making a personal connection.

It was already late when we finished, and Howard said anyone who would like to take part in brewing the medicine with don Rober could meet him at 6 am the following day at the same place. I couldn't sleep from all the excitement, so I was on time the next morning. But, there were only two of us at the meeting place, don Rober and myself. He made a gesture with his hand, like "follow me," and we moved a little deeper into the jungle, leaving the retreat behind. When we came to what was called the Ayahuasca kitchen, he showed me a place to sit and started to do his work. I watched a big metal bowl on the fire and fought with mosquitoes who I knew would eat me alive if let them. Don Rober didn't seem to be bothered by them at all. Around noon, one of Howard's staff members brought food to don Rober. Shamans never leave their pots during brewing, protecting their brew from evil spirits, so I went to have lunch in the retreat and then came back to spend the rest of the day with don Rober. Regardless of bloodthirsty mosquitoes, I felt comfortable, watching him do his work in silence.

Our ceremonies usually began around 9 pm. After everyone was seated, don Rober stood up, gave his thanks to Jesus Christ, Mother Mary, the Holy Spirit, and Ayahuasca, and then proceeded to set a protective field around each of us called Arcana. One Arcana was given to the maloca (a circular ceremonial place); the others were personal for everyone. After that, he went back to his rocking chair and carefully opened a plastic bottle. He directed a silent song and a mapacho smoke (a sacred tobacco used for communication with the spirits) into the bottle of freshly brewed Ayahuasca, which was patiently waiting to be freed. These songs, called Icaros, are magic songs given to the Ayahuascero by Ayahuasca. They serve as guiding tools with which the shaman communicates with the medicine, instructing it and working with it. It reminded me of the flutes with which an Indian fakir control Cobras.

The group was made up of 22 people including 16 gringos, 4 Indians from the Bora Tribe, and 2 shamans, Howard and don Rober. After medicine was poured for everyone, we were then called by name to an

53

altar. Don Rober drank last and blew out the candles. The taste of the brew was extremely unpleasant, and to drink the whole cup was not easy. The first effects of the medicine came on quickly, bringing nausea. I felt like the medicine unscrewed my head from my neck and shoulders, cracked it in half, and spread pieces of my brain all over the Universe, flooding passing stars with vomit. Then, the magic songs of don Rober followed, seeming to harness Ayahuasca like a wild horse and ride it.

A spinning vision like a kaleidoscope appeared thru which I now saw the scenes of my childhood, followed by the tears and vomit of the group. The boundaries between dimensions disappeared, and I felt other, new beings in the room. Some of them I could see in darkness, some I could hear, and others I could only sense. They were flying by like honey bees, seeming to get closer, then suddenly departing.

As all of this was going on, I wondered when it might end, and found that my sense of time was completely gone. Time was just a concept, which I could no longer grasp. Thinking about tomorrow was really scary, since tomorrow was no longer accessible. Past, present, and future appeared as concepts, stretching thru eternity. This new sensation was overwhelming and quite frightening. I started to panic, mentally calling for don Rober, asking him for help. To my surprise, he somehow heard me and came to blow mapacho over me and sing a song. That somehow switched off the kaleidoscope, bringing me back to a realm that was more familiar. But after only a short break and a bit of relief, I was reliving my life in the cult and I could see in the liquid coming from my mouth, expelling it from my very soul like parasites being cast away from my intestines. What followed was the regurgitation of an old relationship with a girl with whom I had spent 3 years back in Israel, and which had left scars in both of us. Then, suddenly I heard a tremendous buzz, which seemed to come from everywhere. It was so loud and disturbing that I thought that if it didn't get turned down somehow, I would become deaf in no time at all. I somehow sent another call out to don Rober, who again heard me and turned it down to a bearable level. But, during that buzz, he began to sing, and I heard amazingly beautiful voices all around us. I thought that if angels did in fact exist, I was now hearing their voices. The most professional choir, in comparison to these angelic voices, would have been amateurs.

The last thing I remember at this first ceremony, was the moment when I felt like asking Ayahuasca: "Who am I?" Her answer unfolded in the form of a vibrational frequency, which was now increasing to a point where I could no longer hold the mental object that I called "I" because it was scattering to pieces. "This is how we die," I thought, and vomited violently while lying on the floor.

Another World

Once, after returning to my room from a ceremony, while still deep in the medicine and far from falling asleep, I lay down in my bed and thought about the unexplainable reality of the Ayahuasca world. Suddenly, I heard the voices of children playing outside. I looked at the clock. It was 3 am. I was surprised because I had not seen any kids in our retreat. I wanted to go out to see, but when I got up to go to the door, it felt like I was held back by an invisible force coming from the next room where don Rober was sleeping. I stood there a second while experiencing this and the voices outside became silent. I lay back down on my bed, and for the first time, thought that I was going mad.

The next morning, I told Howard what had happened and asked him what the meaning of this could be? He said these were river sirens, water spirits. I told him I thought that sirens were mythological creatures from ancient Greece, to which he replied that the jungle was a mystery, indeed.

This was a rest day, and we went to visit a neighbor Bora tribe where we spent all day, observing the lives of the native people. I was especially touched watching their kids running around and playing with happy faces, regardless of an indescribable level of poverty. It seemed like they were in total harmony with their surroundings, living their lives fully, despite having so little. I didn't see in any of them a worry for what tomorrow might bring—which one sees so often in western people. I thought about the person who had once told me that she would get depressed if she did not buy something at least once a week. Here in the jungle, this seemed so funny.

On the return trip to the retreat center in our boats, I asked Howard whether there were cannibals in jungle like those in movies. He smiled and said that I had just spent a full day with them. I reflected on how exotic, positive, and bright it was. With the "primitive" indigenous tribes we were eating, drinking, dancing, and being taught how to shoot from a wooden blowgun, and I remembered giving the kids electronic watches and lighters.

My thoughts were interrupted by Howard's words, "This could be the last day of your life if you came here with bad intentions." This made me think about justice as being an objective concept, which was the same all over the world. I would do enact some form of justice if someone came to my home with an intention to hurt my family. I might not eat them, but I'm fairly certain they would not leave alive.

During that same conversation, I told Howard that after last night's ceremony, I wasn't that excited about drinking more. He said it was my choice to make, but warned me that by not continuing, a heavy feeling of incompletion would most likely go with me when I went home. I understood the meaning of his words. We started the next ceremony that evening at the same time, around 9 pm.

I was sitting next to Howard, on his right. I put a voice recorder next to me to make a recording of don Rober's songs, and on my other side, I placed a bottle of water. In front of me there was a ceremonial bucket in which new friendships were bonded and formed between all participants.

Don Rober was an Ayhuascero from the Lama tradition, or as it is called, Lamista, and was living deep in the jungle surrounding Iquitos, a native village where he was a known healer. He was 11 years old when he drank Ayahuasca for the first time with his father who was also an Ayahuascero. Between his daily duties, don Rober was working with Howard's group as well, healing them with Ayahuasca while Howard was doing healings afterward with Huachuma. Both of them were great maestros; both shared one another's medicine, and both gave one another great respect.

Deeper Into Myself

The second ceremony was even harder. Right at the beginning, after I had already drunk my cup, we all heard a groaning sound coming from the forest and getting closer to our maloca. A moment later, I saw two Indians at the entrance holding a woman between them. Don Rober came to them, and they told him something. He then looked at Howard, who nodded positively. They brought the Indian woman who, at this moment looked whiter than I was, inside the maloca and seated her on the mattress in the middle, which Howard humorously had called the surgery table. This was the mattress for special needs, where don Rober performed his healing on those who needed it in this way.

Now, don Rober came to her, sat down, blew smoke all over her with mapacho, drew nearer to her stomach, sang a song, and then start sucking up air through his half closed hand. He returned to his place and continued to give more medicine to people who had not yet drunk. Then he drank himself and blew out the candles. We sat in darkness waiting for the medicine come up, hearing heavy groaning coming from the woman on the floor.

It wasn't a very pleasant start for me. Soon came the familiar feeling of my head screwing out of my shoulders, cracking in half and being sent right back to my relationship with my parents, my sister, my back-then wife, and others I had known. I saw my wife waiting for me with a divorce. The probability of us getting a divorce was not new to me; I had understood that earlier when I was thinking about leaving the cult. But, now I could feel her feelings and hear her words. That brought deep heartache.

In the next vision, I saw my parents, who knew where I was, and were thinking about me. I felt their love and thought about all the pain I brought to them during my early years. That hurt very much. Then, I saw the gap between me and my sister, who was completely lost living in Israel, and to whom I could not even talk. Our lives were distant from each other, both literally and figuratively speaking. I tried to open my eyes to stop the visions, and when I did, I saw two silhouettes around don Rober, who at this time was in the middle of the room performing healing on the sick woman. I thought these were his helper spirits, closed my eyes, and went back to the next visions.

As the groaning ceased, my attention was caught by something else. I was focusing on the sound of crickets chirping outside. I always liked to listen to them at nights, and now they were effecting me in a calming manner. Listening to them, I start thinking that I was just about to decode their chirpings, but out of excitement for this possibility, I couldn't focus. Trying more, I had the feeling that those crickets were not exactly crickets, but more like transmitters of information.

Following that thought, I tried to see what kind of the information it was and where it was being transmitted to. Following the sounds, my inner vision was climbing up toward the light, which for some reason, I now didn't feel like seeing. Then I started to sense this information was concerning me and was actually passing through me. I experienced myself as a computer on which a powerful anti-virus was uploaded and a start button was clicked. That caused more purging, during which I thought how much could be learned if our DNA would be decoded. At that particular point, don Rober lit up the candles and thanked everyone, announcing that the ceremony was over.

I had barely opened up my eyes, thinking that don Rober had ended too early. I left the maloca last, asking Howard to stay with me a little longer. He stayed, we talked, then he led me to my room where I purged more. He stayed with me until 4 in the morning, and even though I was not feeling very good, I enjoyed our private and special conversation, which left no doubt that Howard saw through me like no one else had seen before.

The next day everyone was curious about what had happened to the sick woman. Howard said she was hit by a magic arrow in her intestines, causing her great pain. He said she was a wife of a Bora tribe leader and was attacked out of jealousy by other shamans. He said that what sounds like fables to western minds is daily life to them. He then shared his personal experience of being hit by a powerful arrow shortly after coming to Peru, but out of respect to him, I will not report on that. Years later, I was hit by such an arrow myself—which I will describe in later chapters.

After the previous night's ceremony, the woman slept until late morning; then she left, walking back home alone. Don Rober had sucked up all the illness from the effects of the "psychic" poison arrow.

As the day began, we gathered together in the circle overlooking evergreen Amazonian rainforest and one of many smaller Amazonian rivers connected to the Great Amazon River, and on which our retreat center was built. After that, we went to visit a local zoo where we were shown different sizes of pythons, pumas, crocodiles, monkeys and huge parrots. One of the parrots confused my ear with something else. Late that night, I informed Howard that the latest ceremony was even harder and asked him to please give don Rober a message to give me less medicine tomorrow.

Path

Healing The Past

In the third ceremony, don Rober gave me the cup with a smile, pouring less as I had requested, which allowed me the rest I needed without skipping a ceremony. It was a beautiful and easy one, but at the end, I realized that I did need to drink full cups. But this welcome break had been necessary.

Once, in a conversation with Howard, I told him that I had heard a lot about the necessity of going thru a psychological death, or ego death in ceremonies. I expressed concern about whether I was ready for it and asked if it could be avoided. He said that it was a desirable thing to go through, adding that this experience is an important step on the path, and with a smile, added that when I was ready for it, I wouldn't be asked.

The final two ceremonies were difficult, but deep and beautiful at the same time. The intolerable buzz cracking my head in half was replaced by angelic voices, which then remarkably transformed into geometrical forms and shapes that melted into understanding of important things. One of these understandings was about my conscience being my only judge and that I was free from the opinions and judgments of others toward me.

I felt my past was getting healed, leading me to a new beginning and leaving forever in my heart the choir of nightly forest voices, the songs of don Rober, the smell of mapacho, and the frightening beauty of this sacred master plant.

During that last ceremony, don Rober had come to me and started to hit me on the top of my head with his chakapa while singing a song. This light-weight, leafy broom felt like he was knocking on my head with a wooden baton, which felt like it would crack my head in half. Then, my thoughts about the safety of my head changed to a specific feeling of my very self I had never had before. It was right in the middle of my head under the bone of my skull. Before that, I had many times sharply experienced myself as pure awareness looking out thru my eyes, but this time was different. I felt the very nucleus of my soul, and as if the core of my being had been sleeping and was now being awakened by the chakapas knocks and the song of don Rober.

After the last ceremony, we were invited to take the boats deeper into the jungle to gather leaves for a chakapa with don Rober. Chakapa is a shamanic tool used for cleansing and comforting the patient with its leafy sounds during the magic songs of the Icaros. It is made out of the leaves of a certain jungle tree.

We took the motor boats and went down the river with don Rober to gather the chakapa. In a little while we arrived, and after parking our boats, went deeper into rainforest. We visited one of don Rober's friends, don Ignasio, who lived in a very simple construction, probably two-by-two square meters, on an elevated wooden foundation. He had a dog as well. While I was thinking about how simply a man could live in the jungle, don Rober called us to follow him farther. Walking on the path I realized that I could see no one in front or behind me. I thought I was lost and started to speak don Rober's name out loud. Within few moments, he appeared, showing me the way to follow. We came to a certain spot where don Rober told us to wait. Then, when he got back with bunches of leaves in his hands, we were directed back to our boats. On the return path, don Ignasio was walking in front of me. Suddenly, it started to rain, a warm and powerful tropical rain. In a second, don Ignasio cut a big leaf using his machete and put it above his head like an umbrella. I didn't care about getting wet, but was enjoying learning the ways of people in the jungle.

To say a few words about don Rober, I would like to mention his humbleness and dedication to his work. Consider the strength it takes to lead a ceremony for 20 people every other night while sucking out of them all kinds of stuff and ending the ceremony at 3 in the morning.

Then, at 6 am he patiently waits for the people who are slowly waking up to come for their flower bath. The purpose of the flower bath is to seal the chakras which had been opened during ceremony.

Usually I woke up last, around 9 and even 10 am, always to find don Rober waiting at the same spot. His dedication to his work became, for me, an example which was worth looking at. Howard told us that once, during a ceremony, don Rober was bitten by a poisonous snake. He didn't stop the ceremony, led it to the end, and only then, began to cure himself. The personal power of this man may perhaps only be understood by those who have been bitten by poisonous things.

Ending the work with Ayahuasca, I silently expressed my gratitude for her deep holistic cleansing and for the trust she taught me, gifting me with an important understanding of myself.

But as they say, Ayahuasca has many faces, and me being shown just one of them, more philosophical in nature, was probably because of my love for wisdom. She can, in fact, appear to others as a miraculous doctor, curing the incurable in mysterious ways. Such a miracle occurred with one of my friends whom I was to meet 3 years later in Peru. For 20 years she had suffered from acromegaly, a chronic degenerative condition which eventually caused a brain tumor. It had gotten so bad that it started to deform her body. When I first saw her, I was shocked and repelled by her appearance, but I recognized a kind heart in her and that overweighed my initial reaction, allowing a connection on another level. To go with conventional medicine would mean surgery, life time monitoring, and heavy medications, all of which she didn't want. She looked for other ways of curing—which fortunately do exist. You can read her story at the following website:

http://www.realitysandwich.com/how_shipibo_healers_cured_my_brain_tumor

Path

Huachuma Call

After two weeks in the Amazon, we continued on our journey into the Andes, working at the ancient sacred places with the master Teacher Healer cactus, Huachuma.

Huachuma is the original name of a certain kind of Trichocereus cactus, rich with alkaloids, among them, mescaline. Huachuma means 'vision' and has been used for thousands of years for healing and spiritual purposes. For the Spaniards, because of its divine qualities, Huachuma received another name, San Pedro. I explained the name change in a previous chapter.

The Trichocereus cactus has many varieties, but only a few of them are traditionally used in Peru. To tell the difference is not easy for someone who has no experience in working with them, since they look almost the same. All can reach 5-6 meters tall with sharp spines; all can have from 6 to 9 ribs. Those who believe in the four-rib Huachuma myth, which is based on a misunderstanding of an ancient Chavin glyph, obviously have never grown their own and are confusing it with another type of Andean cactus which has no relation to Huachuma whatsoever.

All Huachuma plants bloom with big and beautiful white flowers that open for short periods of time, gifting the lucky ones with a gentle smell, and spreading seeds for new growth, then disappearing before you know it. Their habitat is high in the Andes from 3000 meters (9000 ft) above sea level. These cacti are survivors, living in extreme weather conditions, burning sun during the day, icy winds and freezing temperatures at night. They endure heavy summer rains and long periods of time without rain—from April thru December.

Also, if a portion of the cactus breaks off and falls to the ground, it will take root, regardless of the position in which it has fallen. This quality can be viewed as one of Huachuma's lessons about surviving, endurance and strength, telling one that new beginnings are ahead after separation. The stillness or immobility of this plant teaches us of a peaceful and non-aggressive existence, but its sharp spines are telling us of its constant state of readiness for self-defense. The beautiful and aromatic flowers of Huachuma symbolize his kind and loving nature, opening to those who come to him with an open heart. Huachuma, growing at high altitudes, breathes in the clouds often. During rainy seasons, when clouds are low, they swim thru the sky, wrapping Huachuma around them in their ethereal essence. This may explain the feeling of longing for the sky when under influence of Huachuma.

My first ceremony with Huachuma was in the Amazon, right after we had finished an intense work with Ayahuasca. Only one Huachuma ceremony was preformed there, creating a transition from rainforest to the Andes. We started the ceremony around noon and sat around Howard's mesa (altar) full of powerful objects. He spoke a few words and then started to call people one by one to the altar for drinking the new medicine. After we all took the medicine, he said we had about an hour to walk around and get ready for the day.

I went to the river and sat down by the bank. But, within the first 30 minutes, I already began to feel the medicine. What was shocking to me was the feeling of familiarity with it. I found Howard and told him that I knew this medicine without having experienced it, and could already feel it plunging me into infinity. In truth, I was scared, and needed to share this feeling with him. He looked at me directly in the eyes and said, "You have been looking for this all your life and now, when you have found it, you are ready to turn your back and run?"

His words cut me like a blade. He was right. I was looking for exactly that, and now that I had found it, I was scared. We climbed into our motor boats and went up river, which began to merge with the Amazon and enjoyed seeing the thriving rainforest on the way. A while later, we arrived at a certain place, parked our boats, and went walking into the forest. In front of us, we saw a long wooden bridge stretched out above a swamp. While walking on the bridge, Howard was telling me something that I felt was very important, but I was distracted by the surrounding beauty and couldn't focus on his words. I was amazed at feeling so much at once—or everything, to be correct. I shared with him that I had never felt myself so big. I was the forest; I was the clouds; I was a part of the whole; and yet I was feeling sovereign. The bridge creaked and swayed gently, and in the sounds, I could hear the thoughts and feel the feelings of the people walking on it. I felt I could understand their lives. Finally, after passing over the bridge, we came to a meadow where we spent a few hours interacting with the locals who were living nearby. Later that afternoon, we all went back to the center.

It was already dark when the driver of the boat turned off the engine, using the momentum, slowly settling into the berth, when suddenly, I heard a whistle by one of the members of our group. It sounded like he was trying to give a sign saying, "We are friends," to those who were on the shore. That was a creepy feeling. I thought this is how people must feel during war when coming to the shore at night. The next day, I felt like talking to this man, telling him about what I had felt. When I shared with him, he said that once in Vietnam, their own side opened fire on them from the shore. Many who were with him were killed. He was a veteran who returned home with two bullets in his body and missing a few fingers. He had spent over 30 years in deep depression, using heavy antidepressants daily without leaving the house much. He said that in his previous visit to Howard and don Rober, he felt like Ayahuasca cured his depression, and before leaving back to the US, he left his antidepressants in the trash. He also said that he hadn't laughed for 30 years. I must admit his laughter was a little creepy, but all things considered, it was great progress and I was glad for the advancement in his healing.

Huachuma is an incredible Teacher Healer plant, who gently brings you into an altered state of consciousness, followed by understanding of anything you are directing your attention to. The feeling of unity and fullness, clarity and harmony with all the surroundings was bringing me tears of happiness. An opened heart allowed a communion with nature of another kind. I felt that if I was not so excited and delighted by this new perception, I would be able to communicate with animals and plants. But, my overwhelming sense of gratitude for being able to see and feel the world in a completely different way, proving that other realms exist and can be accessed in certain states of consciousness, was more important than new abilities and possibilities. Huachuma is a very kind spirit plant who gifts so much for so little. All that was required from me was to relinquish fear. What happened that evening back at the retreat, after spending the day walking on the long bridge and out in the meadow, I will share at the end of the book. As I understand it now, it was the most important guidance on my path.

The next day, we returned to Iquitos, flew to Lima, and from there, began an exploration of ancient cultures of the coast and did ceremonies in their sacred places. We went to Tucume, a city of a pyramids still resting under thick layers of sand accumulated over a thousand years. Then, we moved on to the pyramids of the bloody Moche, whose ominous carvings on the walls are very telling.

Then we visited the adobe city of Chan-Chan of the Chimu culture. Finishing with the coast, we went up to Andes, back in time, to the source of Andean cosmology and knowledge, on a pilgrimage to the great, ancient culture of Chavin, on which I will expand in later chapters.

While traveling, I was thinking that Peru was actually the cradle of the ancient world of South America. And shamanism, as it's called today, whose history goes back before recorded time, was at the very core of Peruvian culture and remains strong to this day in the Amazonian jungle and magnificent Andes. I was stunned with the beauty of nature, visible in all its fullness on Huachuma medicine. Through this beauty, I could feel the immense potential for healing and awakening, which I had been looking for in all the wrong places.

Path

A New Beginning

My first visit to Peru became a new foundation on which I now felt like building a new foundation for my spiritual house. Leaving Peru was hard, since I felt like half of my heart remained there.

Upon arriving back home to California, just as I saw during the Ayahuasca ceremony, my ex-wife met me with the words concerning her wish for a divorce. I felt exactly as I had felt in the jungle when I had seen this event during the Ayahuasca vision.

Daily life upon returning was trivial and boring, possibly because I couldn't share what I had experienced in Peru with hardly anyone I knew. Some of them would laugh, others were afraid, and others were showing zero interest. I felt alone with an explosion of new thoughts and feelings that I brought back with me. The way I had lived the last 5 weeks was so different from what I came back to, so getting integrated was not easy.

But, Howard's words were helpful. He had told me that what I was experiencing in Peru was only one part of the story, with more to unfold later. That was true. As time passed, I developed a deeper understanding of the events I had experienced in Peru. That helped me survive in the spiritual desert of consumerism—a North American religion that I returned to. More and more I felt like I had to go back to work with

Huachuma soon, since he was closer to my heart.

During all these years, I had never stopped thinking of going to Mexico to look for true shamans. In fact, I did go, but wandering around the pyramids of Teotihuacán wasn't the place to meet shamans; instead I met a lot of carpet sellers. I didn't speak a word of Spanish, and looking deeper into indigenous communities spread all over Sierra Madre mountain range wasn't possible at this time. But interestingly enough, the first thoughts about making contact with Peyote came to me in Peru during a Huachuma ceremony. It wasn't so much intellectual, it was more like the feeling that now it had become possible. I thought that if I could find Huachuma, which was known even less, why couldn't I find Peyote too? I decided I would start the search immediately upon my return.

Going back to the US I remember feeling that Castaneda's world was now closer and within my reach. For many years I was wondering whether don Juan was a real person, or just a collective image of many people whom he had met on his way.

Searching for Peyote People

One night, shortly after coming back from Peru, I googled [peyote] and found a lot of information. I mostly scanned the information without reading it. Then, I found a website of the Dance of the Deer foundation with a picture of an American man together with an old Huichol Indian, don Jose Matsua, who was, I learned later, a known and respected shaman in the Sierra Madres. I contacted the foundation immediately and asked if they did Peyote ceremonies and if I could join them—something I had wanted to do for years. But their response echoed the familiar taste of disappointment in my heart. They wrote that their seminars were "drug and alcohol free." I could not believe my eyes reading this email.

"Drug free"? Why were they speaking of drugs and even worse, of alcohol? Peyote is a sacred Teacher Healer plant used in Mexico for thousands of years for healing and divination, just like the way Peyote's brother, Huachuma is used in Peru. To Mexican Indians, Peyote was always a sacred plant, divine spirit, teacher, healer and protector. So, how could someone who called and advertised himself as a Huichol shaman, speak about Peyote in this way? I am not saying that he said it personally—most likely the response came from his secretary but regardless, secretaries do not generally set policy. I sent another email asking them how they connected to the spirit without using sacred Peyote, especially since use of sacred plants is essential for spiritual communion in every indigenous shamanic culture of the world, whether in Siberia, where shamans in the past used fly agaric mushrooms, in Africa, where an Iboga bark is still used, in Peru, where shamans work with Ayahuasca in the jungle and Huachuma in the mountains, and in Mexico, the only place on Earth where Peyote grows wild.

Their response was: "through drumming and singing."

"Oh, I see," I thought. "I've been through that already and met musicians of this kind." I was aware of "shamanic workshops," where people paid money for spending few days drumming and singing and then went home with an empty heart. Of course, what changes in their lives they could expect when doing this kind of shamanic work? And since I had just come from Peru, where I had been working with real shamans and real medicinal plants, it didn't take more than two emails to disregard this website and move forward.

Immediately, I found another website: http://www.peyoteway.org. Right from the start, just looking at the homepage, it was clear that these were people who actually knew about Peyote. They spoke about the plant with great respect, as if it was the center of their work. I contacted them immediately and asked if I could come to work with the Peyote. They responded "yes" and explained the way they worked. They were up front about the membership fee, which was $50 annually and gave a person the right to work legally with Peyote on the property of their registered church. They also said there was a separate fee for the Spirit Walk, where a person was left alone with the Peyote tea and firewood to keep him warm at night. A few overnight stays were included. I appreciated the direct answers and up front disclosure of all fees. It was clear that these were real people. I made up my mind right away and decided to take a friend with me, who was the only one who understood what I had been through in Peru. At that time, he couldn't go to Peru, so I thought that taking him with me to Arizona would be great.

We flew to Phoenix, rented a car, and began driving, following the directions we had received. In about three and a half hours, we turned off the main road and drove across the desert. Both the navigation system in the car and our cell phones went dead. All we had was the dusty road in front of us and the hope that we were going in the right direction. It was getting late, and we didn't want to get stuck in the middle of the desert, spending a cold night in the car without gas to run the heating system. While thinking of that possibility, we saw a red mail box that read "Peyote way," and took a right as we had been told to do. We came to the gate, opened it up, drove onto the property, parked the car, and entered the little adobe house. We were greeted by Anne Zapf, one of the founders of the Peyote Way Church of God. We were shown our rooms. Then, we shared a cup of tea with Anne, while getting to know one another. We talked about Peyote and the fact that they had to fight in court for the right to use it for non-Indians. I thought this was a miracle, considering that Peyote is a controlled substance and is included as a Schedule 1 drug in the US. Only native Indians can use Peyote in America, but they have to be members of the Native American Church, which is protected by the constitutional right of religious freedom. Going to bed that night, I reflected on how far we have to go sometimes in life, to find the next step, and how interesting are the times in which we live, when a dream world can become a reality with just a few clicks.

Immanuel

The next day, shortly after our breakfast, we were fortunate to meet a very special man and one of the founders of the Peyote Way Church—Immanuel Trujillo, a native American, of the Apache nation, with a re-markable biography and life. At this point, I am going to borrow the biographical material on this man directly from another source—so that the facts will be here, and not just my impression. The following information was taken by permission from the Peyote Way Church of God website.

> Immanuel was born to an unwed teen mother and a WWI vet-eran Apache father, and was given up for adoption and raised as James Coyle in Phillipsburg, New Jersey. In 1942, at the age of sixteen, he ran away from home and joined the Royal Merchant Marines. In 1944, he became a British Royal Marine and fought in WWII. He suffered a traumatic brain injury from a bomb blast on the North Sea island of Helgoland, which required facial re-construction and a metal plate to replace a missing piece of skull.
>
> He transferred into the United States Army Rangers, where he served as a sergeant, training soldiers at Fort Ord, California. He discovered the crafts room in the military hospitals and began to focus his talents on artwork as a means to support himself that

would also allow for spiritual expression.

Upon his honorable discharge, Immanuel followed a lead in his father's will to find an uncle and two of his father's closest friends in the Southwest. His father's friends gave him his father's Peyote medicine box and encouraged him to join the Native American Church.

Immanuel served as an officer within the Native American Church for ten years. He was tried and acquitted in Denver in 1966 for possession of the Holy Sacrament Peyote, a controlled substance. Legalizing all-race Peyotism became his life work. In the early 1970's he signed a purchase agreement with two other couples on the Peaceful Valley Ranch, 160 acres of sacred land in the Aravaipa Valley, and founded the Church of Holy Light. He spent the next eight years conducting a drug rehabilitation pro-gram and securing the property for his vision of a Peyote-cen-tered church. In 1978 he co-founded the Peyote Way Church of God with Rev. Anne Zapf and Rabbi Matthew S. Kent, and the three spent the next 15 years paying off the land and practicing the bona fide religious use of Peyote. Since his sailor years, he had been known as "Mana." He founded "Mana Pottery," which was later incorporated in 1984 to allow this cottage industry to survive him.

In 1986, Immanuel was again arrested in Globe, Arizona— charged with unlawful possession of Peyote—but again acquitted. Immanuel's constant refrain immortalized as Article of Faith #1 is "Peyote is a sacrament for all—no one church, race or govern-ment can 'own' it."

In 1994, his Peyote Way pottery was placed in the permanent col-lection at the Smithsonian Museum of the American Indian.

That morning, he came out to greet us, while connected to the oxygen containers via plastic tubes, which supported his life. As we later learned from Annie, he was not getting out usually to greet people, since his health condition was not allowing it. For us he made an ex-ception and an extra effort, possibly because we were the first Russian guests and members in the Peyote Church, with whom he wanted very much to talk. He greeted us with a clear look and soft smile. He welcomed us and asked what had brought us to this place. I said that I was hearing a Peyote call in my heart for many years, but never knew where to find it until I found their website. We talked about different things, among them, I mentioned that as much as Peyote was calling me all those years, at the same time it was also frightening me. Even though my fear was unable to keep me from coming closer, it had not left me alone and still was present inside, pushing me back from moving forward.

Immanuel looked quietly off into the horizon and asked us to excuse him for a moment. He went to his room and came back with something wrapped in the cloth. Slowly unwrapping it, he began to show us his medals, which he received during the Second World War. He looked into my eyes and said: "This is scary," emphasizing the first word. In his simple sentence I felt so much truth that I became silent and just kept looking at his medals. His message was clear and powerful, and has since been one of the most important guides on my Path.

This was my only conversation with Immanuel, a truly remarkable man and a teacher. He passed away shortly after that, leaving behind him a very bright memory.

Path

First Peyote Meeting

 Following years of working with peyote, the founders of the Peyote Way church came to the realization that it was better to leave people alone with the spirit while providing them with all they needed to spend the night alone. The church land had 160 acres on which there were only two houses and a greenhouse where Peyote grew. In one house, Anne and Matthew lived, and the second house was for visitors who were coming for a Spirit walk.

Immanuel, the founder of the church, about whom I wrote in the previous chapter, lived in this house as well. Anne gave the visitors a brewed peyote tea while Matthew provided firewood, bringing it to the place of the visitor's choice to keep them warm at night. After that, the Spirit walkers were left alone. I was struck by such a method, because in Peru, all ceremonies were led by a shaman from beginning to end. Here, it was quite different. There was not anyone to rely on, except yourself. I felt great confidence and trust which Anne and Matthew were giving to

Peyote and the people. We went to bed with a high expectation of tomorrow.

In the morning we had a light breakfast. The ceremony was scheduled for that evening, after sunset. We spent all day in conversation, exploring the territory of the church, accompanied by three friendly dogs. Quite quickly we found a place with views of the low mountains.

Matthew brought us firewood, and then we talked with him about peyote. He calmed my growing anticipation of the night.

It was late evening when Anne gave each of us a glass container with the tea, smiled and wished us a good night. We went to our places. I set an altar and dug a hole in the ground for a campfire.

It is common to see the desert full of rattlesnakes and poisonous scorpions, and Aravaipa Valley wasn't an exception. We were supposed to sit all night on the ground, so for safety reasons, I put protection around our space as I was taught to do in Peru. With the advent of darkness, I lit a fire, we sat down around it and began to mentally express our intention to the opened jar of peyote. The tea had a pleasant earthy smell, reminding me of something from a distant childhood. We started to drink in small sips, as advised by Anne. To my surprise, after the first few sips, I felt some kind of overwhelming fear and could not continue, while my friend had already drunk the first half. As time went on, night sank into silence. This was my first night in the desert. The shining stars were stunning. I start to feel a warm feeling in my heart. Peyote was slowly revealing itself. We both put on headphones and started listening to music each of us had brought. I was listening to my favorite, *Dead Can Dance*. The fire became alive, and the crackling firewood began to tell stories. I found myself beginning to think about many things very clearly. It was easy to sit by the fire without talking throughout the night. But my clear thinking was periodically interrupted by a painful feeling of fear, which stopped me from drinking more. I tried to understand why. Indeed, in the Peruvian jungle, I had gone through worse. Why now, could I not transcend this inexplicable fear?

These worrisome thoughts distracted me from fully engaging in the magical desert night, sitting under the breathing and dancing starts. It came to me that we commonly think we are looking up when we are watching the sky, and that it might be a misconception we have had since childhood. This "watching up" could also be a "watching down" or "into the side" of our Galaxy. In fact, we live in a vast space we call the Universe, where ups and downs are just the references we use here on Earth, and which actually become illusive in open, limitless space. For us it always feels like we are looking up—probably because we not aware of the rotation of our planet as we rotate with it. But, this night, within Peyote's light, I could actually feel this planetary movement on a massive scale. Following on those thoughts, I have begun to feel our solar system as a giant cosmic organism with its cycles, and to feel the magnitude of our sun in its center—which before only seemed a speck of light in the Milky Way, the Galaxy in which we live. I felt that if I could focus longer in that direction, I could understand something very important about the ways of the Universe, which was incomprehensible in normal states of consciousness. Who can really tell what's up and what is down in the Universe? Where is its beginning and its end? It is like when we think the Sun is rising above the horizon in the morning—which is in fact an illusion created by the movement of the Earth. My thoughts about all of this were entertaining and took me far beyond my fear, which was only evident when I paid attention to it. Thinking even deeper, I began to feel the gravity of our planet in a physical way—as never before. After all, riding on a planet is like on a cosmic horse; it felt good to be so tied to Mother Earth. If ups and downs were only terms used on Earth, they were related to the "here and now" (on this planet at this time), and to our daily lives—a subject which now felt important to penetrate with further thinking.

I didn't finish my tea, and what I had left—about half—I gave to my friend. I had taken enough for the first meeting. We waited for the sunrise, both amazed and happy even though my fear that night had given me some discomfort.

We returned to the church, went into the studio, and met Anne and Matthew. They were making pottery, cups, plates, jugs, on which they were depicting their Peyote visions. It was their business, giving them a means to live. They explained that this allowed them to not sell Peyote and work with it cleanly. Even though we paid a reasonable fee for Peyote tea and a three or four day stay at the church, the concept was clear. I told them that I had an overwhelming fear, which did not allow me to dive deeper. Matthew smiled and explained that the fear would step back at the right time. All day we rested, slept, and the next morning, after saying good-bye, we left with a feeling of warmth and lightness within. On the way to the Phoenix airport, we shared our experiences.

Second Visit to Arizona

Back home in California, I was confident that I had come across the right people, but a feeling of incompleteness was haunting me. Then, I remembered the words of Howard, who had told me about this back in Peru. Now I understood his warning better because I could actually feel it. Reflecting on that Peyote night, I began to feel that my trip was more for my friend than for myself. After all, his night was unforgettable. He had realized some important things for himself, and said that now he would not live as he had lived before. Most of all, he was struck by the simplicity of being present in the moment. Many books have been written on that subject, but printed words are one thing, and a personal experience is quite another. Also, during that night, he gained a new understanding of biblical scenes, and he gladly shared his thoughts on the matter. We decided to go there again in a few months.

Our second visit to Arizona was different. The relationship with Anne, Matthew, and with Peyote had become much warmer. We drank at the same place as the first time. The night was cold, but the fire warmed the body, and peyote warmed the heart. This time, we talked a lot about everything. I talked about my trips to Peru, understanding more about them while sharing. I told my friend that besides the fact that I had found real shamans there, I felt that a part of my heart had remained there forever. By that time it had been almost a year since leaving the

Fellowship cult, to which my friend was still connected. I told him how hard it had been to leave, to go through a divorce, to be alone in a foreign country and shared with him how, in the jungle, I had been purging my cult life out of my bones. During our conversation, more things cleared up for me. The more I poured out my soul, the more I understood it.

My friend shared with me his discoveries, which impressed him with their simplicity. He said that the truth was simple, which is why it gets overlooked by the complicated Western mind.

The night stayed cold, but we sat around the fire talking about different things. The feeling of fear was still present, but I tried not to think about it because I did not want to waste the valuable time I was having with sacred Peyote. Our second visit penetrated into our hearts more deeply, and while my friend thanked me, I was grateful to fate.

A few months later, I returned to Peru to work with Huachuma, who continued to overwhelm me, showing me an infinite depth and a heightened level of comprehension. Each ceremony was becoming a new adventure into the spiritual realm. That state of consciousness—when you are fully aware of yourself and the world you live in, free in your spirit, merged into one with the Nature—was not the end result of grueling spiritual work, but only a beginning, a welcome note. Each ceremony brings awakening to the heart and clarity to the mind. In this altered state of consciousness, I perceived my life as a precious gift and a miracle that I was fortunate to experience. All this caused many tears of gratitude and a strong desire to live life properly, since this I now felt was my duty. During that trip to Peru, I tried to understand the nature of the fear which had followed me to Arizona, and the only answer I got was that I had to go there yet again. I decided to make a third trip to Arizona.

A Saving Fire In Arizona

It was September 2007, when for the third time, my friend and I went to Arizona, with three other friends, who were still cult members. That trip was a fate-changer for my friend.

Again, he and I drank together, while the rest were scattered around in different places. My friend drank a whole jar almost immediately, and I took only half. We would talk for a while, then get silent, and then speak again. During our dialogs, I noticed that a certain drama was unfolding in him. I realized that all three trips to Arizona were mostly for him. My experiences with other sacred teacher-healer plants were helping him to understand himself better. At one point during that night, he said that he had nowhere to escape. I responded immediately saying that there is never anywhere to escape, and if there were any place to go, everybody would be running there. My words were followed by our belly laughs, both thinking of Peyote's sense of humor.

We were having fun until he suddenly realized that he was wearing a sweater given to him by the Teacher (leader of my former cult), which he had bought in Beverly Hills for $800. Looking closely at my friend, I saw on him a shapeless blob of energy with energetic threads coming from it. These threads represented the Teacher's intention when he gave my friend this sweater. They were actually ties that held him in the cult. This was an amazing vision of an intention manifest on the level of energy.

In that same instant, I had a memory of all those people, the Teacher's entourage, who had silky clothing and gold chains, gifted to them by the Teacher, gifts that were actually energetic shackles holding them in the cult. These shiny objects were actually quite dark, because they were never given to people out of love. All this schlock had been purchased by the Teacher in the expensive stores of Beverly Hills with the money that his students were paying, raising and donating to him for the so-called "big fortune" which allowed them to be in the range of a "conscious being" (our Teacher). Unfortunately, he was wasting contributions and donations for the infinite satisfaction of his vile desires. Seeing all that in the moment, I suggested that my friend burn the sweater in the fire. He paused for a moment, probably thinking about the cost of the thing, then took it off and threw it in the fire.

Right after that, a terrible stench arose. We both had to plug our noses. As this thing was melting in the fire, it was shaping into a skull with crossed bones on it. My friend took a stick and began to smash the sweater deeper into the fire. I did not know what he was thinking at the moment, but I had a picture in my head about the collapse of the entire cult. Back at this time, the teacher's authority was still unshakable, and the cult had existed for over 30 years, so no one could have imagined the collapse of such a well-functioning money-making mechanism.

The stench became unbearable, so we moved away from the fire, sat down and shared our thoughts about it. I told my friend that I had seen the collapse of the cult and that soon people would start leaving it in waves. He nodded his head, probably seeing the same thing. In the morning, when we were all gathered together in the house, our other friends asked us about the stinking thing we had burned last night. My friend replied that it was a sweater given to him by the teacher, which they did not seem to believe, shaking their heads in surprise.

In California, my friend did not return to his home. He remained in my house and began to implement the vision he had in Arizona, at the same time taking actions to ensure his legal defense. His sudden disappearance from the cult was quite shocking to many people, since he and his wife were both well-known and respected musicians. They played violin on a daily basis at the Teacher's events, which were recorded and shown later for a fee. His departure from the cult had shaken many members and left them to wonder. People were perplexed, and as we later learned, had talked about it for a whole month. The only thing some people knew was that he and I had gone to Arizona to do something and then that he had disappeared. He stayed at my place for a while, then rented a room somewhere and did what he truly wanted to do. I'll leave out the details of what happened next, because it's part of his personal life. I will say only that after six weeks of drama, his life began to change for the better, all aspects of his life, including the previously deteriorating relationship with his wife, which had been severely damaged by life in cult.

During his departure from the cult, he found a good immigration lawyer who made sure he and his family would not be affected by threats and efforts to disrupt the immigration process. By the time the Teacher's lawyer contacted his lawyer, it was too late, and my friend already had a strong defense. Soon after that, he and his family moved to Sacramento. There they started making professional connections in the musical world, which turned into permanent work in a few orchestras and finding many students who took private lessons with them.

Not much later, we learned that in October, a month after our last trip to Arizona, a group of six people, who had spent over 20 years in the cult, had left. Some were part of the administration. It was a shock to everyone except us—as we had seen it coming in Arizona. At the last ceremony, speaking of the school, we both had "seen" the teacher as a little dwarf appearing to be large, behind a curtain in a theater of shadows. This scene had been funny and sad at the same time. The big, scary, and "enlightened" teacher had appeared in the Peyote light as merely a malicious goblin!

Soon after that first group of six left the cult, waves of resignation in the membership followed, totaling about 700 people during the first year—most of whom left from Apollo. The truth about the teacher flowed everywhere. People were openly sharing their experiences on internet sites created by former students. All the administration's efforts to block the flow of information ended in complete failure. People were talking, telling the truth, and helping others to wake up.

It was interesting to watch the students, who just a few years back, had been telling me that the reason for my disagreement with the "doctrine" and the teacher was within me and that I needed to give more time to the school and to work harder on myself. Some were ashamed of themselves, and avoided contact with me, others, who were more courageous and sincere, asked for forgiveness. I respected these people, and forgave them the past.

The first year after their departure, former students had begun to gather together to share their experiences. It was a great advancement, since in the earlier years, as the students had left, they lived in silence, simply disappearing, fearing retribution. I supported this ex-student movement thru the first year or two. Then, when their social lives got back on track, and they gradually began to realize that their lives had not ended, but had just begun, I went in my own direction, engaging in my life.

That last night in Arizona, toward the morning, as my friend had lain exhausted by the fire, I mentally thanked the Peyote for everything and asked him to help me find other Peyoteros with whom together I could go deeper into the Peyote realm. Apparently at this time I was not mature enough to fully benefit from the way in which the Peyote Way Church had worked so successfully with the medicine.

I Have Been Heard

It was early January when I went to a Chinese restaurant to have a meal, something I rarely did. After dinner, I asked the waiter for the check. He brought it on a small tray, which held a fortune cookie, usually served as a dessert in Chinese restaurants in the United States. The cookie contains a piece of paper with phrases and numbers. Breaking the cookie in half, I took the piece of paper out and saw the following: "Listen to your friends with ear to future." I read the words and wondered who could say something that important to me? Was it real that I was given a message written on a fortune cookie in a restaurant I don't usually go to? What were the chances of me being there at this time? To believe that some higher forces were talking to me in this way would be equal to believing that I could win the lottery without ever buying a ticket. And yet, while rationally thinking of the absurdity of that, those words left a trace of anticipation in my mind.

A week later, January 12, 2008, I received a message from Anne. She told me that their old Peyote friend, whom they known since the 70s and had not been in touch with for many years, had written her, telling her that he was now living in Mexico with the indigenous tribe of Huichol Indians. As I learned later from Anne, I was the only one of more than 500 members of her peyote church to whom she had forwarded his e-mail address. Years later, when I asked her why I was the one, she said that the Peyote chose me.

I immediately wrote a letter to Anne's friend and asked him if he worked with the plant and if I could come to work with him. He spoke about the Peyote with love and great respect, said that he had worked with it for 40 years, and would be glad to meet me. I was thrilled. Was I really heard back then in Arizona, when I asked to meet Peyote people with whom I could share this sacred medicine? I was overwhelmed with emotion, knowing without a doubt that my lifelong dream was becoming a reality. Two weeks later, I flew to Mexico for the first time. Since I didn't speak Spanish, I asked my new friend if he could meet me in the airport in Puerto Vallarta. He agreed and met me there with his wife dona Maria, the granddaughter of the don Jose Matsua, the legendary Huaichol Peyotero, known and respected in many parts of the Sierra Madre. Upon learning this connection, I again wondered whether this don Jose Matsua might be the one mentioned as don Juan Matus, in the Castaneda writings? The initials matched, but the rest remained to be found out.

Rattlesnake

The man who waited for me in Mexico, Eldon, was one of the most interesting people I had ever met. In shamanic circles, he was known by the name "Rattlesnake," which was given to him after his shamanic initiation during which he was bitten by a rattlesnake. The life experiences of this man were rich, but he usually answered my questions concerning his past reluctantly. Although I still don't have a full picture of his life, there are things I can share about him without infringing on his privacy.

Rattlesnake had his first Peyote at 16 years of age, with a North American Indian. This encounter with peyote gave him direction for the rest of his life. I feel I must say here, that the premise that all Native Americans are carriers of knowledge is a myth. Many of them are suffering from alcoholism and have no apparent connection with the sacred Path of their ancestors. But, among them were and are people who are true carriers of knowledge. One of them was Immanuel, founder of the Peyote Way Church of God, of whom I spoke earlier. As it turned out, Rattlesnake knew and respected Immanuel for who he was. The circle of people like him is small, however, and getting into it is only possible by the will of fate. Another man of knowledge was an Indian by the name Kingfisher. Rattlesnake always spoke of him with great respect, and was convinced that he was one of those people who could change your life if you were fortunate enough to meet him.

The biography of Rattlesnake is impressive. He served in Vietnam and Panama, was sent to Alaska, then back to North America where he worked with Peyote for 30 years, 10 of which he served as a road man, a title given to a leader of the Peyote ceremony in the Native American churche. Now, for the last 10 years, he had been living in Mexico with the family of don Jose Matsua. He married don Jose's granddaughter, a Huichol Peyotera named dona Maria. How he came across these people, I do not know—possibly the same way I found him.

When Rattlesnake and his wife, dona Maria greeted me at the airport in Puerto Vallarta, we exchanged a friendly handshake and a hug, then went to the station to wait for the bus to Tepic. After 4 hours, we arrived in the capital of the state of Nayarit. They were renting a small apartment there, spending a few days during the week when coming to town to buy provisions to carry back to the Huichol village where they permanently lived.

Here, in Nayarit, they had the Internet, thanks to which we had talked previously. However, mostly they spent time in their village in the foothills of the Sierra Madre, an hour's drive away from the city. It didn't take much before we talked about Peyote and our coming work. Dona Maria didn't participate in our conversations, since she didn't speak any English. She only smiled and did some work in the kitchen preparing the traditional blue corn tortillas to wrap up our meal. With Eldon, I spoke English in which I was fairly fluent. I thought, "At least I did something useful while living in the States. I learned English."

We talked all day, and the next morning we rode to the ranch, as he called it. When our ride arrived, I wasn't feeling much excitement. It was an old truck full of Mexican Indians in the back, which was already pretty crowded. I was invited to join them. My expectation for a pleasant trip melted right from the start. I climbed into the truck and greeted the others. They greeted me, nodding their heads, looking at me with appraisal, and with some surprise. I obviously did not fit into their world. The mountain road was beautiful, and we were surrounded by green hills and peaks of the Sierra Madre range. I rode standing up,

observing the stunning views. The truck took a turn off the road, going over bumps and holes.

We arrived at a typical Mexican slum. I saw adobe houses with thatched roofs, chickens, geese, donkeys, and pigs running around. On one hand, I felt the authenticity of the place, and on the other, I had been spoiled by the benefits of civilization, I was worried about whether I would find at least some comfort here. My worst fears were confirmed soon; it turned out that the common way to bathe was in the river. I was supposed to sleep outside in the tent, which I had taken with me, and was given a thin mat to sleep on. Waking up the next morning, I felt completely shattered—with a stiff back. I wasn't very excited to think that I would be sleeping a whole week like this.

After a meal, I took the soap and a towel and went to bathe in the river. Actually, I had a very pleasant time. I was alone there, a naked gringo. The water was warm, and I didn't want to get out. It was a small river,

around 30 feet wide and about 3 feet deep, and was surrounded by green trees and bushes. I stayed until sunset. The ceremony was set to begin at dusk, so I had time still for a cup of coffee. Bathing in the river was comforting and helped me focus on the upcoming ceremony.

While sitting outside on plastic chairs, drinking coffee, I asked Eldon about who was who in the village. Accepted polygamy made the answers somewhat complicated. Yet, I managed to find out that his wife, dona Maria, was the granddaughter of don Jose Matsua, and that don Rufino and don Catarino, two Huichol shamans, were her uncles. As was explained, the Indians were allowed to have as many wives as they could support, which I thought was quite fair, even though very different from our western views. The fact is that in the western world, quite often, relationships between people often resemble the relationships between street animals who, after meeting, forget about one another. And it has gotten so bad in the US, that family law was created to obligate the men for child support. Well, these people did not need to have a law, they simply had morals.

Don Rufino, an 80-year-old Huichol Peyotero, had sympathy for me from the start and had attended our first welcoming ceremony, staying on the periphery. Despite his age, he worked from morning until night with his wife on his plantation of hibiscus and corn.

Don Catarino, also an 80-year-old Peyotero, on the contrary, had been a constant guest in our company, even though he lived in another village two days walking distance away. I felt like he was coming to the ceremonies to support me. The first ceremony was attended by don Rufino and his wife, don Catarino and his wife, dona Maria, and Eldon. Their presence was a gesture of their greeting and blessing.

Thank You for Having Me Here

Eldon told me to choose the place for the ceremony and to bring fire-wood, mats and blankets. I went downhill, walked around and quickly found a place where it felt good to be. As it grew dark, Eldon asked me to start the fire. He arrived, sat near the fire, poured water into his

drum, and began to pull on its deer skin. He said he had been inseparable from this drum for 40 years. He then laid the other ritual artifacts
around.

Dona Maria brought a bucket, picked up a stick from the ground,
slipped it into a glass cup, and put that on the bucket. Don Catarino
and his wife sat on my right, next to don Rufino, with his wife near
them; then came Eldon with Maria and myself. At first I thought there
was water in the bucket to be used for a certain purification ritual before the ceremony.

 But, it soon became clear that Peyote was in
the bucket, not water. I had a sudden mem-
ory from childhood when my mother used
to soak our clothes in similar buckets before washing them. That memory was followed by the idea that there might be too
much peyote here for seven people—but I discarded this thought right
away.

It turned completely dark. The fire crackled as everyone sat in silence. I
was nervous. Eldon went through his medicinal bag, took out a handful
of cedar and threw it into the fire, and with hawk feathers skillfully tied
to a wooden stick, dispersed smoke from the burning herbs.

Then, for opening the ceremony, he sang the first song. While he was
singing, I was thinking: "Is this really happening? I'm in Mexico right
now, sitting in a circle of Huichol shamans, with a bucket full of Peyote!
How did I get here? How many millions of people around the world
have read Castaneda's writings and how few of them have actually been
here, especially Russians? "

My thoughts were interrupted by a full cup of Peyote given to me by Eldon. I took it in my hands and began expressing my intention into the cup, trying to list all my questions with which I came. But, at that moment, I realized that the most important action was to simply express my gratitude and thank Peyote for having me there. Little did I know that this first cup of medicine was just a beginning, and that every other song was accompanied by another one.

Somewhere around midnight, I felt like time had stopped. A little later, I felt like time had started moving backwards, creating a feeling inside that this night would never end.

As the medicine unfolded, it brought with it bliss, crystal clarity to my mind, and deep inner peace and love to my heart. It was the same state that I experienced in Arizona, but with more force, since I could now drink more. As the ceremony continued, I was trying to think about all those questions I had in my mind, without noticing that I was slowly being immersed into a world of absolute magic, which could not possibly be described in worlds, but surely could be experienced.

I looked at the sky above. The stars were hanging like ripe fruits, asking to be harvested with my mind. Looking up, I thought it well could be that in the universe, there is as much light as darkness—a cosmic balance, so to speak.

Listening to the crackling wood, I thought about my earlier trip to Mexico a year before. There, I visited the pyramids in Teotihuacan, presumably related to the ancient Olmec culture, looking for the shamans and Peyote. But instead, I only met carpet dealers. Thinking of this event and remembering those impressive pyramids, I felt like I was going back in time and was now sitting with the Aztecs, sharing sacred Peyote around the fire. I looked around at their faces, which were very calm as they looked into the fire. I could feel their hearts and their longing for their roots in their distant ancestry. This feeling was painful, knowing all I knew about the conquest of this ancient culture, which was brutally destroyed by Spaniards 500 years ago. But, how could such a strong and honorable people fall to barbarians, coming from the old world and motivated by their greed?

I began to feel sleepy as I thought about this. I added more wood to the fire and lay down. I was warm and cozy. I had already started to fall asleep, when someone from the group released a melodic fart, followed by laughter. I was embarrassed and did not dare to open my eyes, pretending to be asleep. More farts followed with more laughter. I remembered how I imagined this ceremony was going to be on my way to Mexico. I had thought that wisdom would descend upon me, filling me with knowledge; but instead, old people's farts and laughter reached my ears. The contrast was such that I exploded with a cracking laughter, thinking about the simplicity of life.

Laughing hard, I didn't notice how differently I could now perceive the world. I was "seeing" it all at once, watching how slowly my mind was trying to catch up. Peyote taught me a new way of thinking through a certain visual perception of the world as it really is. This new communion with nature was exciting with its sharpness, speed and ease. "What an experience!" I thought at the time.

Then, I remembered a lot of the debate about the so called modern healing and teaching practices, which are for sale in the spiritual markets, flooded with new age psychics, healers and teachers, who are always ready for a payment to "seal" imaginary holes in one's energetic field, while mysteriously moving their hands over them (sometime even touching). These movements remind me of a search for the light switch in a dark room. Intellectual windbags, a.k.a. new age teachers, appeared in the same light, tirelessly juggling esoteric ideas while enjoying their status and admiration from those who they "teach," instead of together searching for answers. What a world we live in, where the blind heal the blind and the deaf teach the deaf. Now sadly, I thought about how people are profoundly mistaken, and how desperately they are clinging to their illusions, because they are not willing to sacrifice their fear for the sake of real healing and knowledge accessible through medicinal plants.

In ancient times this was how people cured themselves, drawing force from nature, which in modern times is forbidden. Back in those days, a ban of using plants for healing would be just as ridiculous as a ban to breath in air in the world of today.

The time was early morning, before sunrise, when silence was disturbed by the plaintive cry of a donkey, in which I felt the expression of the pain and suffering of his fate. He was joined by other donkeys. Their moaning was about their shared slavery, which was devoid of love. Then, I made myself a promise that if I ever had the conditions under which I maintained a donkey, I would have him simply live, without ever working. Thoughts about the donkey drifted into thinking about the people who ruthlessly treat their fellow human beings like donkeys, forcing them to work, leaving them exhausted in the night, alone with their own pain.

A fire was already smoking and we were resting quietly, waiting for the coming sun. As dawn broke, don Rufino and his wife left. Don Catarino, Eldon and I went up to the house to drink a cup of freshly brewed coffee prepared by dona Maria. When it became warmer, I went swimming in the river where I spent almost all day, reflecting on the night before.

Other Dreams

The ceremonies that followed were more profoundly immersed in the way of Huichol Indians and Peyote. During the ceremonies, usually in early mornings, when the magic of the night feels most powerful, we talked with Eldon about life and many other things. Once, during one of these talks, he told me that my real reason for coming was to find out whether the Peyote tradition of Mexico was real. I was shocked by such a penetrating vision. It was true. Behind all my questions, thoughts and feelings, was an intention that I couldn't formulate in simple words. I had come to Mexico to do precisely that.

Between my trips, I noticed how my dreams had begun to change. Back in my youth I thought about how much time we spent sleeping at nights, letting our lives pass in unconscious dreams. I then thought about the possibility of lucid dreaming, without wasting our lives in them. But my efforts were in vain, gradually extinguishing my desire. The ninth book of Castaneda, *The Art of Dreaming*, which I had read 16 years prior to coming to Mexico, aroused my interest in lucid dreams again. I remember trying to see my hands in my sleep, and the disappointment with which I woke up in the morning from getting no results.

But my dreams began to change by themselves between my journeys to Mexico. I was having dreams in which I was aware that I was sleeping. Therefore, even in a nightmare where I raced a car off a cliff, I was not afraid of my death, because I knew that when the car flew off the cliff, I would just wake up at home. Sometimes, I had a belly laugh during my lucid dreams, realizing their absurdity. Other times, I had dreams in which I ran across the field with my German Shepherd Alpha—to whom I will devote a separate chapter. I always tried to make those particular dreams last a little longer, knowing that in the morning she wouldn't be near.

The level of awareness in my dreams was not constant. Sometimes during a dream, I believed it was real. Afterwards, I would wake up noticeably excited and pleased that it was only a dream. Overall, I started to pay more attention to my dreams. The difference before and after participating in Peyote ceremonies was obvious. I tried to find a practical application for this new awareness.

Once, in Mexico during a ceremony, I plunged into an unusual dream. I lay down by the fire, hearing the crackling of wood and the quiet conversation between Eldon and don Catarino. I felt the pleasant warmth from the fire. But at the same time, I was sleeping and seeing a dream in which some people were arguing among themselves. I silently participated in their conversation, drawing for myself conclusions, after which I would awaken. This dream was surprising with its liveliness. I thought that I had unwittingly entered into someone's life, without getting noticed.

I thought that if I had dreamed that during the Peyote ceremony, it must have been an important dream. Trying to find the meaning in it, I suddenly realized that nothing in the dream, the people, or the conversation, was of any importance at all. What was important was my reaction to it, my feelings and thoughts that were reflected by my subconscious mind—which, thanks to Peyote, was aware of itself in the dream—allowing me to register my reaction to what I saw in my dream. This dream awareness felt as being of great importance. Carl Jung, a Swiss psychiatrist and founder of analytic psychology, argued that the unconscious mind of man sees correctly even when the conscious mind is blind and helpless. I felt there was a truth to it.

I was pleased to find a practical use for lucid dreaming. But thinking more about it, I realized that dream interpretation which nowadays is offered in books is useless, since at the very best they could only have a meaning to the person dreaming them. To try to fit a personal interpretation onto other people's dreams seemed meaningless.

After this ceremony, I waited every day for the night. I continued to have dreams in which I was aware of myself sleeping, and tried to remember the emotions and thoughts about what was happening in these dreams in order to understand myself better.

As a child I often flew in my dreams, but I always fell down after a short spurt of enjoyable flight. These crashes always brought disappointment. But after working with Peyote, I began to fly again, and now, I could consciously and willfully maintain it. These dreams did not bear in themselves any new knowledge, but brought me more of the joy of flights.

Mexican shamans say that in their dreams, they can call the spirits of the dead and consult with them. I wonder now why I never asked them more about it. This seemed to be a doorway to another room if consciously approached. But, even though I saw in it potential for healing and understanding of one's self, I got quite tired of this constant nightly mind activity and began to prefer a good rest over mental work at nights. Often in my dreams, I was leaving America and going back to Israel, then from Israel back to the States, then going somewhere else again. These dreams tormented me with a sense of emotional discomfort. The stress of immigration was playing a part in it, and even though in daily life I was somewhat adapted to new changes, inside there still were bleeding scars, which on a subconscious level, I could see and feel in my dreams.

While still living in Israel, about once a month, I visited my parents and my friends coming to them from Tel Aviv. But after spending the weekend with them, I always felt some sadness in my heart, since no one was truly waiting for me back in Tel Aviv. This same sadness was present in my dreams. It was only later, after I had moved to Peru, that I had a similar dream in which I was going somewhere again, and I felt at ease realizing I was going to Peru and was awaited there by someone. Then I knew that things had truly changed for me.

Alpha

Once I was asked if I wanted to have a dog? I said yes. The next day, the person brought a German Shepherd who leapt from the car and immediately rushed toward me, jumping up and licking my face, as if we had just reunited after a long separation. Her name was Alpha, and she was about a year old. As a sign of respect for her, I decided not to change her name. She was very thin, looked exhausted, and was limping on her back leg. I had the feeling that the owner had decided to get rid of her. I immediately liked her playfulness and friendliness. I took her home and called my vet to whom I was periodically taking my cats. I wanted him to check her to see if any treatment was needed because she didn't seem to be in good shape.

I got an appointment for five days later, but on the day of the appointment, Alfa broke that very leg she had been limping on by jumping out of the truck in which I was taking her to the vet. Now the visit was no longer just for the check up, but for an x-ray as well. The vet said that surgery was needed and a surgeon would have to be called from San

Francisco. He also said that it would cost me $3,000.00 dollars. I agreed immediately, wondering where to get the money. They said that I should leave her for the night in the clinic so they could prepare her for surgery the following day. The surgery went well, and I took her home with a metal pin in her paw. I became her nurse for the next 3 months; cleaning up her ears, giving drops, making sure she didn't lick the paw, and tending to a special plastic collar around her neck. A few months later the metal pin was removed from her paw and Alpha started to recover. Every day I took her for a walk, which she liked very much. We walked around without the collar because she did not like it, and I respected her free spirit even though I understood that it could be dangerous.

When I took her to play with other dogs in the park, I felt that other dog owners didn't like us, possibly out of jealousy because she was the most beautiful dog out there and also for the bond we had with each other; which was more like a bond between two humans. Some people asked if she was a fox, others thought she was mixed with a wolf. I didn't care about her ancestry or whether she was pure bred or mixed. I just loved her and called her "my wolf." She wouldn't let me touch the other dogs. If they approached me, she growled and bared her teeth.

Her love for me taught me patience and forgiveness, even though I often screamed at her after coming home to find shredded shoes or a torn-up water hose in the yard. Once I even spanked her with the collar, and for few days, kept her in the garage without letting her in the house. That was punishment for shredding into pieces a very important artifact given to me in Peru by a shaman. Afterward, I could not forgive myself for being so harsh with her, since she always forgave me right away.

She whined when I went to work in the mornings. When I came home, she jumped around and peed on the floor from excitement. I really missed her when I had to leave, so I hired a dog sitter who stayed days and nights in my house, feeding her and taking her for walks. Once, I even came back from Arizona a day earlier than planned, driving for about 18 hours without rest, after a Peyote night, because I missed her so much.

She was growing strong as time passed by. I was living alone then with her and two cats. I was divorced already. I had been her owner for about a year when one day we went on our usual walk. We walked for a long time. Around 7 pm, while looking at the rising moon, I realized that Alpha had not been with me for a while. I went looking for her, calling her name. As I was walking, my neighbors drove their car past me and they looked at me somewhat strangely. They knew me, and had seen Alpha and me often on the streets. I came home, took the key to the car, and drove around the neighborhood to look for her. I spent a few hours looking, stopping in different places where she liked to be the most. She was not there. I came home around midnight feeling chilly in my heart. I took a hot shower to relax, but couldn't sleep. Every now and then, I got up to see if she was waiting by the door. She was not.

The next morning I took her picture and went out into the neighborhood. The first thing I did was to go to the neighbor's house, whom I had seen driving by me the night before. I knocked on the door, and a woman opened. I didn't even need to ask, seeing her backing up a bit and closing her mouth with her hand. I only asked her: "Where?" She said at the traffic light. I went there and found a puddle of blood. I knew it was Alpha's. I began to look for her in dog morgues. She was not in any of them. Arriving at the last of them, I gave a description of her and the place and approximate time of the accident. The girl said that yesterday, about seven in the evening, they had received a call telling of a German Shepherd that had been hit at that location. She asked me if I wanted to identify her. With fear and pain, I agreed to see her. I already knew it was her, but still, I was hoping for a miracle. We walked inside the yard and from afar I recognized the tip of her tail and paws, lying on a cart, covered by a sheet. Removing the sheet was so painful; I sat down on the ground in tears.

I decided to cremate her and keep her ashes with me. I said that I would come back tomorrow to pick her up. The next day I called my friend who was coming with me to Arizona and asked for help because I couldn't drive that day. He came and picked me up, and we went to the morgue where I received her frozen body in a black bag. I gently put it in the trunk and asked my friend to drive to the mountains, in the direction of Lake Tahoe.

Turning off the highway, we drove uphill. I asked him to stop the car and wait for me. I got out and took the bag out of his trunk. Then, I went a little farther to find a level spot. I unwrapped her and put her on a sheet, which I had taken from the house. We sat together on the snow. With tears in my eyes, I washed her and blew herbal smoke over her, removing her fear and pain before her death. Pictures of our time spent together swam before my eyes. After a while, I wrapped her in the sheet and carried her back to the car. I was so exhausted that I fell on my knees and called my friend to help. Together, we put her in the trunk and drove to the crematorium. Parting with her there was extremely hard. My friend patiently waited outside. I was told that they would call me when I could pick up the ashes. Those were agonizing days as I waited to bring them home.

This all happened in February 2008, 9 months before I was to meet my own death in Mexico.

The following year was so difficult; I missed her greatly. I couldn't even look at pictures of her for about two years, and even then, only for a very short time.

Asking for Advice

This photo (taken with a poor camera) is very special to me. I have chosen to include it here in spite of it's quality level.

My last visit to Mexico surpassed by far any expectation I could have had. In fact, if I had any idea what was waiting for me there, I honestly don't know whether I would have gone. I had two things in mind this time. First, I wanted to get rid of my addiction to smoking, which after 10 years of abstinence, I had begun again following the dramatic death of my dog. And the second concerned a difficult relationship I had begun not long prior to my last visit to Mexico. We had a passionate affair with true feelings for each other, but we had also a problem that had no solution that did not leave me feeling compromised. This problem grew into heavy tension, which we seemed to release only temporarily through having sex.

The cause of this tension was my deep interest in shamanism and related work with sacred plants, a subject of no interest and viewed actually negatively by her as well. She was studying to become a doctor; and it would seem that we shouldn't have had so much controversy, since we both were motivated by service for people. But it only appeared that way. In fact, alternative ways of healing have long been unacceptable by the medical establishment, and she was no exception. One day, while having dinner, I shared my experiences in Mexico and Peru with her. She was listening with much attention for a long time, giving me hope that finally, she had begun to understand. However, she suddenly asked me what I knew about schizophrenia—that drained the last drop of my patience. I decided to ask Peyote for advice on how to live my life further. After that last conflict, I flew to Mexico.

Between Life and Death

This visit was different from the start; I could feel tension in the air. Eldon and Maria seemed a little dry toward me, making me feel somewhat uncomfortable. As usual, after sunset, Eldon told me to bring firewood, but this time to another place, near a structure of wooden poles supporting a thatched roof. He told me to build a horseshoe-like wall on the ground around the fire, facing the east. He also said that my future would depend on how well it was made. These words were somewhat intimidating. I carefully lined up a semi-circle, worrying about what he'd said about my future. When I finished, I rammed it with my hands few time over. I hadn't seen don Catarino at the ranch this time. I asked Eldon whether don Catarino would be joining us to which he briefly responded: "No." This created even more inner tension. After all, don Catarino had always drunk with us, and now he was absent. Dona Maria refused to participate in the ceremony as well. This time, only Eldon and I drank.

It was about 8:00 pm, when Eldon decided to start. Usually we talked a lot before the ceremony, but this time Eldon was silent. He began by throwing herbs into the fire and opened it with a song. We had a lot of medicine in the bucket, so I knew the night would be long. We started to drink. Between songs, we were silent. At a certain point, I felt it would be the right time to ask Peyote a question about the troubling relationship I had in the US. I mentally expressed the situation, asking for advice.

A moment later, in the flickering fire, I saw myself in the future with her. But it wasn't really me; it was my empty body. My spirit wasn't in it anymore. I felt sorry for myself. Then this picture melted in the heat of our blazing fire, and I sat, enjoying the stars and the nightly silence, reflecting on my life in the company of real shaman and drinking real medicine. This filled my heart with inner joy and a sense of spiritual contentment.

Peyote's answer was obvious to me, so was my choice. With a heavy heart I mentally said goodbye to my girlfriend. Peyote also showed me that in fact, we do not have a predetermined future; we only have probabilities of future trends, which we form in the present moment, defining and shaping them by the different choices we make.

Well, one problem was solved; now it was time to solve another. I pulled a pack of Marlboros out of my backpack and threw it into the fire, mentally asking Peyote to help me quit smoking. This was the last pack of cigarettes I held since then.

On this night the moon was full. I was the fire keeper. In Native American tradition, the fire keepers are the ones who have to bless the water at midnight, sipping from it first, sharing between all participants, and then offering it to mother earth and grandfather fire. But before this ritual, Eldon told me to look into a pot of water and remember my face. I took the pot and looked at my face, which was shimmering in light coming from the fire. I only saw a rough outline, blurred by the dark. Trying to see my face in the dark water, I suddenly felt that someone else was looking at me through my own reflection. It was clearly not me looking at myself. This was another entity who knew me. I felt uneasy, thanked the water, took a sip, offered some to Eldon, and then poured the rest on the ground near the fire.

I put a pot of water nearby, added more wood, took my wooden sticks and tapped on them, and repeated several times: Peyote is real, Peyote is real.

These were my last words that night. Soon after saying that, I jumped up, feeling stings on both thighs a few inches below my genitals. I took off my pants and tried to see what had happened there. Eldon told me not to panic, saying it would only make it worse. But how do you not panic when you find yourself in a remote Indian village, far away from the city, with no car or ride to a hospital and knowing nothing of what lies ahead? It felt like something was circling under my skin in the places where I had been stung. I was getting nervous. Eldon was sitting quietly. My instinct was to cauterize the stings, but I realized that it wouldn't really help. But when subcutaneous whirling began climbing up my body, I became seriously concerned for my life.

About 20 minutes later I was knocked out on the mat. I began to feel like I was losing my body. Maria woke up and was talking quietly to Eldon, as my condition grew worse with each passing minute, getting to where my body almost ceased to exist. I could not move even a finger or open my mouth or eyes. I had lost saliva and was breathing just through my nose. Suddenly, my body started to itch and burn terribly. Maria was gone, and just the two of us remained. Eldon told me that I had been stung by scorpions, and there was nothing he could do to get the venom out. He said I had to go through it. I lay there motionless, frozen on the inside and yet in burning agony. I had never felt like I was truly dying before. I began thinking about how sudden death was. Had I come back to Mexico for this? Despair began to overwhelm me. I desperately wanted to leave, to get out of my body, spend time somewhere else, and then come back when this was all over. But I couldn't get away from my body. I was totally awake and chained to it.

Nearby, I heard a crying donkey. Listening to him, I had the realization that my body was this donkey, which had dutifully carried me all my life. And now, in suffering, I wanted to leave it alone to die. I started thinking of my past, when I was spiritually ignorant. I realized I had been practicing a form of asceticism, depriving my body of food and rest for the sake of imaginary spiritual achievements, which I had heard about or once read somewhere. I knew for certain, in that moment, that I was living in a world where blind men were leading the blind. Regretting everything, I asked my body to forgive me for my stupid attitude toward it, for how long I had been devoid of understanding.

I could feel how the venom and medicine had mingled in my blood. The physical reality of my illness, poison from the deadly stings of scorpions, and my absolute powerlessness to control anything, arose in a wave of seemingly boundless despair. I was lying just three feet away from the fire, but couldn't feel the heat. I held on to the hope that if I just made it through the night, the sun would warm me. My mind remembered that nobody knew where I was: my parents in distant Israel, my friends in the USA. I suddenly pictured my cats in California, who would be lost without me. I thought about everything that I had wanted to do in my life, but had not yet done. I could not believe that my life would end like this, abruptly, in the middle of nowhere.

Eldon sat in silence, keeping the fire going. It was somewhat comforting knowing I had drunk enough Peyote to last through the night. There was such a mixed feeling: the power and ecstasy of Peyote and the burning agony of the venom—two extremes experienced at their peak—in the same moment. Somehow, I knew that as long as Peyote was active in me, I would have the strength to fight for my life.

At one point, Eldon came up and put his pipe in my mouth—saying that smoking it would help me pass the time. I inhaled as best I could. I felt a little better, but then, things got so bad that I once again started to give up. The thought of my impending death was killing my will to live. It did occur to me that human death comes when a person is no longer willing to fight for life.

My death was nearby, sitting, waiting. Somewhere in my forehead, behind my closed eyes, I could see the even darker tunnel, which I sensed we walk through when it is all over. I wondered: where was the "light at the end?" Instead there was a black hole of non-existence, and death was the last guide on my journey. A flurry of thoughts and feelings rushed inside, but I saw no pictures of the afterlife; my consciousness was flooded with scenes from my life. My body grew cold, turning my soul into stone. Now, I knew how people felt who were freezing to death. I spent all night like this, waiting for the morning sun. But when it came out, I continued to lie motionless, suffering from the freezing that had somehow overtaken my body, even under the burning Mexican sun. Later, I would learn that the venom of a scorpion is a powerful neurotoxin that targets the central nervous system and paralyzes the prey while the scorpion feeds.

It was already morning, and I was not getting any better. Eldon covered me with a blanket and left. I stayed alone, lying there until evening. As the sun was going down, I realized that if I did not start regaining my body, I wouldn't make it through one more night. Thinking how dearly I loved life, I started to gather the will to push death away. I knew this battle was the most important battle I would ever face, since I was now fighting for life itself.

Having made the choice to live, with an incredible effort, I began to try and sense my body, to get a grip on it, and after a while, I could roll over from my back to my stomach. A little later, I forced myself to bend my knees; but to sit more than a few seconds was very hard. My head was spinning terribly, making me feel even sicker.

Eighteen hours had passed since the stings, and now it was getting dark. I tried to get up by holding on to the wooden columns of the  structure. I could now rise to my feet, but only for a few seconds. Then I could get up again and take a few steps. Slowly, trembling all over, I walked around the building and fell again to the mat. In that moment, I knew that I was not going to die. The battle for my life was over, but the frightening thought remained that perhaps I would have to live in this crippled condition.

I tried to open my eyes, but saw nothing except a blur of colors. Loss of sight suddenly became a frightening possibility. Dona Maria brought me some water. I parted my lips, and she splashed water into my mouth. The water had an acidic taste, so I couldn't drink it. I spent about two or three hours in this condition of trying to gain my strength, to see, to move, to do whatever I could to live again. It was already quite dark when I found the strength to walk slowly to the house where Maria sat with Eldon, enjoying the night air. On the way up the hill, I thought about old age and how life force withdraws from the body, leaving it to die. I was experiencing my old age—after I had lived my own death.

Seeing me, Eldon said: "You got what you wanted after all. You were looking to meet your ally." He was right, I really was looking for my ally, but I had imagined it to be a little different.

Thinking about it later, I realized that Death, which had scared me when I was a child, now had become my friend, reminding me of the miracle of Life and the importance of focusing on living in the present, fully engaged with what is, rather than worrying about what might be after one is dead.

It was now 22 hours since the stings, and my condition was still bad. I made an effort to drink some coffee and force a corn tortilla into my mouth. Eldon shared with me that his shamanic initiation was accompanied by the bite of a rattlesnake and that Peyote had saved his life as well. He said that he had spent five days near death, alone in the hills. He also told me that even though I had received more than enough venom to kill me, I was lucky that my guide to the spirit world had not been a rattlesnake. Eldon and I now shared something very real and very deep that would not need to be spoken about. Later he and Maria told me that when I jumped that night from getting stung, they had seen six stings on my thighs.

The second night was still hard. I could not sleep, tossing and turning while my whole body itched. The next day was also not easy, but I was able to walk, even eat. I wanted to take a bath, but I didn't feel like I could make it to the river—a five-minute walk away. So I asked if there was another way to bathe. Eldon showed me some big barrels of water. I undressed and started to pour water on myself, which felt strange and unpleasant—my body was literally hissing like a kettle pouring out steam from boiling water.

I managed to get some sleep on the third night and even went to the river during the day. My senses had finally returned. I could see and talk well and was getting my body back. But I could feel electric voltage surging through my arms, from my elbows to my fingers. Even on the fourth day, this sensation of electricity was still there.

Trusting the Vision

I am reminded about this one time, during one of the visits to Mexico, I was given a very special gift. Usually, upon arriving, we would go to visit don Rufino after the Peyote night, and he would donate a few Peyote plants for our ceremonies, which then were added to by Eldon. This time, don Rufino, as usual, was glad to see me. Before I left, he went behind the house, and came back with a very large Peyote plant, saying it was his gift to me. I asked him how old this Peyote was; he laughed and said it was probably older than he was. According to Eldon, it was about 100-120 years old. It was one of the oldest Peyote don Rufino had ever found during his lifelong pilgrimages to the Sacred Wirikuta, the legendary homeland of the Huichols, and holy place where Peyote grows wild.

I was very touched by his gift. For a shaman to give someone Peyote, especially that old, indicated a personal invitation into their culture and their life. But then, before departure, Eldon told me that don Rufino had advised me to leave the Peyote at the village, and not take it with me to the states. I asked him why and he said that don Rufino thought it would be better. I was very disappointed with this turn; I even thought that the old man had become greedy and didn't want to let go of such an old Peyote. But I still trusted his vision and told Eldon that I would leave it with him.

Sure enough, when I arrived at the Houston airport, I was literally turned inside out at customs. I was thoroughly checked; even my used socks got inspected. It was obvious that there was no way I could have smuggled a large Peyote; it would have been found and I would have been charged with possession of a controlled substance. As the TSA agents relentlessly inspected my personal items, I mentally thanked don Rufino.

Chavin de Huantar

"There are two kinds of art, one quite different from the other—objective art and subjective art. The difference is that in objective art the artist really does 'create,' that is, he makes what he intended, he puts into his work whatever ideas and feelings he wants to put into it. And the action of this work upon men is absolutely definite; they will, of course each according to his own level, receive the same ideas and the same feelings that the artist wanted to transmit to them. There can be nothing accidental either in the creation or in the impressions of objective art."

G.I. Gurdjieff.

Only upon return to America, from that previous Mexico trip, and waking up the next morning, did I finally believe that my three-day nightmare was over. Before traveling to Mexico, I had already planned another trip to Peru, and a month later, in December, I went there. I wanted to understand what had happened to me in Mexico. In the ceremonies with Huachuma, I tried to see into the Mexican situation, but that adventure was still shrouded in impenetrable mystery. Before leaving Mexico, Eldon had

warned me that it might take years to understand the significance and importance of what happened to me there. And he was right; it's only now, looking back four years later, I am beginning to understand what happened to me in Mexico—and yet the first glimpse into it I already had during that journey to Peru, a month later.

This next two-week journey to Peru—which occurred three-and-a-half months before I finally moved there—was very significant. We visited an ancient Chavin tem-

ple, located high in the mountains of the Central Andes. According to archeologists, the Chavin culture began to form around 1200 b.c.e. and lasted for about 1000 years until its mysterious disappearance. It is important to note that no warfare tools were ever found associated with the Chavin culture, which makes one wonder how an ancient culture could rule for a millennia without warfare? Chavin culture can be understood on many levels, or more depending on one's personal level of understanding. This has little to do with academic training. So while mainstream archeology is trying to offer a coherent theory of ancient enigmatic culture by examining the stones, another view exist, in which the full meaning is revealed when the language of symbols is understood.

It is quite obvious that Chavin's shamans and priests drew their power from their connection with the supernatural world, a guardian of which was sacred Huachuma cactus, whose images are clearly present in Chavin iconography carved in stones in order to avoid misinterpretation of it by future generations. But what is not so obvious, and what in fact is hidden, is the Chavin understanding of evolution of consciousness, which they symbolically depicted as a process of transformation from animal to human, from human to a deity that now points to our own divine nature. This deeply spiritual understanding was however understood by scholars as "shape shifting due to use of psychotropic drugs," a view which makes me shiver. The Chavin Huachumero diety—an anthropomorphic creature—a combination of serpent, feline, condor and human—with an ecstatic smile on his face, holding Huachuma cactus in his hand, representing three worlds of existence in Andean cosmology, in my opinion, most telling glyph from all hieroglyphs known. It is a symbol of spiritual transformation which can be achieved through work with sacred Huachuma (when focused) whose spiritual force is still unknown to the world and is revealing itself due to the urgency and spiritual crises humanity is now facing.

There is another question in regards to dates which archeologists are giving us in relation to different cultures and sites. Their method at best is based on radiocarbon dating of the artifacts found in different sites—indeed a scientific method but a method only pointing to the fact that a particular culture was occupying a particular place in particular time. But it's important to remember that having evidence of a cultural presence living in a certain site does not necessarily prove that this is the culture that has built it. Radiocarbon dating can only date organic remains, and these findings only demonstrate the fact that a certain cultures lived in that place at a certain time. So oftentimes, it could be that to seal a historical hole, mainstream archeology "forces" an association between the culture and the place its evidence of living was found, which might or might not be the same. A good example of cultural mixture is evident in vast portions of the Inca culture of the Andes.

Sites like Pikillacta for example, near Cusco, give a very good picture of that, clearly showing differences in stone work of the same structure, in terms of content, quality, construction methods, etc. This leads to further thinking that a later culture could simply adapt the previously built sites and make an attempt to reconstruct it.

Other sites such as Ollantaytambo, Sacsayhuaman, and Machu Picchu in the Cusco region, also indicate this. Early 16th century Spanish chronicles reflects the amazement in regards to the ancient archeological sites found in Cusco, and when they asked the Incas whether they had built them, the Incas laughed and said that these sites were built by their Gods. Whatever they meant by the Gods is not the point here.

The point is that these places were not built by the Inca, which even they themselves are admitting, nor it was built by the Killke culture, a pre-Inca culture who lived in the same area before the Incan empire. A Killke's culture, whose ruins are all over the place, built between 900 AD to 1200 AD before the Incan empire, are quite primitive and are completely different from the archeological sites I mentioned above. Furthermore, I was lucky enough to witness all the new archeological findings made by archeolo

gists who had discovered a Killke culture cemetery near an ancient Killke culture city in the Sacred Valley, with ancient mummies and lots of artifacts like ceramics, war tools, and other tools which are exactly the same as those of the Inca displayed in various museums.

And who was living in this region before the Killke culture? A Wari culture, which begin from 500 AD and fell about 900 AD. There are many archeological findings from the Wari sites, which are exactly the same as the following culture of Killke, and later coming Inca and the Wari constructions are built exactly the same with regard to style, design and methods. So it is quite obvious that no technological progress

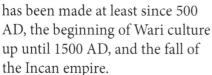

has been made at least since 500 AD, the beginning of Wari culture up until 1500 AD, and the fall of the Incan empire.

These are the words from the Spanish Conquistadors expressing their amazement: "The most beautiful thing that can be seen among the buildings of that land are these walls because they are of stones so large that no one who sees them would say that they had been placed there by human hands, for they are as large as chunks of mountains....These are not smooth stones but rather are very well fitted together and interlocked with one another. And they are so close together and so well-fitted that the point of a pin could not have been inserted into any of the joints. Neither the bridge of Segovia nor any of the structures that Hercules or the Romans made are as worthy of being seen as this. We can assure your majesty that it is so beautiful and has such fine buildings that it would even be remarkable in Spain." — *Arrival of the first Spaniards in Cusco in 1533*

Thus what we are fed by mainstream archeology as a scientific fact, that some of the greatest archeological monuments like Machu Picchu, Ollayntaytambo, Sacsayhuaman and others are only 500-800 years old—is more of an assumption than a fact. For example, a relatively recently discovered Caral culture, near Lima, which is now thought to have been built around 3000 b.c.e., is presented as the culture which actually built the complex of Pyramids it occupied—again a scientific assumption rather than a fact. The organic, datable remains found there only point to the fact that people lived there around that time, but whether the people who lived there 5000 years ago, were the once who also built this ancient city—remains a question. So to say that the Inca built the most famous and majestic sites in Peru, like Ollantaytambo and Sacsayhuaman, based on the finding of Incan textures and primitive tools found on the sites, would be like saying that the cathedral in Cusco's central square built by the tourists, because the footprints of 21st century shoes are found on the floor during rainy season.

Rocks and stones of ancient (or non-ancient) ruins cannot be radiocarbon dated. Do we really want to be advancing theories (some of which are even ludicrous) about these marvelous historical sites and their origins when we still have no extensive or verifiable scientific knowledge how they were created and developed? Doesn't it somewhat insult our 21st century intelligence? Could we believe without question that the Incas, who apparently hadn't invented the wheel yet, played with the megaliths like we today play with Rubik's Cube? And also that complex brain surgeries, were carried out with the primitive tools that have been found at these sites? I must raise these questions to the reader, and I further encourage readers to investigate for themselves these subjects with an open mind.

Sadly, with regards to the Chavin culture, through thousands of years, its spiritual practices have been forgotten for the most part; and now the local population in this region is barely aware of the vast shamanic knowledge of their ancestry and the healing and spiritual properties of the sacred Huachuma, for example. It would be fair to say that a foreigner has more respect and faith in this sacred teacher healer plant than the locals do. This disparity of remembering the old ways and the knowledge that is only recently "discovered," is so evident in the contrast between the ancient temple and the village surrounding and is striking. Inside the temple, one can still feel the positive, energetic charge and power of the ancient shamans. Meanwhile, outside, almost the entire the present-day local population is suffering from alcoholism and extreme despairing poverty—the atmosphere is one of depression.

Speaking of the Temple itself, one cannot be anything but surprised by its design. The walls are inclined at an angle toward the inside, and its stone layers are built in rows of large blocks followed by rows of small blocks, then large blocks again. Five- foot wide walls separate the world from the underground labyrinths, creating an incredible acoustic insu-

lation, within which, if one is silent, he or she can hear the beating of his or her own heart.

There is gate in front of the temple, but it leads nowhere; behind it you see only a wall – constructions of that type called "portal" in Peru. Nearly all of the objects which have been found during archaeological excavations are ceremonial; thus a spiritual usage of the Temple seems quite obvious, and the deadly silence of the labyrinth could well have been utilized for deep meditation—which can be

achieved with the help of the sacred Huachuma, a central image of Chavin stone art. Looking at the objects found in Chavin, it has become apparent that people were coming there from afar, bringing their gifts and offerings. Those pilgrims were coming for the spiritual purposes like divination and the blessings for their people, as they go to the site of the Oracle in ancient Delphi.

A Huachumero, whom we went to meet, was one of only two shamans in the area. The man who led us to him was Martin, who I met in the jungle in December of 2005; shortly after he had moved to Peru. He was over 50 years old when he made this bold step. He did not have enough money to move and didn't know the language. He only followed his vision, which he had while drinking Huachuma at one of the volcanic huacas (power places) in the Andes and traveling with Howard, who I mentioned in earlier chapters. As Martin told me later, at this ceremony, while deep in the Huachuma, he was plunged into a prophetic vision in which he saw himself living in Peru, married to a woman with many children. It was a surprise to him, since at that time he was tied to America, was married, had his carpenter business, and did not intend to either get a divorce, leave his business, or move to Peru. But, a year later, things changed to exactly what he had been shown by Huachuma—was now living in Peru and married to a Peruvian woman with seven children.

After he moved to Peru, we did not speak for several years, but as it turned out, we both remembered our two weeks spent together in the Amazon back at the end of 2005. I contacted him in 2008, between trips to Mexico, asking him if he would like to travel with me and my friend from St. Petersburg, to Chavin and other ancient sacred places in the region. He gladly agreed and organized the journey. In December, my friend came to California and we flew to Peru. Together, we planned to do a pilgrimage to the ancient temple of Chavin culture, a cradle of the Andean civilization. The journey was very special for all of us, but for me it became a certain break thru. After coming back to

California from this pilgrimage, I had a lucid dream in which I was preparing Huachuma. I woke up the next morning and right away went out to my Huachuma garden, which I had been growing for three years prior, but had never once cut. For the first time, I cut a few plants and started preparing them like I had been shown in my dreams, surprising myself, watching my hands doing something they had never done before, but already knew how to do. I will describe in detail how this ceremony went for us in later chapters.

It was quite surprising to enter the ancient temple of Chavin de Huantar and see armed guards with bullet proof jackets. The reasons for this were not very clear; it was hard to imagine what they were guarding from tourists armed with cameras. Everything anyone could take from the temple had long been removed and was being kept in a museum, located a half-hour walk from the temple. There, instead of armed guards, visitors were met by a nice receptionist who smiled and gave out a number from the box where they had to leave their personal things.

Was such protection required for the over four-meter long carved of granite Lanzon monolith, a Chavin deity depicted as the jaguar-man? It weighed more than three tons and was dug in like a spear, surrounded

by labyrinths—perhaps placed there before the temple was completed. To carry it out, one would have to first destroy the temple—so what was the reason for such an armed presence—other than absurdity?

According to local shamans, the ancient shamans approached the Lanzon, the anthropomorphic central deity of the ancient entheogenic Chavin culture, always with proper honor before and after ceremonies, which were held at the central square, in front of the temple. Hundreds, perhaps thousands participated. Extending outward from the Lanzon's statue, are numerous tunnels presumably used for ritual initiations. According to one version, the participant was given a Huachuma concoction and then led into the dark tunnels where he was supposed to find his way to the deity. During ancient times, initiates had to go through stages of apprenticeship before they were allowed to see the Lanzon.

In 2010, during one of my visits to Chavin, we almost got into trouble for playing a little mystical music inside the temple, for trying to express our respect for the ancient shamans. As my German friend began playing his didgeridoo, a guard approached and told us that all rituals were prohibited in the temple. I tried to explain to him that this was not exactly a ritual—we just wanted to play a little music to honor the ancient ways. But, apparently I was not convincing enough, and he told us to leave. More guards joined the educational process outside. I patiently repeated to them that playing soft, mystical music could hardly be called a ritual, considering the history of this place. Soon I realized I was talking with people who were committed to carrying out orders and not to thinking, so I stopped trying to educate them. I could see us possibly being arrested and spending a while in the police station, so we left. On the way back to our place, I shared my thoughts with my friend.

"It truly is absurd to ban rituals in the temple, where they were the anchor and spiritual core of the whole culture. In ancient times, people drank Huachuma here and sent their message to eternity, imprinting their sacred process on the stone. And in the world of today, we almost got arrested for peacefully and respectfully playing a few minutes of mystical music."

It reminded me of a similar incident that had occurred in California, just before I left for Peru. It was around the time when I met wild Owl—a story to which I will dedicate a later chapter. But, that was in North America, where shopping seems to be a cultural ritual, and we were in Peru, the center of the ancient shaman's world of South America.

Over the years of traveling and visiting historical, archeological and sacred sites, it has become quite evident to me that the cultural establishment of the modern world has a fear of letting people learn too much new information that is being discovered about the history and practices of ancient world. They seem to want to suppress spiritual kinship to sacred places and ancient cultures in those people who, in fact, have more respect for these sacred places than the people guarding them. What is so dangerous about letting people freely express their feelings and desire to commune with ancient ways?

Discussions about who, when, how, and why have built the temple, where they built it and the way they built it and why it is so heavily protected by armed guards today—would be interesting dishes made of

speculation with science-fiction gravy on the top. Yet, the fact is that another esoteric aspect of Chavin culture and its objective art persists. When understood, this inspires admiration and a desire to spread Chavin Consciousness worldwide, thus contributing to an archaic revival and to the meaning of human life in a bigger sense.

Path

Can Loyalty to Science be Unscientific?

"Those who control the past, control the future." – George Orwell

There are archaeological findings which are not widely or publicly recognized because they do not fit into the officially accepted version of the development of life on Earth. Objects of this kind—which archaeologists cannot attribute to any of the known cultures – are hidden from public view so that they do not challenge the picture of the creation of the world imposed on us by the scientific and cultural establishment and its servants—for whom academic titles and honorariums are more important than the truth.

Throughout history, the ruling elite have tried all sorts of ways to keep people in darkness in order to maintain power and control over them. By getting rid of hundreds of thousands of papyrus scrolls created by ancient scholars and philosophers, the Roman patricians replaced ancient knowledge with Christian dogma. Perhaps, the seed of the Inquisition was planted then, which reached its heyday in the Middle Ages, and continues even up to the present—even if somewhat less bloodthirsty.

One of the victims of the "scientific inquisition" has been Dr. Virginia Steen-McIntyre, who was sent to an archaeological site in Mexico to help determine the age of artifacts found there in 1970. She used the best equipment and verified the data obtained using four different methods. For the scientific world, the results were shocking. Archaeologists had expected a date of 25,000 years or less, and Dr. McIntyre has insisted on the figure of 250,000 years or more.

Estimation of the age of the finding of 25,000 years or less was convenient to confirm an existing theory that the peoples of Asia "crossed" the Bering Strait, and appeared in North America about 20,000 years ago. However, it contradicts the oral tradition of indigenous inhabitants of North America, according to whom no migration ever happened.

Jesuit priest José de Acosta was the first who proposed the theory of migration of peoples from Siberia to Alaska across the Bering Strait. In 1856, Samuel Haven, on the basis of this theory, put forward the hypothesis that during the Pleistocene Period (about 20,000 years ago), due to freezing of large quantities of water, the sea level dropped significantly in the Bering Strait and formed a land mass that became a land bridge between Siberia and Alaska.

It is not known for what purpose these ideas were put forward, but I would not exclude a political motive to justify the Spanish conquest of the New World, arguing that therefore the indigenous peoples of America were also immigrants. (But, even if this is so, is 20,000 years of living on the land not enough to be considered a native people?)

Steen-McIntyre conducted tests three times and each time got the same results. She was given a chance to renege on her conclusions, but she didn't. As a result of her loyalty to science and the truth, she lost her teaching job at an American university and subsequently faced big obstacles in any future publication of her work.

Another sad example of an important discovery that was ignored by mainstream science is connected to the name of William Niven, a mineralogist and archaeologist. This scientist discovered a number of minerals—one of them even named in his honor. In 1911 he discovered ancient ruins buried under volcanic ash in the Federal District, north of Mexico City. The following two decades of his life were devoted to archaeological research in the Valley of Mexico, and, in agreement with the government, he financed his own excavations, resulting in the sale of the artifacts found. Niven has created a private museum in Mexico City, which exhibits more than 20,000 items. In the process, he found unusual stone tablets with icons in several places in the valley of Mexico. This discovery eventually included more than 2,600 stone tablets and gained fame through the work of James Churchwood, starting with his *Lost Continent of Mu*, first published in 1926. In 1929, the scientist moved to Houston and gave a number of Mexican artifacts to the large museum there. Interestingly, official science simply did not take notice of the stone tablets of William Niven—perhaps because he never published a "scientific" report.

Finally, I can add that a friend of mine, an anthropologist named Renato Santiago Davila Riquelme found stone tablets with petroglyphs and stones in which clear evidence of mechanical work is present, in a museum in Huaru near Cusco. These tablets were found in ancient graves next to mummies, where he also found incredible skulls resembling human ones. After making his discovery of the Waiki ('brother' in Quechua) as he nicknamed the particular skeleton—which is quite interesting and unique when examined closely, he attracted all the major Peruvian television channels who came to Cusco, filmed it and broadcast it on national TV. Renato offered his view that the extraterrestrial beings whose remains are now in his possession, were involved in construction of different archeological sites around Cusco—a bold statement that brought upon him a heavy hit. Two days later he was "grilled" in Ministeria de Cultura of Cusco. I will provide the pictures of his finding in later chapters.

In our private conversation, after giving him my thoughts on the subject, which made him notably exited, he shared with me some personal stories about his encounters with the cultural establishment. They served only to reinforce my own thinking in these areas. It well might be that this encounter and his finding would become a subject of my second book, along with lab results of the remains.

In 1993, NBC aired "Secrets of the Sphinx," a documentary film, which presented geological evidence that the famous Sphinx is at least twice as old (9000 years b.c.e.) as was commonly believed and claimed by

Egyptologists. It all began with the fact that a self-taught Egyptologist, John Anthony West, studied the age of the Sphinx using data on water erosion. He then acquainted geologist Dr. Robert M. Schoch with his method. They traveled together to Egypt and conducted a thorough examination of the ancient structure. After studying the Sphinx, the geologist agreed with the conclusions of John West, and they announced their findings.

They were immediately inundated with criticism from Egyptologists, who managed to bypass the scientific argument strait to a personal attack. Sometime later, Dr. Shoch was invited to discuss the question at the American Association for the Advancement of Science. West was not invited because he had no degree, and had to forfeit the right to express his position. Well, following the logic of the representatives of modern science, we can say that only a theologian can discuss issues of a religious matter, only licensed doctors can have opinions about health, and only politicians can vote for a president!

Whatever the true reason, West was unable to speak to the scientific community. Since then, the debate about the age of the Sphinx has not yet ended with a concrete conclusion and has instead developed into a dispute about when, how and by whom the pyramids of Giza were built. In fact, this important question could have been solved a long time ago by creating a group of independent engineers and architects who could refute the controversial theory that the pyramids were built with primitive tools and techniques about 2500 b.c.e.

It is hard to imagine that highly educated people can really believe that 2.5 million accurately placed stone blocks that make up the pyramid of Cheops, each weighing multiple tons, could be transported to the desert and perfectly constructed into a gigantic pyramid. Not to mention the carefully stacked multi-ton stone slabs forming one hundred-meter-long corridors and passageways inside the pyramid. This with manual labor? And all this massive construction of millions of tons was built as a tomb for the pharaoh who could die at any moment, long before his tomb would be ready to host him? But the purpose of the construction is a different question. And here we are talking about its methods.

I introduced a friend of mine, an experienced Peruvian engineer, to the parameters of the Egyptian pyramids. For over thirty years, he specialized in road construction in the highlands of the Andes. His latest project, in the course of which I met him, was building 22 kilometers of winding, mountain, asphalt roads at a height of about four kilometers above sea level. Piercing the rocks in some places required the use of the latest heavy equipment. The project cost the state $30 million, which most likely, would not be given to a person with doubtful reputation. So, acquainting him with the characteristics of Egyptian pyramids, I asked him if he thought that such buildings could be built by primitive people with primitive tools. His response was unequivocal. He said that even though he was not a structural engineer, he still thought that this was impossible. He said that the pyramids had to be carefully designed, and their builders had to have instruments of measurement and to employ contemporary techniques for the delivery, handling and lifting of blocks to the required height. Then, I drew for him, from memory, a picture from my Russian childhood, when we were taught in school that slaves pulled ropes to move the huge blocks across the desert and then used wooden shims to raise the blocks to the height needed. He remarked that in Peru, when young children ask where they came from, they are told that the stork brought them. I replied I was told that I was found in the cabbage. Then, we had more tea and talked about our childhood.

I was in Egypt when I was 20 years old. I remember visiting the great temple of Karnak in Luxor, the Pyramids of Giza, and the Sphinx in whose expression I could hear an echo of a distant past about which we know nothing. I remember walking around the pyramids trying to imagine exhausted slaves, dragging tons of blocks through the desert, cutting them precisely with hand tools, then putting them together in a way that would withstand the test of time, creating the greatest structure in the world. This theory, I felt, had to have made even the camels laugh.

The efforts to hide the truth is obvious, but why? Could it be that if it were proven the Egyptians did not build the Great Pyramid in 2500 b.c.e. using primitive methods, or that the Sphinx appeared about 9000 b.c.e., or earlier, then the whole carefully constructed house of historical cards would collapse? This would destroy the hypothesis of a cultural evolution that started with the Sumerian culture in southern

Mesopotamia, which arose not earlier than 4000 b.c.e. This view excludes the possibility of the existence of advanced civilizations before that time. What would archeology and history mean without a fixed date, as well as the theory of "cultural evolution" connected with the theory of Darwinian evolution? Seems as if there is a lot at stake. Does this perhaps explain why the facts are hidden; why anomalies and enigmas are ignored? In my opinion, it does.

A few related thoughts on this: Aside from the obvious cultural and scientific suppression, a religious one seems also present to me. A sea of evidence pointing to a systematic destruction of the ancient architecture, fueled by an egomania and religious fanaticism can be found throughout Peru and some places in Mexico, which I have seen. There are churches built on the foundation of ancient temples clearly destroyed by conquistadors, who not only robbed the native people of their possessions but also robbed them of their faith.

And the same appears to be the case in Egypt, with the attempts of destruction of the pyramids and the sphinx. I see the evidence of conquerors (usually military) arriving who obviously could not accept the greatness of any others before them. These destroyers of original cultural symbols great architecture, and timeless writings were conquering leaders, whose vanity, often wrapped in religious context, would be pitiful—if it were not so destructive. Human grandeur and ego, —these were the powerful forces behind cultural annihilation—new leaders competing for "divine status"—each one threatened

by the great achievements of the past, both intellectual (in case of ancient manuscripts of Greece) and architectural.

And then if you add the part about "If you don't believe in my God, then I will either force you to or destroy you...." Well, what more needs to be said about the history of new cultures being built on the old and the truth of how that happens? I leave the reader to ponder this.

Ica Stones

This particular story is most telling in my opinion, if one is able to look at it with an open mind. I will only focus on some particular facts taken from the book of Dr. Cabrera, *The Message of the Engraved Stones of Ica*, which will be enough to make my point—leaving the rest of the story for research by an interested reader. I want to go on record here by saying that I admire the personal and professional integrity of Dr. Cabrera and his courage to challenge from scientific point of view the official version of evolution on Earth which excludes the possibility of highly advanced civilizations existing in the remote past.

I also have to say that the parts of the story I have included here are essentially as they were written in his book. No facts were altered, but I paraphrased to the best of my ability. To make a long story short, I will start from beginning in May, 1966, when Felix Liosa Romero, a childhood friend of Dr. Cabrera, arrived at the doctor's home. Romero brought a small stone and offered it to the doctor, who took it and was surprised by its heavy weight for being so small. Oval-shaped, it had the carving of a type of fish the doctor did not recognize and thought it was extinct. Some thirty years earlier, family-owned land in Sala, in the district of Ica, was cleared for planting and a similar stone had been uncovered. Workers at the time attributed the engraving to the Incas. It was common in this zone to find ceramics, metal and wood objects, textiles, and human remains of the ancient civilizations that had once inhabited the area.

Felix reported that his brother had a huge collection of such stones and had given it to him. Cabrera was surprised since he knew that in Ica, many artifacts had been found—but none that were carved. Felix added that the huaqueros (grave robbers) of the Ocucaje desert had for many years been removing and selling such stones to private collectors. He also mentioned the names of several of the collectors and told the

doctor there were more stones in the regional museum. Cabrera visited Felix's brother, where he saw "a collection of engraved stones with carvings of birds, lizards, spiders, snakes, fish, shrimp, frogs, turtles and llamas....drawings of men in scenes of hunting and fishing, animals with different characteristics from those of the species as we now know them, snakes with wings on their spines; birds with horns; insects with pincers as long as their bodies and fish covered with wings."

Dr. Cabrera felt the need for a scientific investigation to clarify their

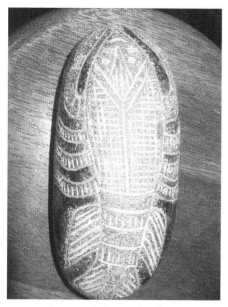

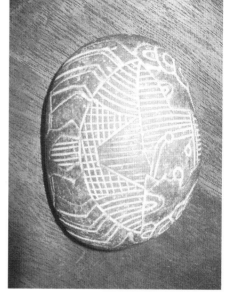

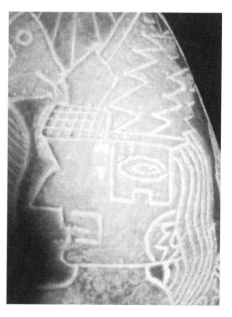

mysterious origin and relation to the classical cultures of ancient Peru. Coincidentally, the doctor was asked to found and direct the Casa de Cultura of Ica, for the promotion of science in the region in affiliation with the institution of the same name in Lima.

With the clout of his new "position" he began to think seriously about carrying out such an investigation. He approached Adolfo Bermudez Jenkis, Director of the Museo Regional of Ica, and inquired about the stones, which on previous visits to the museum, he had never seen. The director agreed and had them brought out of storage. But when the doctor broached the idea of an official study, the director brushed him off saying that the stones were carved by the huaqueros who had sold them to the museum. When asked if laboratory tests could confirm this, the director said that such tests were not called for.

Continuing to try and awaken the interest of Peruvian and foreign

scholars in the stones, Cabrera decided to form a collection of them to exhibit in the Casa de Cultura. With his own funds, he began to purchasing specimens, eventually accumulating over 5000 stones. During that time, he learned that nearly a year before his friend Liosa had given him his first stone, Herman Buse had published a book in which he acknowledged the existence of the Ica stones. Buse had written that in 1961, Ica river floods had unearthed a large number in Ocucaje, and that it had become a big commercial venture involving huaqueros who had found them. Cabrera named the Soldi brothers, saying that they had tried in vain to get archeologists interested in conducting a study. Cabrera increased his collection and began organizing them into a series based on the themes of astronomy, anthropology, biology, zoology, transport, and use in fishing and hunting.

He noticed that the animals, while bearing resemblance to modern

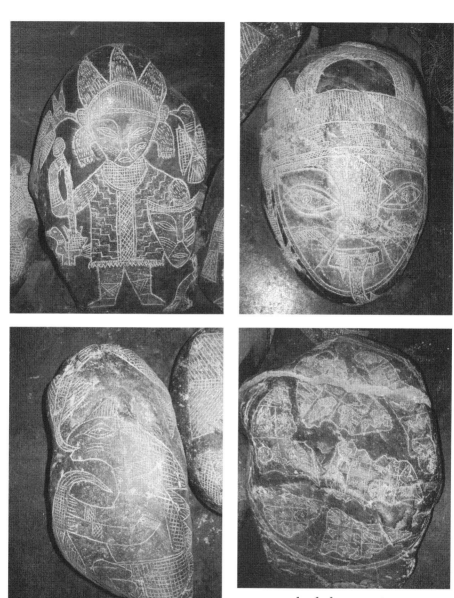

creatures, had characteristics which set them apart. Using Paleontology standards, he found that they had a morphological affinity to prehistoric animals; they showed, for example: The "…horses and llamas with five toes, megatherium (huge giant sloth bear) alticamellus (a mammal with the head and neck of a giraffe and the body of a camel, Megaceros (giant deer) mammoths (primitive elephants) diatrymas (giant carnivorous birds) and other animals."

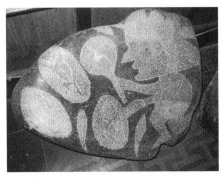

This could only mean that the people who had carved these stones came from a much earlier time period than the Incas, even Pre-Incas. Furthermore, other items in Cabrera's collection reveal even more ancient animal species, which lived in the Paleozoic era (405 million years ago). The stones series shows images of humans together with pre-historic animals, which only existed millions of years ago. Among them, and easily identifiable, are Diplodocus, Iguanodons, Tyrannosaurus Rex, and several others.

Some were depicted as if they had been domesticated, while others appeared wild. Some were harnessed and appeared to have been used like horses; and others looked as if they were possibly dangerous to humans.

Cabrera understood that the men who carved these stones not only had seen these animals, but knew them well in a biological sense: i.e., noting that their reproductive cycle, eating habits, and their physical vulnerabilities were clearly portrayed in the drawings. He concluded these people were highly evolved intellectually, as was evidenced by their understanding of biological processes.

Cabrera's continuing studies of the stones revealed that this ancient humanity left a testimony of vast and deep knowledge of medical science. The information revealed through the figures and symbols in the engravings deals with different aspects of this science, not the least of which is surgery. Cabrera's series contained engraved stones attesting to the fact that gliptolithic humanity was able to solve surgical problems that still baffle our present culture. Groups of stones reveal information about techniques used to anesthetize, cesarean surgery, and transplants of both cerebral hemispheres and of the heart.

Himself a surgeon, Cabrera identified evidence of the existence of an anti-rejection hormone and the double transplant of both a kidney and the adrenal gland. This double transplant, and the use of the anti-rejection hormone, indicated procedures used in the phase previous to the transplant of the organs, to prepare the body to receive a transplant without subsequent rejection. These people not only had the required knowledge for highly technical surgery, but had solved the problem of rejection using the blood of a pregnant woman. The receptor of the organ transplant received the blood of the pregnant woman and the organ to be transplanted was irrigated with that same blood before the operation took place.

Such precise knowledge of anatomy required for more complex surgeries, like full heart and brain transplants—which even today remain highly problematic if not impossible—overwhelmed Cabrera. He needed lab analysis to verify the antiquity of these stones. He selected 33 stones, among them a few that showed the reproductive cycles of long-extinct animals, which he knew would be controversial if their authenticity could not be confirmed. He went to his friend Luis Hochshild, a learned mining engineer and Vice-President of the Mauricio Hochshild Mining Co., in Lima, and asked if his laboratories could determine the nature of the stones and the antiquity of the engravings.

A month later, he received a report, in a document signed by the geologist Eric Wolf which stated: "This is unquestionably natural stone shaped by fluvial transport (river rock). Petrologically, I would classify them as andesites. Andesites are rocks whose components have been subjected mechanically to great pressure which causes chemical changes to take place. In this case, the effects of intense sericitation (transformation of feldspar into sericite) are obvious. This process has increased the compactness and specific weight, also creating the smooth surface that ancient artists preferred for carving. I will try to confirm this preliminary opinion by means of a more detailed test in the laboratories of the Engineering School and of the University of

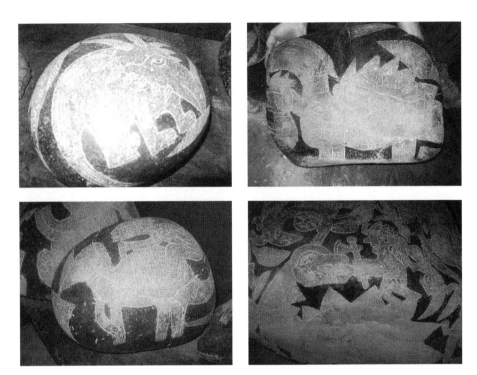

Bonn, West Germany. The stones are covered with a fine patina of natural oxidation which also covers the engravings by which their age should be able to be deduced. I have not been able to find any notable or irregular wear on the edges of the incisions which leads me to suspect that these incisions or etchings were executed not long before being deposited in the graves or other places where they were discovered."—*Lima 8 June 1967; Eric Wolf*

For Cabrera, the analysis revealed three important facts: (a) The engraved stones have a higher specific gravity than common river rocks found in riverbeds and beaches, which he had guessed as soon as he first held one in his hand; (b) The engravings are old, to judge by the coating of natural oxidation that covers the incisions as well as the stones themselves; and (c) The stones were engraved not long before being deposited in the spots where they were found, to judge by the absence of wear on the edges of the incisions, which means that the stones were not engraved for utilitarian or even artistic purposes, but rather to be deposited in a safe place - for some unknown reason.

One year before, Santiago Agurto Calvo had published the results of a petrological analysis of the engraved stones in his collection. These re-

sults were part of the newspaper article mentioned earlier, in which he discussed the discovery of engraved stones in the Ocucaje zone. Specifically, the article dealt with some specimens that he had purchased in 1962 from huaqueros which, according to him, contained "unidentifiable things, insects, fish, birds, cats, fabulous creatures and human beings, sometimes apart and other times shown together in elaborate and fantastic compositions." He had entrusted the analysis to the mining Faculty of the Universidad Nacional de Ingeneira and it had been performed by two engineers, Fernando de las Casas and Cesar Sotillo.

Learning that, Cabrera deciding to compare the results of the analysis he received from Eric Wolf with analysis published by Agurto Calvo which read:

"All the stones are highly carbonized andesites, despite their coloration and texture, which suggest a different nature. The stones come from lava flows dating from the Mesozoic era, characteristic of the zone where they were found. The surface has weathered, and feldspar has been turned into clay, weakening the surface and forming a kind of shell around the interior of the stones. This shell measures an average of grade 3 on the Mohs scale (which measures the comparative capacity of a substance to scratch another or be scratched by another) and up to 4 1/2 in the part not so affected by weathering. The stones can be worked with any hard material such as bone, shell, obsidian, etc., and naturally, by any pre-Hispanic metal implement."

On January 28, 1969 Cabrera received word from Eric Wolf that the results of the laboratory analysis conducted by a Professor Frenchen and his assistants at the University of Bonn were available. He had sent some of the same samples from his collection which he had analyzed in Lima, and the results of this second analysis merely confirmed his own:

"The stones were andesites and were covered by a patina or film of natural oxidation which also covered the etchings, permitting one to deduce that they are very old. The report added that it was difficult to

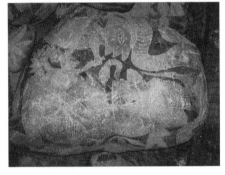

determine precisely their antiquity, and that in this task the comparative methods used in stratigraphy and paleontology should be employed."

As regards the comparative methods of stratigraphy, Wolf pointed out the need for excavations, in order to establish in which geological strata the stones are found. The antiquity of the strata would determine, by the principle of association, the antiquity of the

engravings. The comparative method of paleontology works much the same way: The age of fossilized vegetable, animal and human remains found in the strata where the stones were found could be determined, and by the same principle of association, could determine the approximate date at which the engravings were executed.

In view of the fact that the patina of oxidation that covered the stones

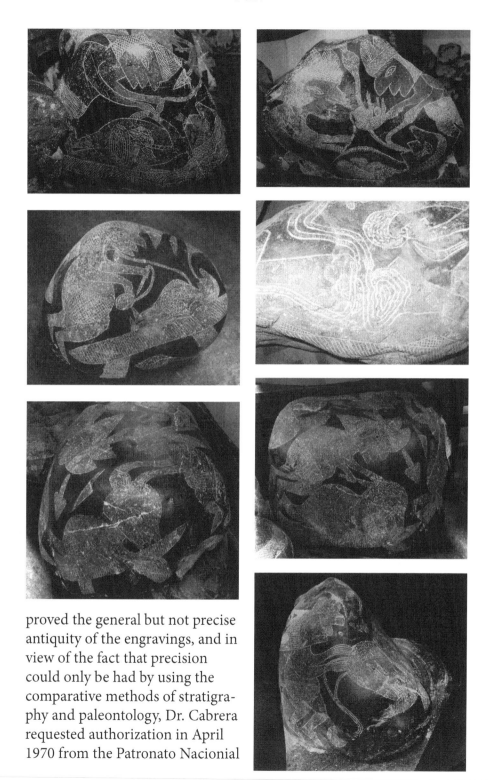

proved the general but not precise
antiquity of the engravings, and in
view of the fact that precision
could only be had by using the
comparative methods of stratigraphy and paleontology, Dr. Cabrera
requested authorization in April
1970 from the Patronato Nacionial

de Arqueologia to carry out excavations in the appropriate zone. This institution alone had the power to authorize such excavations. On July 16, 1970, his request was refused.

The laboratory results that he had painstakingly sought, fit with Cabrera's own conclusion that man coexisted with prehistoric animals. At the very least, it seemed clear that the stones had unusual archeological significance. He was convinced that this significance would be appreciated with the collaboration of Peruvian archeologists, and decided to publish the results of his investigations. He hoped to awaken their interest and set in motion a plan to preserve the Ocucaje zone and stop the illegal removal of stones. He began to give lectures, interviews, and to publish results of his studies in the periodical press, which reached throughout Peru and beyond.

He soon succeeded in getting the attention of the archeological establishment of Peru, but only to feel their viciousness. They claimed dogmatically that the coexistence of man and dinosaur was something that had not and could not be proven. They declared the Ica Stones fake. Dr. Cabrera was later accused of being a falsifier and mentor to a group of peasants who were "helping" him to fake the stones.

Peasants at Work

On January 17, 1975, Lima magazine *Mundial* published a long article trying to prove that the engraved stones of Ica were falsifications. Thirteen of the seventy-two pages in this issue were devoted to this task. The article claimed that the engraved stones in Cabrera's museum were not old, but were carved by two peasants who lived in the region of Ocucaje: Basilio Uchuya and Irma Gutierrez de Aparcana. The article stated that a group of reporters from the magazine went to the city of Ica and then to Ocucaje to look for Basilio and Irma Gutierrez, the alleged stone carvers.

Basilio Uchuya's wife told them that several days before, they were taken away by the police to make a statement as to whether the stones were false or real and whether they carved them or found them. Basilio told the police that he had carved all the stones he had sold to Dr. Cabrera and that he hadn't dug them up.

It seems obvious to me that he would say exactly that; otherwise he would be sentenced to jail for illegal excavation in search of archeological treasures—an activity severely punishable by Peruvian law. It is easy to picture the situation in which Uchuya and Gutierrez found themselves. To say they were legitimate meant admitting they were huaqueros. And it is understandable that they wanted to avoid jail and to continue selling, which they could not do if the stones were part of the national patrimony.

In another part of this article, an interview with Uchuya was reproduced:

Reporter: "He knew that you were carving the stones?"

Peasant: "Well, yes, he knew. I told him that I made all of them."

Reporter: "And he bought them anyway?"

Peasant: "Yes, always."

Reporter: "And why did he want them if they were engraved by you?"

Peasant: "Well, he told me he wanted to study them. He said he was doing some kind of study, and he asked me to get him more."

Reporter: "To get him more or make him more?"

Peasant: "To make more, then. It's the same thing, right?"

Coincidentally, two days later, on the nineteenth, the Lima daily *Correo* published a supplemental interview with Adolfo Bermudez Jenkis, Director of the Museo Regional de Ica. Adolfo Bermudez Jenkis holds, among other opinions, that the Engraved Stone of Ica were stated that the stones were indeed made by Basilio Uchuya and his relatives and that it had not been necessary to solicit the opinion of an expert because his friend, the north American John H. Rowe, had assured him that the stones were fakes.

Back in 1966, when Dr. Cabrera was Director of the Casa de Cultura of Ica, he had heard Adolfo say that investigations were pointless, since a friend of his had told him the stones were carved by the huaqueros of Ocucaje. But this was the first time that Adolfo had named his "friend." To declare in public that the opinion of a specialist was not needed and thus to assume that the stones are fakes struck Cabrera as completely unscientific.

But there was more. In the thirteen pages *Mundial* devoted to the engraved stones, as examples of the "innumerable" stones that Uchuya and Gutierrez had supposedly carved, only seven photographs were displayed, and all were of the same stone. Also strange that Adolfo's interview, published only two days later, should also be illustrated with only two photographs—of a single stone. This perplexity began to clear up for Dr. Cabrera and reveal the true nature of things when he could clearly see that the stone in the *Correo* photos is the same one as in the Bernudez Jenkis article. So, both publications used the same photographs. It was clear that while the article was busy trying to discredit Dr. Cabrera, it didn't mention other facts; it said nothing, for example, about the fact that engraved stones had been found all over Peru by different people at different times, information which alone would force one to give it a second thought.

My research on this revealed the following: the first mention of the stones was made by a Spanish priest journeying to the region of Ica in 1535.Father Simon, a Jesuit missionary, accompanying Pizarro along the Peruvian coast, wrote about his amazement upon viewing the stones. And in 1562, Spanish explorers sent some stones back to Spain. Also, the famous chronicler, Juan de Santa Cruz Pachacuti Llamqui, wrote at the time of the Inca Pachacutec, that "many carved stones were found in the kingdom of Chincha in Chimchayunga, which was called Manco." Chinchayunga was the low country of the central coast of Peru where Ica is located today. Other, more current evidence of the stones was discovered in ancient tombs at Paracas, a culture dated between 800 b.c.e. and 100 b.c.e. and the succeeding Nazca cultures dated from 100 to 800 c.e. Archaeologist Alejandro Pezzia Asserto, who was in charge of archaeological investigations in the cultural province of Ica, and a trustee of the Ica Museum, conducted official excavations in the ancient Paracas and Ica cemeteries of Max Uhle and Toma Luz. On two separate occasions, engraved stones were excavated from Pre-Hispanic Indian tombs dating from 400 b.c.e. to 700 c.e. The engraved stones were embedded in the side of the mortuary chamber of the tombs next to mummies. Asserto's degree was from the National Archaeology Department of Peru. In 1968, he published his work with drawings and descriptions of the stones, including a five-toed llama that was supposed to have been extinct for over forty million years. Other stones were of a fish that allegedly had been extinct for over 100 million years. These stones became the possession of the Ica Museum as part of the Colca Collection. Were these stone also carved by Basilio Uchuya and his wife thousands of years ago?

In the early 1960s, architect Santiago Agurto Calvo, a former rector of the National University of Engineering, was expanding his collection of engraved stones. He never gave any of the stones to the Ica Museum. The Calvo family still retains that collection of stones in storage. Calvo published an article in the El Comercio Newspaper in Lima about the fantastic things engraved on the stones. He also submitted stones for laboratory analysis to the National University of Engineering and to the Maurico Hochshild Mining Company.

Another name that was not mentioned was Colonel Omar Chioino Carraza, who was the Director of the Peruvian Aeronautical Museum, in which was revealed that he had no doubt about the stones' authenticity. After official government tests, Carraza declared in 1974: "It seems certain to me…that they are a message from a very ancient people whose memory has been lost to history. They were engraved several thousand years ago. They've been known in Peru for a long time and my museum has more than four hundred of them." It should be noted that the Aeronautical Museum's collection of engraved stones, including dinosaurs, was acquired from various locations throughout Peru; very few were from the region of Ocucaje.

In the late 1950's, Commander Elias, curator of the Callao Naval Museum, acquired some stones from huaqueros—including individuals who resided in Ocucaje. Deposits of stones found about twenty miles south-southwest of Ica near Ocuaje and the Rio Ica, and were documented to have been discovered in caves and graves. Commander Elias was a man with an ardent interest in archeology, and by 1973, he managed to have approximately three hundred stones displayed in the Naval Museum.

Nothing was mentioned in the 1975 *Mundial* article about other archeological findings either, such as: In June,1970, Dr. Richard Macneish, anthropologist and head of the Department of Archeology at the Phillips Academy, discovered, during a dig in the basin of the Montato River (a tributary of the Amazon), to the southeast of Lima, in Ayacucho, "….utensils used by humans positioned next to fossilized skeletons of prehistoric bears, horses camels, deer and various feline species. These utensils, as well as the skeletons of extinct animals (smilodon), were found across five geological strata."

According to Dr. Cabrera's extensive writings on the stones, (which had become for me, an important source of credible scientifically-based information) paleontologists tell us that the megaterio, or prehistoric bear, became extinct 1 million years ago, that the prehistoric horse and camel became extinct 13 million years ago, and that the prehistoric deer and feline became extinct 1 million years ago. Unquestionably, writes Cabrera,

"Macneish found himself faced with evidence that ancient man had co-existed with prehistoric animals and that, at the very least, this coexistence must date from the epoch in which the animals became extinct, and probably earlier. Nevertheless, Macneish did not dare reveal the true implications of his discoveries, and insisted that the tools belonged to a people who lived but 20,000 years ago. His statements reflect a very strange application of the comparative method, but they cannot hide the transcendent significance of his find."

In April 1971, in El Boqueron, in the state of Tolima, Colombia, a fossilized skeleton of the dinosaur Iguanodon, twenty meters long, was found next to a human skull.

"The fossilization process had turned the skull into gray calcareous stone with whitish striations; the eye sockets were almost obliterated; the nose was elongated; and the skull had a crest from the top of the forehead to the base of the cranium. The chin was slightly angled and the jawbone vertical, like a simian. The cranium measured 25 centimeters in length."

The find, made by Homero Henao Marin, a professor of anthropology at La Universidad de Quindio, Colombia, was of tremendous paleontological significance, for several reasons. For one, it was the first time a human fossil had been found anywhere in the world next to that of a dinosaur. Second, it was the first time in America that a human fossil was found next to this particular species of dinosaur, which allowed for the conclusion, by association, that they lived at the same time. The Iguanodon appeared at the beginning of the Jurassic period, 181 million years ago, and became extinct 63 million years ago, at the end of the Cretaceous period. In the same dig, Marin found skeletons of other animals: "a huge serpent, an animal with the head of a dog and an open gullet, as well as some petrified fins." Six years earlier, in the same area,

Marin had found a megaterio fossil, an animal that dated from the Oligocene period, 36 million years ago, and became extinct in the Pleistocene, 1 million years ago.

In 1974 Dr. A. A. Zoubov, a Russian anthropologist and a member of the Academy of Sciences, travelled at the invitation of the University in Ica to give a series of lectures. In conversation, he told Cabrera that in 1973, Hindu anthropologists had made a surprising paleontological find in India: human fossils in Mesozoic rocks. The discovery, reported to the Academy of Sciences of the USSR, established beyond doubt for Cabrera (and for me) the existence of man in the Mesozoic (in other words, between 230 and 63 million years ago). Cabrera was not only surprised by this distinctive discovery, but also that the information was hidden from the world.

All of these discoveries topple the traditional chronology of paleontology and destroy the idea, cherished by anthropologists and archeologists, of the recent origin of man.

More of the Same

In October 2001, Philip Coppens published an article in *Fortean Times* magazine entitled "Jurassic Library" in which he discredited Javier Cabrera as a clever hoaxer who worked as a team with the peasants, Basilio and Uchuya, from Ocucaje, for the purpose of attracting the tourist industry.

(The original article by Coppens can be read here)

http://www.forteantimes.com/features/articles/259/jurassic_library_the_ica_stones.html

The article begins with the following words: "Our story has several possible beginnings, but we'll start on May 13, 1966 in Ica, the capital town of a small Peruvian coastal province...."

Why not start with the facts, rather than from "possible beginnings"? Does truth have different versions or 'possible beginnings'? Or is truth what it is—with itself being the only beginning it can have? Would it be so hard for anyone who claimed to be "an investigative journalist" bold enough to claim that he also investigated the JFK assassination to avoid making premature conclusions before even beginning the investigation?

Later in his article, Coppens says the following: "Even if we assume they are genuine and millions of years old, they do not necessarily contain the type of information Cabrera maintains; the heart and brain transplants could just as well be mutilations or acts of cannibalism."

However, Dr. Stanton Maxi, a member of the American College of Surgeons had a different opinion: "….in the photographs of stone carvings depicting heart surgery, the detail is clear—seven blood vessels coming from the heart are faithfully copied. The whole thing looks like a cardiac operation, and the surgeons seem to be using 8 techniques that fit with our modern knowledge."

In addition, the Peruvian Times wrote an article about the stones in 1972, in which they concluded that the Ica stones "give a very clear picture of the operations which twentieth century surgeons are only just now contemplating." R.L. Moodie, the great paleo-pathologist, summed up his study of ancient Peruvian surgery in following words:

"I believe it to be correct to state that no primitive or ancient race of people anywhere in the world had developed such a field of surgical knowledge as had the Pre-Columbian Peruvians. Their surgical attempts are truly amazing and include amputations, excisions, trepanning, bandaging, bone transplants, cauterization and other less evident procedures."

Next, Coppens quoted the American archaeologist and publisher, David Hatcher Childress, who said, half-jokingly, "the scene showing ancients using telescopes could equally show them playing a game of prehistoric tennis."

After reading the thoughts of Coppens and Childress, I decided to consult my Peruvian nephew, who had just turned 10 years old, asking him what he saw in the images of both the surgical procedures and a man looking thru a telescope. Without any hesitation, my nephew said: "This is operation of the heart. This is operation of the brain. Here is a man with a telescope looking at the stars." (my translation of his Spanish.)

If the depictions were so obvious and so easily interpreted by a ten-year-old, how then was it ambiguous to two educated adults who are authors? Coppens also suggested that a tribal shaman could "date" a bone by entering into a trance—which showed me how little he knew about shamanism. His statement is another contribution to a common misconception of what shamanism is all about. Having done hundreds of ceremonies with Huachuma and other sacred plants, I would never claim that I could do anything like that. Shamanism, if simply put, is about getting well and finding meaning in your life—not identifying the origins of objects. If I did announce that I could "date" a bone, or stone, or any other found object, I would, by my own standards, become another charlatan with zero integrity—but perhaps with a large amount of money in the bank!

Coppens takes yet another shot: "Cabrera considered that his hypothetical ancient people–Gliptolithic Man–had larger brains than ours (even though no skeletal remains exist) and were therefore more intelligent than us."

His contempt for Cabrera is clear. Yet, I myself photographed elongated skulls in a museum in Cuzco that were clearly much bigger than those of modern mankind. Besides the one shown here in my photograph,

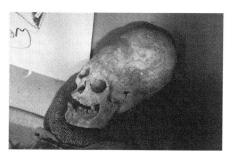

there are many other similar skulls, which have been found in the regions of Ica, Nazca, and Paracas, and are currently on display in regional museums throughout Peru.

Interestingly, one can also see trepanned skulls with evidence of circular and linear cuts, scraping and drilling techniques—which point to a surgical procedures rather than acts of mutilation or cannibalism. The clearest proof of trepanned is a skull with a frontal cranioplasty, with a gold plate and perfect healing of the bone around it. This is the view expressed by a panel of contemporary neuroscientists, whose academic titles wouldn't fit on this page.

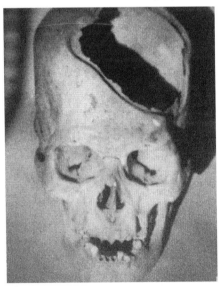

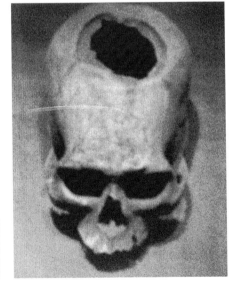

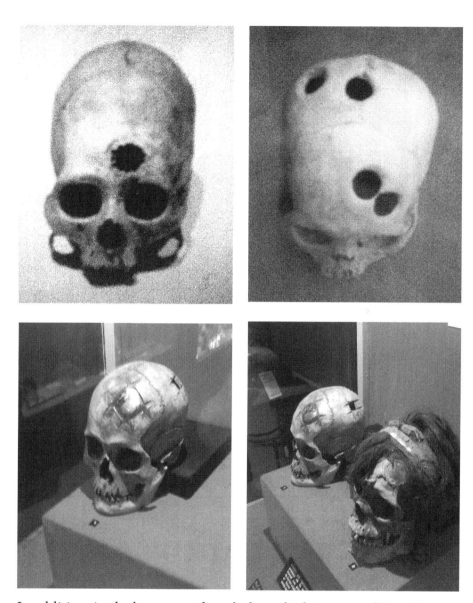

In addition, in the language of symbols—which is not traditionally regarded as "scientific," but is, in my opinion, no less informative when understood—there are engraved stones showing a patient with an opened eye during his operation, suggesting that the patient was alive and not a cadaver intended for dissection. Besides, I have to wonder, would a corpse need anesthesia or a blood transfusion as depicted on some Ica stones?

It gets better: in 2011, Coppens, along with Childress, starred in "Ancient Alliance," a television series, in which they both passionately promoted theories about ancient astronauts—the very theories which Coppens had made fun of ten years earlier in his Jurassic Library article! I must admit, his passionate defense in the series would have been quite convincing—if I had not read his first article in *Fortean Times*.

Did Coppens truly change his views so radically in a decade, and come to believe in the same theory that Dr. Cabrera had come to long before through a decade of studying the Ica stones, for which he had been discredited by the scientific establishment—and smeared by Coppens himself? Well, Coppens might have, but I have yet to see a retraction.

A final note on Dr. Cabrera: he gave the two largest engraved stones of Ica stones from his collection, one of which weighed a half ton, to Queen Sofia of Spain and Queen Silvia of Sweden:

www.museodepiedrasgrabadasdeica.com.pe/MuseoIca_Museo0111.html

They honored these gifts by placing them on exhibition in Zarzuela Palace in Madrid and Drottningholm Palace in Stockholm. How absurd it would be for a well-respected scientist and sergeant, with roots in Spanish nobility, to give forgeries to European nobility, who would subsequently put them on display in royal palaces.

I have to conclude in all honesty that certain scientific and religious dogmas have long been and continue to be maintained and well-guarded, and anyone who dares to challenge them is likely to be attacked and even their careers ruined. Nevertheless, as was so obviously true of Dr. Cabrera, it is also clear to me that there have been, and are still, honest scientists who have knowingly risked their reputations and careers—in their deep loyalty to the true meaning of science.

Meeting with Eugenia Cabrera

In July, 2010, I had a meeting with Eugenia, Dr. Cabrera's daughter, who showed me the stones in the normally closed museum of which she was now the caretaker. For this, I flew to Lima and took a five-and-a-half-hour bus ride to Ica. In all, counting all connections, I spent eleven hours in a bus that day. We met in the Plaza de Armas de Ica, the town central square; it was thrilling to enter the museum where all 11,000 stones were collected in several rooms. They were everywhere, on the floor and covering the shelves.

I had very limited time, just few hours, so I asked Eugenia to show

me what she considered the most important stones. They were more impressive than I had imagined. The people depicted were similar to modern men, but with different body proportions—the head was unusually large in comparison to the body. Seeing that, it was easy to speculate that extraterrestrial intelligence could have been at the origins of life for this ancient civilization. It was while visiting numerous museums of Peru, that I had been able to see real elongated skulls, twice as large as our modern skulls and resembling the depictions of those same figures on the Ica stones. (I spoke about this in the earlier chapter.)

The official version for the reason of these strange, elongated skulls is that this was intentional deformation achieved by ligation of the human head from an early age by a bandage in order to point out the nobility of the child. As we know, however, a hallmark of aristocracy, anywhere in the world at any given time, has been the clothing, which distinguished the rich from poor.

Let's consider the examples of this reshaping that can be seen in some African tribes—where children's heads have been bandaged to change the form of the skull. It is most likely done as a form of imitation of the ancient Egyptian deities such as Atum, Amun, and Osiris, as well as pharaohs Thutmose II, Akhenaten and his wife Nefertiti, and all their daughters. But a closer look at the skulls strapped in modern African tribes, and a comparison with the elongated skulls found in Peru, will reveal something of great significance. Even with the prolongation, the African heads are not twice as large and do not larger at the top as were those found in Peru. (The latter reminded me of an inflated balloon projecting through a fist.)

In addition to this view, another one exists: cone-shaped skulls were examples of hematoma, a swelling of the brain, which caused the patient's skull to become enlarged. Following this logic, it would appear that the ancient Egyptian gods and kings depicted on the walls of temples and tombs were merely medical text books left by a previous dynasty to be used as study material for its successors….I would wonder about that.

In addition, in the same museums, as I mentioned in the previous chapter, one can find trepanned skulls, obviously opened with surgical cutting instruments—indicated clearly by the cuts around the cranial holes. The notion that these operations were carried out with the use of primitive, volcanic, sharp rocks—which are often exhibited lying next to the trepanned skulls, seems just as ridiculous to me as the notion that megalithic ancient cities were built with primitive tools.

In conversation with Eugenia, my attention was drawn to an object lying on a table. I learned that it was a magnet from Nasca, given to her father, Dr. Cabrera, by a friend. The magnet had a flat surface, and was about 2 inches thick, 5 inches wide, and 8 inches long. Eugenia said that she treated her headaches with the help of this magnet, passing it slowly near her head for a few minutes. She reported she received the same effect from an unknown liquid, which had been seeping for years from one large, engraved stone lying on the floor near her father's desk. She said that Dr. Cabrera considered this one the most important stone in his collection. It wasn't really leaking, like an irrigation hose would, but had a spot that was always wet. The substance looked to me like oil or grease of some kind.

It was an unexplainable anomaly. She said that her headache pain went away after moistening her finger in it and putting it to her head. I also remember her saying something about the fluid affecting her state of consciousness. I do not remember her exact words, since my Spanish back then was not good, so I won't try to repeat her words (to avoid a distortion of what was said), but what I do remember is that she spoke about it quite positively and with surprise.

Eugenia was a city person who lived in Lima and was far removed from shamanic practices. She had experienced the healing properties of stones and a magnet by intuition only. I told her that the sacred plants have infinitely greater potential for healing and I asked her whether she had ever experienced shamanic plants, and she said no. I invited her to my home in the Sacred Valley to participate in a ceremony, and at that time, she agreed to come.

There were other large, engraved stones lying on the floor. On one, I saw a man looking at the sky through a telescope. Other stones represented ancient maps of continents, including the two lost continents of Mu in the Pacific Ocean, and Atlantis in the Atlantic, each continent depicting representations of different life forms. On some of them I saw pyramids and dinosaurs alongside the faces of animals and men. By association, I was remembering the story about Gurdjieff, who said that he trembled when he was shown an ancient map of Egypt by the monk in one of the monasteries of Central Asia. Gurdjieff did not say what he saw there exactly, but perhaps the map he saw had a recognizable sphinx and pyramids with a completely different landscape background, possibly not the desert, which would indicate a much earlier time period for the sphinx and the pyramids than is commonly believed. Or, did Gurdjieff perhaps see a Sphinx with a lion head instead of a body disproportional to the Sphinx's human head—which according to Dr. Robert Schoch, was re-carved during the dynasty time from its original head—which according to him, was "severely weathered and eroded" thus after re-carving becoming naturally smaller." Or, did he tremble because he perhaps was looking at a Sphinx without the pyramids at all? Whatever he saw, it made him tremble, and we can assume that it might not have been coherent with the "official" history that we have been taught about ancient Egypt.

On the subject of the magnet again, I was surprised by its force:

www.museodepiedrasgrabadasdeica.com.pe/MuseoIca_Museo0111.html
(On home page click Museo > Visitas al Museo de Ica > picture 217)

The metal paper clips were literally flying toward it. As a child, I had been passionate about the power of magnets. I loved to play with them, especially with their negative force, pushing another magnet away without touching it. But never before now had I seen such a strong one. I do not have the habit of asking for gifts, but I asked if I could take a piece for myself. Eugenia thought for a moment; then said I could not take all of it because it was the only one she had, but that I could take a piece of it. She handed me a hammer. For the next few minutes, I sat on the floor and breaking the magnet into several pieces. I asked whether I could take two pieces, and Eugenia nodded approvingly. Holding the little magnets in my hands, I was again surprised by their negative force. I shared as best I could my assumption that the presence of a large number of magnetic plates, beneath the surface of the earth, under the Nasca area in Peru for instance, could create a very powerful magnetic field, which could be used for a magnetic levitation, technology, which, for example, does exist today. (see Maglev system) Eugenia pointed to the wall on which there was a painting of a UFO taking off with a beam of light toward the constellation Pleiades. The artist had depicted the accumulation of seven shining stars in the upper corner of the painting.

This was interesting since I myself was always fascinated with the Pleiades and thought about it as a possible location of other life forms, from whose seeds our life on Earth might have flowered long ago.

In the temple of Chavin, which I mentioned in an earlier chapter, I had seen the big stone with seven holes in it, representing the Pleiades Constellation. We don't know for certain what it was used for, but if those holes are filled with water under a full moon, the reflection of moonlight creates an image very much resembling the constellation as seen by the naked eye in the night sky.

After our friendly talk, we went to have dinner, and then I took a night bus to Lima. Eugenia gave me the impression of being an honest and humble person, who I felt was like her father—although I knew him only through his book, which I wrote so much about in earlier chapters. Dr. Cabrera, as surgeon, a university professor and a member of many scientific societies, had earned the respect and credibility of so many. Using logic and science, he was able to understand the meaning of the mysterious stones of Ica, which, according to him, depicted the life of an advanced civilization of the ancient world. The Stones of Ica, as claimed by Cabrera, were not just a picture of the ancient world, but a message for future worlds. His radical theory about the emergence of life on Earth, as farfetched as it might sound, yet is not impossible, when other things considered.

As I rode on the night bus, I thought about the darkness in which we live, based on Darwin's theory of natural selection, which says that life on Earth slowly evolved through biological changes as a result of random genetic mutations. Various species gradually evolved over time, adjusting to the changing conditions of life in which the strongest species survive and multiply. Thus, according to Darwin, marine life appears from micro-organisms, then reptiles, mammals, birds, animals and finally primates, who developed into homo sapiens—as we are called today.

But, does such a theory withstand a scientific argument, which points to the fact that in molecular biology and genetics, mutation is still viewed as neutral or negative changes in genomic sequence of DNA—an error during the DNA replication? Based on this, doubt has to arise that the primitive and simple body is capable of mutating into a more complex organism and a more beautiful body. A good example of this can be seen in the nonflowering plants of the distant past, which have been found in fossils and then compared to the incredibly complex and beautiful combinations of colors and design of tropical and subtropical plants of a later period.

Or, imagine a monkey, slowly "mutating" into a beautiful, intelligent, and artistic human being, who can perform surgeries, play violin, write poetry, or create timeless paintings—all due to genetic disorder!

Let's take a slightly deeper look at this idea: Paleobotany, a branch of Paleontology dealing with the evolutionary history of plants, is telling us that before the early Cretaceous period (145 million years ago) the vegetation on our planet primarily consisted of gymnosperms—seed-producing—and ferns—seedless, both nonflowering plants. We have also been told that these plants were suddenly replaced by an entirely new group of plants—the angiosperms (flowering plants), which made their first appearance in the tropics, then spread around the world toward the end of the Cretaceous (65 million years ago) replacing the non-flowering plants. This sudden increase in diversity of flowering plants was one of the greatest puzzles faced by Charles Darwin, who in his letter to Joseph Hooker, dated 22 July 1879, referred to an "abominable mystery." Perhaps he called it this because this mystery was contradicting to his own theory of gradual evolution on Earth. The great diversity of fossil flowering plants from the late Cretaceous, and virtually no fossils known from the early Cretaceous, was completely in conflict with his version that the emergence of new species could only take place very gradually. While Darwin was baffled by this question, perhaps trying to fit this fact into his evolutionary theory, over one hundred years later, we have now been offered yet another theory, which says that perhaps these massive sudden changes "could be attributed to the plant's capacity to transform the world to their own needs and simultaneously evolve with the insect species that had to pollinate their flowers in order to reproduce."

Well, it sounded like good theory and seemed it could put the debate to rest, but looking at Entomophily—a form of pollination where pollen is distributed by the insects who are attracted by the colored and/or strong scent developed by the plant, another question arises. Logic tells us that the plant had first to develop the necessary qualities, or to evolve in itself, in order to reproduce with the help of the insects through pollination. So how were these plants reproducing before that and what were these pollinating insects supposed to be doing while waiting for the plants finally to evolve so they could get busy working? Or could it be that plants have given birth to pollinated insects who weren't there before? To what absurdity would we get to if we to follow this line of thought?

To me this idea looks more like adaptation to the world rather than a transformation of the world—which makes me think that modern evolutionary science has not evolved that much since Darwin's time, who in fact was leaning more toward adaptation of the species. In my mind, this indicates plants do have a certain type of intelligence (which we need to consider and factor in) while studying evolutionary process—

which in itself leads to whole another subject of consciousness in broader sense. But, in the interest of staying on the subject, it becomes evident that this question is similar to the one about who came first? the egg or the chicken? Whichever answer is the correct one, one thing is certain—one of them had to come first! And that alone should put the idea of simultaneous evolution to rest. If my logical conclusion debunks the idea of simultaneous evolution of plants and the insects, then what else could cause this sudden change which baffled—and still baffles scholars?

And what about the primates? Why did only some of them supposedly evolve to human and others didn't?

I must admit that Darwinian theory-based ideas about how we can trace our ancestry back to the primates and their migration and adaptation, to me sound a bit like a scientific fables. So if both Darwinism, and Creationism—which say that the world was created in six days—does not hold water or make a solid case, then what does? Could it be that "genetic" interference, from outside the bounds of our planet, at the universal level, into organic life on Earth, took place in the distant past, and thus "intelligence" was seeded into the biomass native to the planet? It is worth considering, is it not?

Can we actually continue to believe that all this transformational evolution of consciousness, which took place, was merely the result of negative mutation and genetic failure to copy DNA? Would a better example be to look at negative mutation due to radiation exposure where the offspring are a clear deviation from the DNA of their parents resulting in ugliness? Or, finally, does

Darwin's theory withstand the striking ancient archaeological monuments, which still baffle scientists in 2012? To this day, for example, we don't know for certain, by whom, when, or how Ollantaytambo Sacsayhuaman and other ancient monuments were built.

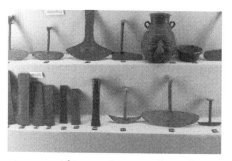

It would be ludicrous to think that all these structures were built by Incas with primitive bronze tools that were found in the tombs and can now be seen in the museums. It would be hard to imagine a person with bronze knives and a hatchet, cutting a 100-ton granite stone as if it was butter, then fitting it together perfectly with another block, then placing more of the same on top—like pillows. It would be like saying that brain surgery was performed with the same tools, without anesthesia or a highly sterile environment in which such operations are performed.

And, if all this was done by people more primitive than us, why then can we not repeat it today? Why can't we even build another modern wall like Sacsayuaman or Ollantaytambo with the modern tools we have? Or why not try to operate on person brain with Inca tools? Who would like to be a patient?

Well, one might think, what if those operations were performed on dead people as a study in practice?

To put this argument to rest would be quite easy by looking at this picture where a gold plate was used for skull reconstruction which was nicely healed by the bones around it. Would that healing take place if the patient were dead? Anyway, I realized that this discussion could go on for a very long time, but as it was already clear, we weren't told the true story from day one and were led to believe in scientific fables that were not based on facts.

I could only imagine how Dr. Cabrera would feel confronting the "luminaries" of modern science.

Eugenia had mentioned constant pressure put on her father by the authorities in order to close the museum, which wasn't a surprise after seeing the stones.

One observation of significant was of interest to me was that the Ica stones were void of religious context. As we know, in the art at the center of nearly every known culture one sees the elements of its philosophies, spiritual beliefs and practices, and its formalized religions. Art of the European Middle Ages, for example, is notorious for its plethora of biblical scenes painted on the walls of churches and cathedrals throughout the world.

An active religious life can be seen in pre-Columbian cultures, depicting worship of the Divine in another form. It is quite obvious that our civilization is rooted in religious ground with roots in the mystical experiences of our ancestors from all parts of our globe. These experiences are considered to be the most important events that occurred in antiquity within different cultures. The sacred rites, the kernels of the different religions, indicate a divine intervention, which becomes a cornerstone for their beliefs. It's not to argue about the validity of it, it's only to show that religious context is the bases of every known culture.

I found myself wondering: Could it be that the absence of religious landscape in Ica stones speaks of an another time, a much more ancient time, when an intelligent life on earth could be genetically seeded by extraterrestrial beings who mixed their DNA with the DNA of Neanderthals native to the Earth? In this respect, the biblical expression that man was created in the image and likeness of God, takes on an entirely different meaning. And if that was the case, then we truly are one with our "Creator," sharing the same DNA.

Regardless of whether these attempts to genetically improve the life on Earth were just a sort of experimental science, like that we practice repeatedly today in labs, or was it already perfected science which served a specific purpose create intelligent life on Earth for a yet unknown reason why. And still, I think it is important to remember that these are only theories which we can't prove or disprove at this point – just like the Darwinian theory of evolution of species is only a theory even though is taught in schools as fact. In this sense, it would be fair to give consideration to other theories which could be equally valid or invalid as Darwinian, but since they have been opposed to—ridiculed and discredited as such.

Or we suppose to believe that life on Earth is the first life form in a 14-billion year old visible Universe (the astronomical number the age our universe has been assigned, and even that estimation may grow older with time and better technology) or should we be speculating (perhaps even arrogantly) that this infinite Universe was created just for us—making us the center and the jewel of it?

After all, just centuries ago, people thought that Earth was flat, and it would appear that now we still are thinking the same way about things like origin and evolution of humanity and other life forms in the infinite Universe. Given the knowledge of basic astronomy such as that our Galaxy contains approximately 100 billion stars and 200 billion planets, of which 100 million Earth-like solid planets can support life – then multiplying these numbers by at least 100 billion known Galaxies, and what would we have? A probability of other life forms of astronomical proportions—to say the least!

Such thoughts and wonderings kept me awake and occupied as the all-night bus made its way across the desert to Lima.

Sometime later, I gave a small sample of Cabrera's magnet to a laboratory in Moscow to see what they could find out about it. A statement came back that no anomalies were found and that the magnet was a naturally occurring magnetite with an element of barite, a mineral that forms at medium to low temperatures under hydrothermal conditions and precipitation, which is quite surprising when you find yourself in the middle of Nazca plateau—a hot and dry desert without any signs of rainfall. Could it be that at one point the climate has dramatically changed in this area in the same way as it possibly could have in the Giza plateau, which is just as hot and dry and yet its famous monument of Sphinx has evidence of water erosion? That of course leads to another subject. But here it was interesting in the sense that in today's world, powerful magnets of this kind are only made artificially. And yet, that night, the one I held in my hand and played with as I mused on the bus, and feeling its huge inherent power, was natural and was found in an area referred to as Nasca—which became famous in the late 20th century for its "lines." Could it be that a magnetic field of Nasca plateau was identified long before us and marked by famous Nasca figures (perhaps an ancient prototype of modern-day crop circles) which can be seen in their entirety only from above? Who knows how much of "latecomers" we humans actually are?

Dangers vs. Benefits

It would appear that knowledge, which could potentially change the usual picture of the world, has long been controlled by those who do not want to lose their power and authority over the masses. In other words, one could say there has been a "cover-up" of some evidence in regards to certain highly developed ancient civilizations; even today, in 2012, the origins of some of these civilizations are still unknown and are open to continuing investigation and speculation. The fact that the suppression of discovery and knowledge continues, indicates that the conventional theories of creation and evolution are, at best, historical efforts to explain, rather than answers to real questions. However, as the previous chapter demonstrated, honest people in science are trying to counter this—often risking their reputations and careers.

There is much written these days about the increasing convergence between religion and science, but we should not overlook the historical reality and nature of their relationship too soon; in fact, for centuries, both religion and science have tried hard to keep control of the story of "how things are" regarding human evolution on Earth.

Given my experience at Chavin (and other sacred places as well), and the story of the Ica Stones, for example, I have to ask: Is there a relationship between a case of forbidden archeology and the preponderance of forbidden rituals?

I began my thinking by coming up with possible reasons for modern-day cultural establishment to prohibit rituals in sacred sites. Originally, I reasoned, these sites had been built for the purpose of rituals. So I hypothesized that in those days, people were able to activate the "power" of the places on which the sacred sites were usually built. This activation would release a certain kind of energy that was then shared among people seeking spiritual awakening. The revival of such rituals today, I realize, might very well contribute to insight and understanding for millions of people, therefore showing them their own mental slavery—potentially leading to rebellion against such enslavement. I am reminded of the drama of Jesus. Did not the authorities of that time crucify him (a human being) who had taught liberating ideas) because they feared losing their power and control over the people? Imagine a liberating knowledge (not human) but rather in the form of energy that cannot be imprisoned, crucified, burned, or stopped in anyway?

Even though today there are still remote countries and spots in the world where people can be persecuted and even killed for religious or spiritual practices, it is generally true among developed nations that we are "free" to believe and practice our religions, our meditation, and to read literature on virtually all subjects, no matter how esoteric. But we should also consider that perhaps the true reason why these activities are acceptable is because in and of themselves, they do not threaten to "trigger" a collective leap in human consciousness—which is in fact necessary for any significant change to occur in how we see the world. It seems that man is safely left in his age-old perceptions that contain still a lot of fear and ignorance. P. Ouspensky called it "tumbling from corner to corner, while thinking you are moving up the floor."

Thus, for example, the propaganda about the dangers of the use of age-old shamanic plants and a negative public attitude towards shamanism, are maintained. The powers that be somehow know that hard core shamanic practice, along with the use of sacred plants, are capable of triggering serious changes in human consciousness and are a potent and real threat to long established power and the ability to manipulate collective thought.

Consider how many stimulant substances such as sugar and coffee, for example, are sold legally without any concern for your health. This should make you think about why other substances with zero toxicity are banned completely and made illegal. Coffee, sugar, alcohol, and cigarettes cause health problems immensely greater than "illegal" wild plants, which have medicinal roots in antiquity. Coffee is addictive and requires larger doses as the body becomes accustomed to caffeine. It also prevents the absorption of nutrients and washes away necessary minerals from the body. It has actually been found to be dangerous for people predisposed to or suffering with diseases of the cardiovascular system. Dependence on sugar is among the most powerful problems in our "developed western" diets. Sugar contributes to a number of diseases such as diabetes, multiple sclerosis, obesity, tooth decay, and it lowers the immune system. Smoking is addictive and triggers cancer. And the devastating effects of alcohol addiction on the human body, psyche, family, and society are obvious and beyond all arguments.

Yet, all of the above are sold easily and freely, without inquiry into your medical, physical, psychological, or criminal history. And why is that? Well, it would appear that to the regulating bodies of government your health does not matter. The only thing that matters is profit. Especially when it comes to pharmaceuticals and medical sales. Profit in this area is counted by tens of billions of dollars a year—conservatively. How naive it would be to think that corporate heads, whose income is billions of dollars a year, care about anything other than the increase in their revenues? In fact, it would seem that they might even be trying to "find" (or invent) new diseases in order to expand markets for their products.

The only logical conclusion I have been able to consistently come to, from the beginning of my search for answers up to the present, is that the goal of a well-functioning mechanism of the market is to squeeze out of us as much money as possible. Anything that sells well and creates a continued demand for it will always be legal for the masses, regardless of its effect on people's health. At the same time, it seems, those substances (such as the sacred plants mentioned earlier), which can help a person to get rid of harmful and destructive addictions will be banned.

One has to conclude that the "bad" habits of some people bring profits to others. Thanks to this kind of mind set, massive numbers of people continue to be sick and do not have a chance of getting healed. To the music of this special interest group, dance the bureaucrats who are writing the necessary laws to protect and promote their unhealthy agenda. I reflect on an all-too-often occurrence regarding the use of cannabis. For example, someone can go to the pharmacy and buy a legal, opium-based antidepressant whose side effects can cause fear, anger, aggression, hostility, hallucinations, psychosis, and thoughts of suicide. No one is alarmed—in fact, often the establishment of doctors convinces even the family of that person that things will go better if pharmaceuticals are used. (I will go into the use of pharmaceuticals a little further on.) And, another person can get a little cannabis and peacefully transform it into blue smoke at home with the intent to re-lieve his or her physical or emotional pain—and perhaps try to reflect on its causes. But, a brainwashed neighbor, alarmed by the smell com-ing from the smoker's apartment, has called the police. Now, the person who may not have completed a necessary alchemical process with the cannabis, is disturbed by the loud knocks of (now I am describing an actual incident that occurred—the swat team who was ready to take him to jail and actually shot the owner's dog in front of his eyes…and then ordered Youtube to "pull" the video (under a copyright claim or other reason). After that, as usual, they spun it in the news about how "dangerous" the man was and how "aggressive" his dog was, protecting the home from a late-night invasion of armed men in masks.

http://www.infowars.com/missouri-swat-team-shoots-family-dog-during-raid-over-%E2%80%9Csmall-amount%E2%80%9D-of-marijuana

There have also been cases when the swat team raid was conducted on the wrong house, killing the pets and traumatizing the family members for life without remorse…but I'm digressing here…my temptation is to get caught up in the injustice of it all.

http://www.wnd.com/2012/08/cops-kill-dog-handcuff-kids-in-wrong-house-raid/

We should remember that in India, for example, wild cannabis grows like a weed and has been smoked by people for thousands of years, in-cluding the old time Yogis who have used cannabis and other plants to deepen and to enhance their meditation. Use of wild plants for healing and for spiritual purposes is deeply imbedded in the cultures of both India and Peru. They have served as good, effective medicine and are superior to any pharmaceutical toxic drugs that can be patented and monopolized—something which is difficult if not impossible to do with most wild plants.

It would appear then, that what kills a person slowly is legal, but what truly helps him is banned. The deplorable reality of Western psychiatry, and its impotence in matters of mental health, is evident, and all of it can be expected, since it uses pharmaceutical medicines. These medicines, by definition, are drugs which only dull the physical pain, or drive a person into an emotional stupor to temporarily suppress the symptoms rather than addressing the causes of the disease—thus eventually contributing to the problem. A temporary blunting of physical pain, or mental discomfort, sometimes can cost more than just money; it can cost people their lives.

In the USA, when a celebrity dies as an apparent victim of pharmaceutical overdose (among the most recently and most notable: Michael Jackson, Whitney Houston, Heath Ledger, Marilyn Monroe, Judy Garland, Elvis Presley…) it attracts the attention of the media, and there is much popular discussion and debate about whether individual character or collective social responsibility is at the heart of the problem. The fact remains that addiction to prescription drugs is currently one of the highest statistics on record in the current medical industry. But celebrities are only a few among hundreds of thousands of people in America who are quietly dying in their beds every year from "prescribed" hence "legal" medication—and either misuse of or adverse reactions to these drugs in their systems. According to the following statistics, the annual death rate in America from adverse reactions to prescribed drugs alone is above one hundred-thousand:

http://www.ourcivilisation.com/medicine/usamed.htm

http://www.ourcivilisation.com/medicine/usamed/deaths.htm

This necessitates a close look at the current approaches to the treatment of mental health in the US. It is widely known that the preferred method of treatment today is the employment of anti-depressant, anti-anxiety, and anti-psychotic drugs. A 2005 study by the Centers for Disease Control and Prevention showed that 2.4 billion drugs were prescribed by doctors and hospitals. Of those, 118 million were anti-depressants—figures that are cause for serious consideration. The alleged effectiveness of these medications is reported to reduce the epidemic of mental illness in America, but, in fact, mental crises and illnesses are increasing every year, is penetrating into all age groups, including children of six and seven years old—who are now being diagnosed and put on medications—which in some cases has caused their deaths.

http://psychiatricnews.wordpress.com/2009/04/23/7-year-old-on-psychiatric-drugs-hangs-himself/

And if you think that drugging seven year old children is an outrage, wouldn't you agree that drugging infants under 1 year old would not be only insanity but a crime? I urge you to read a testimony before Congress by Gregory D. Kutz, Director Forensic Audits and Investigative Service which can be found here:

http://www.gao.gov/new.items/d12270t.pdf

This testimony admits that such practices do exist in different states beginning from paragraph: "Psychotropic prescriptions for infants" page 15 and forward.

More facts on the subjects can be found here:

http://www.infowars.com/18-crazy-facts-which-show-that-no-nation-on-earth-is-more-doped-up-on-prescription-drugs-than-america-is/

Available data for 2010 shows the number of prescription drugs sold has increased nearly 60% since 2005 and hit 3,703,594,389 drugs sold totaling $220,338,509,960. If taken, even at the same rate proportionally as it was in 2005, then the total antidepressants sold in one year would be around 190,000,000. Below is a website showing the total number of retail prescription drugs filled at pharmacies in 2011. If you don't think it epidemic then I don't know what is! We're talking astronomical proportions here!

http://www.statehealthfacts.org/comparemaptable.jsp?ind=265&cat=5

Why is there such a rise in demand for medication to "treat" mental illness? In early 2011, there were 44 million Americans receiving monthly food stamps, but by September of the same year, there were already 46 million people below the poverty level. This figure is equal to the population of Spain and 13 million more than the entire population of

Canada. Coincidentally, these tens of millions of Americans who are now below the poverty line are also eligible for free prescription drug coverage thru Medicare part D, a federal subsidiary program for below-income households that covers both anti-depressants and anti-psychotic drugs. Is it really coincidence, or dare one speculate that huge masses of people, dissatisfied with the loss of economic security along with the hope for any improvement in their situations might "rise up" in some form of rebellion—if not for the "calming" effect of such readily available chemical agents. Except, the calming effect these chemicals can also lead to very negative consequences.

In December, 1994, Professor David Healy interviewed Jonathan Cole, Director of Psychopharmacology Research at the National Institute of Mental Health. Healy asked: "What about a group of patients who may get worse on Prozac? Cole responded: Yes. I'm one of the authors of the suicide paper. Yes, I have seen people, at least a handful, who clearly got more agitated and got weird thoughts and developed a suicidal drive."

Another researcher, Tony Rothschild, found three people taking Fluoxetine who had jumped off something and survived. They agreed to take it again and the same desperation driven quality was re-created with Fluoxetine (Prozac). Also, many other well documented cases show extreme violence associated with antidepressant use. This article below lists just a few of them:

http://www.infowars.com/antidepressant-drugs-causing-epidemic-of-mania/

More antidepressant nightmarish stories are here:

http://ssristories.com/index.html

It is important to take a look at the chemistry (the actual active ingredients) of these dangerous drugs. For example: A key ingredient in Prozac is fluoride (fluoxetine), a toxic industrial waste product which was used for mind control by the Nazis. A scientist names Charles Elliot Perkins was sent by the U.S. Government to take charge of the I.G. Farben chemical plants in Germany following WWII. He concluded that the real purpose behind water fluoridation was to reduce the resistance of the masses to domination, control and loss of liberty. In his report to the Lee Foundation for Nutritional Research in October of 1954, he stated: "Repeated doses of infinitesimal amounts of fluoride will, in time, reduce an individual's power to resist domination by slowly poisoning and narcotizing a certain area of the brain, thus making him submissive to the will of those who wish to govern him." One can't help but wonder if this may have been at the base of the shocking "obedience" to Nazi tyranny, brutal torture, and surgical procedures carried out on prisoners without anesthesia.

To highlight the scope of pharmaceutical intoxication, we can look at another study, which may appear somewhat comic, if not insignificant and yet, is actually quite tragic and has great evolutionary and environmental implications: Research out of the University of Portsmouth in the U.K. has found that pharmaceutical waste runoff, and particularly that of anti-depressant drugs like Prozac, is causing shrimp and other exposed crustaceans to change their behavior in ways such that many more of them than usual to die off. According to the study, shrimp exposed to anti-depressants from waste runoff are five times more likely to swim towards light—which means they are far more likely to encounter fishermen's nets and birds that are hungry for a meal. While they would normally stay in more protected areas, these drug-induced sea creatures appear to be basically committing suicide.

Alex Ford, also a leading researcher, said this in a press release: "Crustaceans occupy a critical place in the food chain. And, if the natural behavior of shrimp varies due to the level of anti-depressants in the sea, it could seriously affect the natural balance of the ecosystem. Most of what people are consuming can be detected in the water in some concentrations. It is not surprising that what we get from the pharmacy is also contaminating the water and sewer ways of the country. "

The report continued that under the influence of anti-depressants, the natural behavior of certain species deviates from the norm. They appear to be losing the natural instinct of self-preservation. In addition, the report added, fluoride blocks the pineal gland which is responsible for the regulation of hormonal background, biorhythms and the human immune system, potentially leading to further depression, obesity, neurodegenerative diseases and cancer.

Standing on occasion in the aisle of the average pharmacy or supermarket, while staring at the overwhelming variety of toothpastes and mouth-"sanitizing" products, I can't help but ask myself: How could a toxic waste product from the aluminum, chemical, and atomic industries, be turned into a therapeutic agent for the prevention of tooth decay? The question seems obvious and necessary. And the answer as well, however, the more inquisitive or even skeptical reader can learn by reading a monumental work by Christopher Bryson "Fluoride Deception" consisting of nearly 10 years research into the facts on this topic:

This chapter, in fact this topic of the dangers versus the benefits of the current pharmaceutical industry and its global effects (in my opinion, more negative than positive) could go on and on—in fact any reader can find a plethora of articles and books written on this and related topics—as many as hundreds of new ones each day. It was not and is not my intention to write an expose on the pharmaceutical industry, but I must go on record as acknowledging a major reason why this situation has reached such a high level of danger for all of us now and in the future. It has to do with power and politics—doesn't almost everything nowadays?

The shocking ties between big corporations and regulatory agencies are neither new nor diminishing. Today the "revolving door" is in full swing just as it was decades ago (the movement of management personnel back and forth between the legislative branch of government and regulatory agencies and the resultant regulatory and legislative effects on corporations). Some good examples can be seen between biotech corporations and FDA—a conflict of interests that is as apparent as the wind behind the ocean waves (you can't see it but you know it's present) and should raise huge questions about safety for the consumer. Government ties to pharmaceutical industry should also be growing concern, and while public is fed genetically modified organisms (GMO), there continue to appear fake studies showing this food to be as being equal and healthy as organic food. Yet, there is fast-growing evidence that it is as potentially deadly to all organic life on Earth in the long run as a nuclear war. At the same time, we are sold on dubious FDA approved vaccines, which have been shown over and over again to cause all kinds of neurological disorders in children such as narcolepsy, paralyzes and death.

As I reflect on "cozy and penetrating" relationships in the world, my mind naturally goes to the ones between the banks and the Treasury

Department—which (coincidentally) is currently headed by a former president of NY Federal Reserve Bank—which is a privately own bank bearing a federal logo. I find myself wondering if open barrels of fish guarded by cats would look any different?

Well, I could continue this musing to the point where you would not be able to read it anymore, feeling disgusted in your guts, but I encourage you to do your own research and find more about it.

In my research I also encounter something that is very close to my own deeply personal concerns for the future of our children and our children's children (I keep seeing my tiny daughter's face before me). In 1970, a Congressional hearing was held on whether or not to fund research into pharmacological drug treatment using amphetamines for children's school-related problems, such as Attention Deficit Hyperactivity Disorder (ADHD). During the hearing, Dr. John D. Griffith, Assistant Professor of Psychiatry, Vanderbilt University School of Medicine, testified:

"I would like to point out that every drug, however innocuous, has some degree of toxicity. A drug, therefore, is a type of poison and its poisonous qualities must be carefully weighed against its therapeutic usefulness. A problem, now being considered in most of the Capitols of the Free World, is whether the benefits derived from Amphetamines outweigh their toxicity. It is the consensus of the World Scientific Literature that the Amphetamines are of very little benefit to mankind. They are, however, quite toxic."

http://www.ritalindeath.com/Against-ADHD-Diagnosis.htm

This type of scientific, honest look at the risks, weighed against the benefits, of psychiatric medications is rare today—though more than ever necessary. The reason for this is that the psychiatric diagnosis and subsequent sale of anti- depressants is very profitable to all who are involved with production, marketing and sales of these drugs. However, the reports are being accurately compiled and are available to those who want to know the truth.

How Two Weeks of Chemotherapy Killed My Mother

In mid-July 2012, right after my 36th birthday, I received the e-mail from my sister. I talked to her same day. She told me that a cancer was found in our mother's stomach. My father didn't want me to find out, but she thought I had to know. I was truly shocked; my mother was known for being a strong hard-working woman. We never knew if and when she was ever ill because she just kept doing her things in the house and never said anything. And even after the cancer was found in her, she made no complaints until the point when she could no longer eat. I told my sister to tell my mom to meet me on the computer (on Skype) as soon as she could.

By the time I got the news about mom's cancer, chemotherapy had already been started. She had an immediate and a violent reaction to it. She was brought home and lay in bed vomiting continuously. The doctor said that it was a normal reaction to this type of treatment and it would take some time for the body to adjust. I wasn't content with that; I contacted my friend, a Shipibo maestro ayahuascero, and asked if he could cure her. He said it would take a month. Great, I thought, now we just needed the money to bring her to Peru. But her condition was already so bad that even going from her bed to her kitchen was too hard, let alone flying from Israel to the other side of the world. I invited my friend to my house anyway to do a special ceremony to support my mother. It was just the two of us. The energy was very heavy that night, and when he looked at her picture and said that she was very weak, I knew exactly what he meant. Tears came to my eyes, and feeling a deep heartache, I sensed the reality that she wouldn't survive.

After that first devastating week of chemotherapy, we talked on Skype. She looked tired, but still pretty much the way I had always seen her. I asked her if she wanted me to come to Israel. She smiled and said, "No, son, don't worry. Do what you need to do. I am not planning to die." Her smile and her words had a calming effect on me—and I somehow began to think there was still hope.

This was our last real conversation. After that, our Skype connection was vastly different….my mom was not responding anymore. It was like watching her body on the screen, but her mind was not there. The setting of these bizarre encounters was in the hospital, with my mom in the bed…staring at the screen without seeming to see anything. My family was with her at all times. My father told me that the doctor had begun to give her anti-psychotic drugs to "help her relax." I didn't know what he was talking about. Later I learned the shocking truth. The problem was that when my mom started her negative reaction to the treatment of chemotherapy, she said she wanted to quit this and go home and be at peace, letting nature take its course. It seems like the doctor decided that this state of mind was "psychosis" and needed to be treated with psychotropic. (I'm thinking to myself: "The doctors want to keep her "relaxed" in the hospital so they can continue to give her the chemotherapy—the drugs that are killing her so fast and so painfully!"

Working on my book became almost impossible. I was thinking about her all the time, and could not believe that this was really happening. It was so out of the blue. I didn't know what to do; should I find the money and go to Israel to visit her or wait? Days were passing. I couldn't sleep at night, and I couldn't work during the day. I was in a kind of stupor. When the second week of chemotherapy began, I was getting a daily updates on her condition, which was getting worse and worse. All this time, the doctor was saying that it was all normal and she needed some time to recover. But I knew that I needed to go, and was able to buy a plane ticket for August 14. That gave me about ten days to take care of things at home. But the condition of my mother was now deteriorating daily. My sister and my father were going every day to visit her in hospital and stay all day. My sister had a laptop with her—so at least I could be with them in this way. Every morning I would wake and see her lying in the hospital bed, looking worse and worse. One day I woke up and saw her with an oxygen mask; that's when I knew I had to change my flight date and get there as fast as possible. The 12th was the earliest possibility. On August 10, two days before I was supposed to fly to Israel, logging into Skype was very slow and somehow felt different. When I finally did get through, my sister said the doctor had told them not to leave because my mom had only hours to live. I could hardly believe it: I was on Skype watching my mother dying, sitting together with my father and my sister listening to the machine above her bed with signals reflecting her slowing pulse. This was the last hour of her life. I asked my sister to put her laptop close to my mom's ear. She did, and I told her last words—that I would love her always and she could go in peace without worrying for anything. Ten minutes later her pulse stopped.

My sister, by my request scheduled the funeral for the 14th, so that I could attend. I flew out of Lima on August 12 and arrived in Israel on the 14th at 5 am. I took a shower after two days of traveling and lay down until people started to come at around 8—after two days of travel, I had only three hours rest before the funeral. It was like being in a nightmare from which you cannot wake up. While still in Peru, I had been looking for excuses not to go; I was afraid to see my mother dead. But I also knew that if I didn't, I would think of myself as a coward and never forgive myself. So I went to face what I had to. We arrived at the cemetery and all stood around as my mom's body was rolled out. That was the hardest moment, but I knew that my father needed me the most, and I had to be strong for him. After prayers were said by the rabbi, we all went to the burial place. More prayers were said, and then the body was slowly lowered into the hole—in that moment her death to me felt final. I had to hold onto my father who had fallen on the grave in tears.

We went home and began shiva. In the Jewish tradition it means the sitting for seven days. No TV....no radio....no nothing. All mirrors are supposed to be covered. During that time family, relatives, friends, and neighbors were coming to visit, bringing food, since no cooking could be done during the first week. The days were passing very slowly and I was in difficulty. Here I was sitting in the house of my parents, after not being there for years, and instead of visiting them in a good way, I had come to escort my mother on her final way. My grief was mixed with anger that my father did not tell me what was happening early enough, thus blocking any chance we had to save her by bringing her to Peru. I didn't want to add to his grief by blaming him for that. After all, his intentions were good and he sincerely wanted to help my mother. But I knew then that this regret about how he handled it would stay with me forever...even after the time comes when it is right to tell him how I feel.

The sad irony is that the chemotherapy, which was supposed to save my mom, became the probable cause of her quick and sudden death......it was scheduled for three weeks....but only two weeks was needed to kill her.

My dear mother, these words of my everlasting love will be written to you in this book. You were a great mother. Your hard work, your care, your love, and your dedication to us will be remembered always. Rest in peace, wherever you are.

Legal Does Not Necessarily Mean Healthy

I have touched only the tip of the iceberg on the dangers of current pharmacopeia (particularly in North America and the rest of the "developed" world), and shared the personal tragedy of losing my mother suddenly through the misguided modern medical system—with its obsessive attachment to synthesized drugs for the treatment of all illnesses—physical and psychological. While this is not a book on that specific subject, I think it was important to explore the ramifications of the uses and abuses of allopathic medicine and to identify some connections to the politics of keeping natural and spiritual healing traditions from entering the mainstream.

So, as part of this exploration, I have taken a brief look at the criminality of the overall "drug scene" from the perspective of comparing and contrasting. At the most general level, if we look at the statistics of crimes committed under the influence of alcohol vs. crimes committed under influence of sacred plants, such as Peyote, Huachuma, or Ayahuasca, a logical question would arise: why is alcohol legal, and sacred plants are not?

For example, among 250,000 participants in the Native American Church, who practice the religious use of peyote, statistics available to the public indicate that there is almost no crime committed among Native Americans working religiously with sacred peyote—a plant that is recognized for thousands of years as helping lead one to prudence and sanity and respect for moral norms and goodness. Equally available to the public are statistics reporting that as of 2012, alcohol-based crime is on the rise throughout the globe. Alcohol is long recognized for its effects on humans—making them aggressive and more likely to commit crime.

One of the strongest links I can make between keeping business as usual about legalization and criminalization of certain substances is the financial one—making money big-time. For example, right now, business is booming for the prison industry. One latest statistic is that for every 100,000 Americans, 743 citizens are incarcerated annually, totaling more than six million inmates. Just to make a comparison, this annual figure exceeds the amount of prisoners held in the camps of the former Soviet Union at any point in its entire history!

Between 1970 and 2009, in the U.S., the number of people in custody increased 772 per cent, due mainly to the influence of private corporations on the legal system. To protect this business model, millions have been spent lobbying state officials and political candidates in an effort to influence harsher "zero tolerance" legislation and mandatory sentencing for many non-violent offenses.

Let's take a look at the booming prison industry in America.

As of 2012, the USA prison population is about six million people a year with each inmate costing the taxpayers nearly $50,000 dollars a year. Multiplying 6 million times, $50,000 dollars a year would equal revenues that would make a non-criminal society an impossibility. Among other interested parties, the owners of private prisons would certainly do anything required to prevent this from happening.

Here are some more links for you to follow:

http://www.lao.ca.gov/laoapp/laomenus/sections/crim_justice/6_cj_inmate-cost.aspx?catid=3

Again, I am especially concerned about these issues when it comes to young people, as I have expressed earlier in this book. A chilling example of how extensive the problem of wrongful imprisonment that occurred in 2008, in what is known as the Kids for Cash Scandal. In

Pennsylvania, judges accepted money from private-owned detention facilities in return for sentencing youth to incarceration. Investigation revealed that the owners of the detention centers received state funds based on number of inmates. During the investigation, both judges pleaded guilty for receiving over two million dollars in bribes from a youth facility operator and were sentenced to long prison terms. The same fate befell the operator, who for personal gain, had shattered the lives of thousands of children and their families. Later, the Pennsylvania Supreme Court ordered hundreds of convictions overturned.

http://www.jlc.org/current-initiatives/promoting-fairness-courts/Luzerne-kids-cash-scandal

Here are few more links that back up my point:

http://www.globalresearch.ca/profit-driven-prison-industrial-complex-the-economics-of-incarceration-in-the-usa/29109

http://www.infowars.com/private-prison-company-to-demand-90-occupancy/

An annual report released by the CCA in 2010 is very telling of the hidden ties I am referring to:

"The demand for our facilities and services could be adversely affected by the relaxation of enforcement efforts, leniency in conviction or parole standards and sentencing practices or through the decriminalization of certain activities that are currently proscribed by our criminal laws. For instance, any changes with respect to drugs and controlled substances or illegal immigration could affect the number of persons arrested, convicted, and sentenced, thereby potentially reducing demand for correctional facilities to house them. Legislation has been proposed in numerous jurisdictions that could lower minimum sentences for some non-violent crimes and make more inmates eligible for early release based on good behavior. Also, sentencing alternatives under consideration could put some offenders on probation with electronic monitoring who would otherwise be incarcerated. Similarly, reductions in crime rates or resources dedicated to prevent and enforce crime could lead to reductions in arrests, convictions and sentences requiring incarceration at correctional facilities."

To bring it to a more personal level, I recently heard from a friend who told me about a person who was sentenced to 3 years in prison for helping hundreds of people get rid of the destructive addiction of heroin, using iboga bark. This bark is from a sacred plant used by African shamans which, of course, in America is prohibited. It is worthwhile to mention that the curing process of this terrible addiction takes just two to three days. I myself have never worked with iboga, but I have a friend who has. He said that consuming it was the most difficult test in his life—which he would not like to go through again. To me this indicates that iboga would never become popular, and it turning into a pill that could be sold on the streets is highly unlikely. Why, then, is it prohibited if it is indeed capable of curing such serious drug addictions?

The same is true with Ayahuasca which is always a challenge to work with. The recreational use of this powerful sacred plant, which means "Vine of the Dead" in Quechua, would be again so unlikely.

In thinking about all of this, I have to ask: Why, in modern western society, are things this way?

Is it because the police need crime like doctors need illnesses, and spiritual leaders need the spiritual blindness of their flock? In other words, of what use would these well-paid professionals be if society didn't "need" them? (Sure enough, it would result in a higher unemployment rate!) That being said, I don't mean that there are no honest doctors, pastors, or police officers. There are, of course, but unfortunately, they themselves are victims of the same sick society they trying to heal, educate, and protect, and they are all employed by the system which restricts their personal freedom.

In America, for example, doctors are not always free to choose what drug to prescribe for the patient. This decision is often made by pharmaceutical companies, who at different times, need to push different products. Thus, the psychiatrist becomes a legal drug dealer, a policeman becomes a fundraiser for the state, and pastors are used to brainwash the flock, telling them what to believe in.

Doctors may be deprived of a license for disobedience and pastors are afraid to lose their tax-free status. Therefore, are they doing what they are told to do and not what they think would be best for the people? The same question goes for scientists who live of the grants given them from our tax dollars, which are rarely used wisely:

http://www.infowars.com/chimps-throwing-poop-and-29-other-mind-blowing-ways-that-the-government-is-wasting-your-money/

Police in America have a quota to fill, they are obliged to bring in a certain amount of revenue every month. Otherwise, they may be demoted or fired. Will they one day begin to ticket us for breathing—by classifying human breath as an illegal activity, possibly a pollutant—fining or taxing us for it? As ridiculous as it may sound now, it could well become a reality at some future date. I recently discovered they have already made texting while walking illegal in New Jersey and can give you an $85 ticket for the offense: http://www.infowars.com/new-jersey-city-makes-it-illegal-to-text-while-walking/

How much farther do we have to go to find ourselves in total madness and tyranny? In the novel *1984*, George Orwell was viewed as a dystopian sci-fi writer. In 2012, he is in fact a realist.

I think Krishnamurti was right when he argued that adaptation to a sick society is not a sign of health. And yet, we are trying to survive in this environment while retaining our sanity and decency. I was never really interested in politics, and have always considered myself a spiritually oriented person. The first time I've heard about all of these things was from the woman I met in the airplane coming back to US. Over the course of later conversations, she told me about the brain sensing nano-technology, a microchip that can disrupt the chemical signals sent by neurons to each other, essentially controlling the brain activity. It sounded like something out of sci-fi movies and I as well as everyone else could dismiss it as fiction, but she held a management position at a major multi-national semi-conductor corporation and said that they were actually making those chips. She also talked about the "class war" and an attack on the middle class, but at the time I knew as little about that as I knew about nano-tech. The next time I heard about the same agenda, on a much broader scale—i.e., to establish brutal, dictatorial, world government, which has been long in the making, run by a banking cartels and huge transnational corporations—was from Eldon in Mexico. He opened my eyes even wider and explained what the "beast" (the system) really meant.

Back then, Eldon's knowledge of global affairs had seemed strange to me, and Mexico would have been the last place I would have expected to learn about such things. At that time, I thought that the spiritual world had nothing to do with politics and society. Only later did I begin to realize that everything is interconnected and the way we look at one thing affects the way we see other things.

Following several years of my own research, in order to cut through the "web" of conspiracy theories and get straight to the conspiracy facts, I concluded that things in the world are actually worse than they are thought to be by many informed people and critical thinkers. The world became revealed as ruled by greed, corruption, and evil, which grows exponentially as people are held up in their trance and fed propaganda and lies.

It was quite shocking to me to find out that this new world government was not the endgame but only a prelude to the vile and murderous plan to depopulate our planet – to "soft kill" humanity by sterilizing and poisoning it using bio and chemical weapon (which is already happening as we speak) significantly shrinking its size to a manageable number of a "slave" class run by a tiny elite running a high-tech neo-feudalistic society—basically making life not worth living.

And it would seem that this horror future is now unfolding before our eyes as intellectual numbness continues unabated in the minds of those who need to wake up the most.

To speak more about it will require me to write another book on the subject. For now, I want to leave you with inner questions and discomforts, if you will, that spur you on to seek truth—without doubt you will be on a path of spiritual awakening that will be filled with the stumbling blocks of so much available information–what you are "fed" in contrast to the stubborn facts of reality. I first felt this many years ago in Israel, and I continue to feel the same way. Change must come, and it must come from within.

Ignorance Is Dangerous

What is really known to Western medicine about the spiritual and healing properties of the ancient, sacred medicinal plants like Peyote and Huachuma? These two plants are brothers in Spirit and share a similar chemical structure—with mescaline as a dominant alkaloid in both.

A history of the West's acquaintance with mescaline is brief; it has been 125 years since the first account of a peyote experience was recorded by Dr. John Raleigh Briggs, the first western scientist to report on the experience of consuming a small amount. This first article was written in the Medical Register of 1887 and mistakenly titled, "Muscale Buttons"—Physiological Effects and Personal Experience."

After taking one third of a fresh peyote plant, Dr. Briggs became scared—suffering a severe panic attack that might have killed him if he had not rushed to his friend, Dr. E. J. Beall for medical aid. Beall prescribed ammonium chloride and whiskey every few minutes, which, incidentally, are both contra-indicated and can be dangerous if combined with peyote.

It is no wonder he experienced what he did by taking the Peyote sacrament without the proper mind set and guidance and completely lacking in spiritual context. Unfortunately, this naive and sadly even comical experience, which can be properly classified as a "bad trip," has become an archetype for consciousness-expanding psychoactive plants that have recently been introduced to the Western world—a culture that has existed for too long without a truly developed notion of spirit.

This first encounter by western science with a spiritual realm well demonstrates the fear of the unknown that dominates up to the present. And even though continued investigations by notable ethnographers of the late 19th century have presented completely different accounts, the Briggs syndrome has unfortunately managed to become ingrained in the collective subconscious of the masses.

But, Briggs failure has not prevented all other people from exploring. Arthur Carl Wilhelm Heffter was a German pharmacologist and chemist who isolated mescaline from the peyote cactus in 1897 and experimented with the substance a number of times.

Still, a systematic study of its impact on human psyche did not begin for another 30 years. It was done by a German-American Ph.D. in physiological psychology from Stanford University named Heinrich Kluver. He later wrote a book, *Mescal and Mechanisms of Hallucinations*, which, of course, had nothing to do with hallucinations, but had to do with the wrong interpretation of a new phenomenon into western terminology. Kluver's book, first published in 1928, discussed the possibility of using of the substance for studying the unconscious mind.

In 1937, British writer and philosopher, Aldous Huxley, shortly after his arrival to U.S, heard about the use of peyote in Native American ceremonies in New Mexico. Later, he became aware of mescaline as an active alkaloid in peyote cactus from an academic paper written by British psychiatrist Humphry Osmond. This paper expounded on the results of using mescaline for the treatment of patients with schizophrenia. In 1952, Huxley wrote a letter to Dr. Osmond, in which he expressed an interest in his research and offered himself as an experimental subject. In his letter, he explained his motivation based on an idea that the brain was a reducing valve that restricts consciousness and that mescaline could help him access a greater degree of awareness, reaching beyond the boundaries of his ego. He reasoned that this could bring him closer to spiritual enlightenment, satisfying his quest as a seeker of knowledge. Two years later, after only 10 experiments with mescaline, Huxley published *The Doors of Perception*, in which he described his mescaline experiences. The book was received by readers with enthusiasm, and began a heated debate on the subject.

By 1970, mescaline had become a controlled substance, which put an end to further scientific research; thus, Western psychology has had only 40 years to study it. Mexican Indians have worked with Peyote for thousands of years, a fact which is supported by archeological findings discovered by George Martin in 1933 in Shumla Caves on the Rio Grande, Texas. These Peyote samples are part of the collection of the Witte Museum in San Antonio. An isotope laboratory at UCLA has radio carbon-dated the well-preserved plants, dating the samples between 3780–3660 BC. This added nearly six thousand years of cultural heritage and ceremonial use of Peyote to the area by native tribes of the Rio Grande of south west Texas, which until 1850 was a Mexican territory.

Dry Peyote "buttons" (a term only used when the plant is sliced and dried) and other ceremonial artifacts were found, among them rasping sticks and a rattle, which are simple shamanic instruments used for creating a rhythm. They are usually made of deer bones or wood. Also found was a pouch containing cedar incense and feathers, which are objects used in Peyote ceremonies even today. A separately done alkaloid extraction analysis from powdered samples led to the identification of mescaline in both samples, which showed, among other things, an incredible persistence of naturally accrued chemical compounds thru many millenniums.

Those 40 years of Western study, moreover, included the Great Depression, which began in most places in 1929 and lasted until 1939 and World War II. That meant another 16 years of difficult times for many—perhaps reducing focus on any such studies to more like 24 years. So, on one side of the scale we have a brief introduction by Western science of one extracted and synthesized alkaloid from Peyote cactus, without spiritual context, and on the other hand, we have a millennium-long traditional use of Peyote by Mexican Indians who held and still hold this sacred plant at the very center of their lives.

In addition, the difference between using a laboratory-extracted alkaloid from peyote and eating the live peyote plant is similar to the difference between baby formula and breast milk. But, even these two types of milk are probably closer to one another than the synthesized substance from peyote—a process which makes extraction nearly void in terms of spiritual connection—and the actual living plant

Understanding that, one begins to realize that what is known by Western psychology about the sacred peyote, and also Huachuma, and their influence on all aspects of human life, is only sufficient to prove the need for further research and everything connected with traditional use. The scientists will need to go beyond the walls of their laboratories and seek out a living culture of native Indians to learn from them about the healing properties of these miraculous spiritual and medicinal plants—and with them as guides, dive into a realm where true knowledge is available and is perceived through direct spiritual experience.

Even the best minds, devoted to studying the human psyche, have stopped half way in regards to the healing potential and influence on the human brain by psychedelic substances. This research could lead to major discoveries in medicine, psychology, and psychiatry. And it is so regrettable to see the general attitude of society regarding the use of psychoactive plants that have been sanctioned by the shamans for many millenniums, which allows you to heal yourself permanently, fill your life with meaning, and satisfy your spiritual thirst with knowledge—thus contributing to the good of all.

The common view on the risks and dangers of the use of psychoactive substances are not supported by any scientific evidence; rather they are based on fear of the unknown.

However, in regards to science in general, and in particular to psychology, we should note the following;

The root word "Psyche" – from Greek means 'soul'; psychology means a soul study or science of the soul. But, how did the founders of Western psychology intend to study something they denied existed?

Wilhelm Wundt, a German physician, psychologist, physiologist, philosopher and professor of the19th century, is known as one of the founding fathers of modern psychology. He tried to understand the physiology of the soul by studying anatomy of the brain and its physical manifestations. In my opinion, that is like trying to understand what a radio host is saying by looking at dissembled radio transistor in your hand. Wundt made a truly shocking statement, showing his misunder-standing of human nature by saying that the 'search for the spiritual nature of man is meaningless, because man does not have a soul,' a view still widely shared in the scientific community today.

Wundt's "study" of the human soul, denying its very existence, did not prevent his work from becoming among the most important work in the field of psychology and referred and recommended to students in universities around the world. Well, to me, an obvious and serious gap exists between philosophy (love for wisdom) and psychology, which views humans as bio-machines without consciousness.

It should also be noted that J.I. Gurdjieff, a founder of the Fourth Way system, shared exactly the same view—regarding people as sleeping machines without consciousness. He considered all human activity, including its creative expressions, such as writing, music and art, as mechanical manifestations that happen in "sleep" where a person spends all his life. And, he argued, only those who were incredibly lucky to find a real esoteric school or teacher, had a chance to wake up from that sleep. Gurdjieff's generalization and labeling of the whole human race as sleeping machines, absent of consciousness and will, resonated well with the prominent psychologists of his time. This, of course, does not make the assertion true, but rather highlights the world view of the West at that given time.

From the beginning I have always been attracted to philosophy and its approach to the study of the human soul, in comparison to the dryness and lack of spirituality of psychology. Of course, religion, which is vastly different than philosophy (although some religions are based in philosophical thought), has quite a history of the supposed "search for knowledge." As we know, up until only a few centuries ago, many people were openly killed for their beliefs. Today, even persecution for beliefs continues but it is usually more covert than in history.

For example, let us recall the Italian philosopher and Dominican friar Giordano Bruno, who was charged with holding opinions contrary to the Catholic faith and found guilty of heresy by the Spanish Inquisition and sentenced to death by burning at the stake in 1600. His crime consisted of his belief that the Earth revolved around the Sun, and the stars we see in the sky were all suns like ours, each with its own solar system whose numbers are infinite in the Universe.

Surpassing the common knowledge of his time, Bruno basically was charged with the crime of knowing, which, in the religious context of those times, was a deadly sin and labeled heresy. Any opinion which was in contrary to theological dogma, was punished by death if was not recanted. But, being a brave and strong man, Bruno did not recant his ideas; so as a heretic, he was burned alive by the Inquisition.

The Italian physicist, mathematician, astronomer and philosopher, Galileo, now recognized as the discoverer of gravity, said that the Bible referred only to the salvation of the soul and had no authority in scientific matters. Galileo was charged with heresy as well, and for supporting the world view of Nicolous Copernicus, whose heliocentric system was condemned as heresy.

Under threat of the penalty of death, Galileo was forced to recant his idea that the sun was the central celestial body around which the Earth and other planets revolved. The hypothesis of the motion of the Earth, according to the eminent theologians of the time, was contrary to Scripture, which spoke of the immobility of the Earth and movement of the Sun. After his recant, Galileo was sentenced to life in prison, which was soon changed to house arrest and life-long surveillance by the Inquisition. The case against Galileo went on to become a symbol of the confrontation between science and religion—the struggle for freedom of thought against dogmatic beliefs. In my mind, this is what intellectual revolution is all about, and this is an important part of the inspiration behind sharing the story of my own path.

Sadly today, when science and religion appear to be progressing toward more realistic world views, there remains one area where both religion and science are coming together in the wrong way, that is, in condemning the ancient shamanic traditions.

From a religious point of view, shamanism is often called paganism and devil worshiping; and from the scientific point of view, it is viewed as primitive and without merit. Science does not seem in general to recognize the spiritual nature of things and reports that it "cannot find the soul in a dissected human body."

I had a friend who became a fundamentalist Christian and told me that

Sun worshiping was an act of the Devil. I love our sun as I love our planet. These are two celestial bodies that support our lives. Without the sun we would die in a moment, frozen in space. How can anyone in his right mind say that loving the sun is bad and satanic? This "Bronze Age" mentality has not changed much, continuing to infect minds throughout centuries. One would have to think that the very same people who were committing crimes against humanity in medieval ages, while thinking that the Earth was flat, are now preaching that Sun worshiping is bad and other nonsense. I remember one occasion, while still living in California. I was coming home from work and gave a ride to a person I knew, who noticed a book on psychology on the front seat. When he took it in his hands, and simply looked at the cover, he began trembling and said that this was knowledge coming from the devil. He suggested that I read only the Bible and become a member of his Church.

According to his views, this book was heresy, despite the fact that it did not relate to religious matter. But, I have seen the same reaction in the followers of other religious and spiritual viewpoints, which have flatly refused to even talk about their beliefs. Among those were Fourth Way followers who fiercely defended Gurdjieff's ideas and views, only some of which were based in reality.

So, who has the authority or even the capacity to deal with the question of the Soul? A blind religion or spiritually ignorant science? Both…or perhaps, neither?

I think the true authority in this matter is within you, using your powers of reason and intuition, extracting all that is good from both religion and science and putting the pieces together in a different order, according to your own experience, understanding and knowledge. The combined effort will lead you to true answers.

Anthropology - (from Greek "antropos"–man, and "logia"–study) seen in this light, seems to be a more inclusive way to study human nature, since it is a combination of disciplines which include a wider spectrum of human life, dealing with all aspects of human existence; physical-biological, social-cultural, archeological and linguistic. In this context, field work is a necessary part in the study of any, its customs and beliefs, and to allow immersion in their world.

However, the question remains about the accuracy of the knowledge understood and transmitted during the so-called "field work," especially the principal accuracies. And, it is important to understand that the sacred plants affect everyone equally, and this is their value. The experiences of different people can differ, depending on the inner content of the person, his cultural background and the society he is coming from, but the essence of all this remains unchanged–it is love.

And as far as shamanic practice goes, it originated with work with medicinal plants, since a shaman without a plant, is like a violinist without a violin. If a musician comes on stage without his instrument, he will only be able to talk about the music—the actual sound of which no one will hear.

In any case it seems to be wrong for any government to claim authority and assume the right to determine which wild plants should be legal and which ones should not, banning, tabooing and prohibiting their use for medical and spiritual purposes.

I think it is critically important to remember that the plant kingdom was created long before us by the same creative force that created us.

If someone has the right to classify certain plants as being illegal, what is there to stop him or her from doing the same with regard to animals—say, for example, prohibiting the keeping of German Shepherds because of their loyalty and love for man? Is there really any difference? Yesterday, we made some kinds of plants illegal, today we might classify as illegal certain breeds of animals, and tomorrow perhaps we will ban certain ethnic groups of humans? And the shocking reality is that this would not be new…as we well remember from the numerous and global incidences of genocide.

Where would it end?

Is this one of the underlying reasons for paying taxes to the government? To keep us safe from ourselves? The role of government in a free and democratic society should be limited to defending individual freedom, and supporting those in real need without undo interfering in people lives. Otherwise, the governing class will become dangerously arrogant and detached from ordinary people giving birth to new versions of old tyrants like the murderers Hitler or Stalin who also said that "it doesn't matter how the people will vote, what matters is who counts the votes."

This leads me to reflect on freedom. One of the founders of constitutional law in America had foreseen the need to include the provisions for medical freedom into the US Constitution, which is one of the most brilliant documents ever written. For instance, freedom to receive medical care is essential in a free society. It should be a natural right of a person to use plants for the purpose of self-healing and learning.

Dr. Benjamin Rush said the following: "Unless we put medical freedom into the Constitution, the time will come when medicine will organize into an undercover dictatorship to restrict the art of healing to one class of Men and deny equal privileges to others; the Constitution of the Republic should make a special privilege for medical freedoms as well as religious freedom."

Well, I believe that this is exactly what we are witnessing today, a medical dictatorship and its war against alternative medicine and healing.

So if this is so obvious, why does the order of things remain as such? What will it take for the people to finally stand up for their natural birth rights? Will it take more tyranny to wake people up or do we have more than enough of that already?

Path

Healing Properties of Sacred Huachuma

Much has been and can be said about the curative properties of sacred Peyote and Huachuma, however, I will speak only to those to which I can attest personally.

With regards to Peyote, I believe it is the best natural scorpion and snake anti-venom—the story about which I wrote in an earlier chapter. I also happen to have a friend who had skin cancer—which may have started with his military service in Vietnam—who used Peyote as a curative over many years and has cured himself.

But, I can say more about Huachuma. When I still lived in California, I suffered from severe back pain on my left side. I had tried everything to cure it, going to the gym, swimming, massage courses, and rubbing my back like a cat on sharp corners and rocks, but the pain persisted.

I usually asked the therapist to work on this particular spot where I felt the intense pain. She worked with her elbows, making her quite exhausted at the end. It felt good and somewhat alleviated the pain for a day or two, but the pain always came back soon after. I was in continuous discomfort during any activities and especially disturbing when I was driving.

As I wrote earlier in the chapter Chavin de Huantar, after coming from

Peru in the end of December of 2008, I had a dream in which I was brewing Huachuma. That morning, I immediately cut a few Huachuma plants, which I had been growing for 3 years, but had never touched.

It was interesting to watch myself doing something I had not only never done before but had only learned the night before during the dream. And yet it felt like I had been doing it forever. During the brewing, I felt I should not drink at this time, but that I should invite a friend who had been with me in Arizona to drink instead.

Well, three of us gathered in my place, and I shared the brew with my friends, but I did not consume any. After that, we stepped outside to breathe the night air and let the medicine unfold. It was a beautiful night with a sky full of stars. As it began getting cold, we came back in and sat down around my mesa. I lit the candles on my altar, and we sat comfortably on the floor around it.

I was curious to see how reality was perceived by my two friends. My friend from St. Petersburg began to roll an invisible ball with his fingers, then gently push it like a balloon to my other friend who then played with it in his hands and sent it back. As they were busy playing, I thought that I should drink also in order to take part in their new discovery. But instead, I got the thought of showing them a picture of me with a previous girlfriend and asked them what they saw in the photo. They looked at it briefly and both said that I was just an episode in her life, confirming something I knew myself. They then said that they didn't want to look at the picture any longer because they did not want to affect anything. I understood what they were saying, and took the photo away.

We were talking about the illusion of time as I was falling asleep on the floor. What woke me up was a pain in my back that felt like it was penetrating to my soul. I literally jumped from the floor and saw my friend from St. Petersburg standing with an out-stretched hand about 3 feet away from my back. Seeing my reaction, he apologized for the pain he had inflicted on me. He explained that he had seen a ray of energy coming out of my back, and felt that he should gently touch it. It was very strange. My friend touched the invisible beam of light, at a distance of not less than one meter (3 feet) from my body, and I felt not only on my back, but also in my soul. I would not have had a hard time believing this happened had I been under the influence of the medicine, but I was completely sober.

After a couple of minutes, I calmed down and went to make tea. We talked about different things and enjoyed our tea. Then, my two cats came in from outside and joined our circle, staring at my friends and getting stared at back. My friends both said that my cats were "seeing" them. I knew what they meant, but I couldn't see the cats in the same way. Near morning, I fell asleep.

The next day, we drove to the airport where my friend had to fly back to St. Petersburg. He later reported to me that while flying home and until his arrival, he continued to play with those energetic balls between his fingers. Some days later, as usual, I went for a massage. The therapist worked hard on my back, but I had a feeling that she wasn't hitting the spot. I went home somewhat unhappy. It took another few days for me to notice that my backache was gone, and I had not been aware of it for a while. I realized that I hadn't felt the pain for quite some time. In fact, I didn't remember feeling it after the ceremony. My friend, with the help of Huachuma, had healed my back without actually touching it. And I did not have the Huachuma in me either!

I had heard that after deep emotional trauma, a piece of the soul gets frozen by the pain and turns into a chunk of ice. Such a trauma for me was losing my dog which I wrote about in the chapter Alpha. This situation tormented me for about a year and a half before I decided to ask my friend to recall the details of that night and to write me about it. Here is an excerpt from his letter: "...and then I saw a green-gray beam of light coming out of your back like wings or more precisely, it was like pieces of a glass with chipped edges. I had an impulse to touch this beam and realized that I could now do it."

Later, he sent me a drawing made by his friend, an artist-animator,

 from his verbal description. It was a funny man with large wings that looked something like sharp tongues of flame. More than four years have passed since then, and my back pain has not returned.

The second case happened two

years ago when a woman came to me from California for Huachuma work from which she expected to find deeper meaning in her life. Almost all of her life had been spent in spiritual search, and yet she felt that something was still missing. I had not been aware of the condition of her health, in particular the fact that she was suffering from hypoglycemia or low blood sugar. I had only learned about this when we had met in Peru. I felt she shared that with me with some uncertainty, possibly because she thought that I would not be sure about working with her because of the possible consequences from long gaps between meals—which is required by this work. There was the possibility that she could have developed a hypoglycemic coma with convulsions and loss of consciousness. Working with me, she would have to abstain from food for about 10-12 hours during the ceremony plus the night before, which would total nearly 24 hours with an empty stomach. Also, the energy required to go through the day spent at high altitude wouldn't be an easy task even for a healthy, but unaccustomed person.

Fortunately, the spirit of Huachuma had mercy, overcoming her health condition and giving her the necessary strength to go through the day by regulating the level of her blood sugar. She said she had only remembered her health condition at night, during dinner. She was even more surprised to see her body getting well during the next 10 days of drinking Huachuma daily.

A year later, I asked her how her health was. This is what she wrote:

"...I feel like the medicine was of such a harmonious frequency that it neutralized my imbalance and helped me feel strong without food throughout the day. In terms of a permanent healing, I can't say for sure. I still have to be conscious of my diet to maintain the balance. The permanent healing qualities that I received from Huachuma were more around emotional healing and an opening of my heart. Life changing really. My inner peace just keeps growing and deepening which allows me to be more open, loving, and even sensuous in ways I've never known before. Of course I continue my own practices to enhance that, but Huachuma gave me a strong base of healing that opened me deeply. The guidance that I could clearly hear on medicine, is now a continuous conversation. I have that guidance and wisdom available to me at any given moment. I have more sensitivity to the continuous love and support and guidance within the spiritual realms. It is deeply comforting and I live my life from that peace for the most part. My relationships with my family and my beloved have benefited the most out of my ten days with you and huachuma"

The third case was a year ago.

I received an email from the friends of the woman, whom I just mentioned above, in which they expressed an intention to come to work with me. They were a couple, and for her, it was a spiritual journey while for him, it was an attempt to cure his chronic form of asthma and related allergies. I explained to him that my work was more of a spiritual nature and that I was not as focused on body healing. I explained that body healing was more of a bonus rather the center of my work. When he described the history of his illness and methods with which he maintained his health, I had a certain hesitation to let him come, concerned about his condition. But believing in the healing potential of sacred Huachuma, I told him that he was welcome to come, telling him all the details about the work I do.

A week before the trip to Peru, during his routine work with his allergist, he got a chest x-ray and wrote me following:

"…Over the past week or so, I've been treated for my allergies and asthma in order to get ready for this trip. In the routine work up, they took a chest x-ray and yesterday they told me that, rather than just straight up asthma, I may have COPD (chronic obstructive pulmonary disease)."

At any rate, my condition may be more serious than we thought. When I told the allergist I was leaving today for Cusco at 10,000 feet elevation, he went ballistic. He wants me to take Diamox before I leave for altitude sickness…"

When he asked me whether he should start taking it before coming or not, I wrote him the following:

"Well, I am against all drugs unless it's a matter of life and death. I personally wouldn't suppress my immune system with resulting adverse reactions just as a preventive measure. But, in any case, if you decide to take it, I would suggest you take it now and get it over with before arriving. I understand your preoccupation and I think that taking reasonable precautions is a good idea, but I also think that you will do just fine and will be very happy here…"

And he did feel good here as I told him. But, I was amazed by his words about his doctor who prescribed him a pharmaceutical that is known for severe side effects that could complicate his journey, turning it into a nightmare possibly resulting in the need for hospitalization. It seemed to me unreasonable to suggest for a person to deliberately suppress his immune system with a pharmacological agent before traveling, all for the sake of battling altitude sickness—which passes naturally within a day or two as the lungs adapt to lesser amounts of oxygen.

Fortunately for both of us, he listened to me and didn't take this toxin. During our three weeks of work, my American patient, who had been using pharmacological steroids twice a day for 25 years, cut his dose in half. Then, after the second week, stopped taking his medications all together. He surprised himself with his vigor, good humor and well-being, while drinking Huachuma and walking at high altitude, even at my pace.

During the last ceremony, he reminded me of a playing child, running through the fields. I enjoyed watching him enjoy himself. In the evening, he told me that in that ceremony, he recalled his memories from early childhood and saw himself as a healthy boy.

Six months later, I wrote him a letter asking about his health. This was his reply:

"My health is doing remarkably well. I've cut way back on the asthma meds. Almost off. My goal is to be off of them completely in a few weeks. But since I've taken them for 25+ years, and since the body can become dependent on corticosteroids, I want to take this slow so that it doesn't backfire on me. I'll keep you posted. My allergy responses are down as well as no asthma symptoms. I AM THRILLED!!! This is what I wanted and had set my intentions for."

Unfortunately, later on, he went t back to using meds again, but said that he could still smell and taste—which was something he had long forgotten because of his asthma meds. I was happy to hear about his health improvement, but at the same time, I felt sorry for his dependency from taking meds for over two decades. I had a feeling that if he would repeat this work, at least once or twice, he could cure his lifelong health problem permanently. After all, 25 years of everyday heavy steroid use doesn't get cured overnight, so the process of removing the dependency cannot be completed with just few sessions.

I could then and still now do see how sacred healing plants could help a person with alcohol and drugs addictions, if repeated over time. And, if the healing process of the two last examples could be ascribe to alkaloids or chemical structures of the plant, then in my own case, curing my persistent backache permanently truly was a miracle.

One a side note, but still important, as a result of working with Huachuma, I only recently noticed that my chronic sinusitis, which has given me headaches all my life, with even the slightest weather change, has all but disappeared. How many pills and nasal sprays I took during the years, all just to temporarily suppress the symptoms. I also had ongoing pain in my knee that was probably the results of so many years given to sport—a sharp pain especially noticeable when I was walking up the stairs. I had forgotten about its disappearance until I began to write about the backache story in this book. But all these healings and others are minor when compared to spiritual healing through which a man can restore his own connection with his soul.

Nevertheless, sacred Peyote and one of its active alkaloids, mescaline, which is also active in Huachuma, are included in the list of Schedule 1 drugs under the Controlled Substances Act for the United States. These "drugs" are defined as having no accepted medical use and having high potential for abuse. The sad and ironic truth is that the dangers exist only with addictive and dangerous drugs such as the opiates and their derivatives, like heroin, for example, which are also listed in that same Schedule I.

Path

Wind of Change

This final trip to Peru was different from all my previous ones. I sensed a premonition for a change in my life, and I felt that this journey could become the culmination of all the stages that I've passed through so far as if it was the end of one part of the path and the beginning a new one. These feelings and thoughts had first came to me in Chavin de Huantar, but I felt the force of them a few days later. It was during the last ceremony in the ancient place of power, located high in the Andes, where we went with don Victor, after a pilgrimage to Chavin.

It was a forest of giant rocks located on a plain between the snowy peaks of mountains, 4,300 meters above sea level. According to our shaman, it was an ancient geological formation that ancient shamans used for special ceremonies. He said it was considered sacred by different cultures, succeeding one another in this area. But this place was little-known, even among the local population. There were no road signs pointed there; it was one of those places you needed to know in order to find it.

We turned off the main highway and drove along the mountain road. After a while, we reached the high land plateau. Leaving the car, we went to the cave to set up the mesa for the coming ceremony.

The cave could not be seen from a distance; it was hidden in the rocks and became visible only when you got very close. Don Victor set up his mesa in front of ancient cave paintings and petroglyphs he believed were about 10-12 thousand years old. I later thought they could be of a

much earlier age, possibly related to the Middle Paleolithic era, which would make them tens of thousands of years older.

One cave painting in front of the ancient stone altar was a depiction of a bird-man near flocks of llamas. I thought these were an artistic expression of that era, when hunter-gatherers used sacred plants and shamanic techniques of remote viewing through the bodies of flying birds to see the landscape from above and find their prey through the vision of the birds.

I've heard similar stories about ancient African shamanism. To the right of our altar, there was a carving on the wall of a hollowed palm of the hand. If touched, an energetic boost could be felt.

After drinking huachuma, we stayed for about an hour, letting the medicine unfold.

I was sitting right in front of the entrance to the cave and staring into the distance, when I noticed a man who was quite far away, but moving in our direction. He was wearing a hat and a bluish sweater. When he was still a good distance from us, he suddenly stopped, and it seemed like he was listening, looking in our direction. It surprised my friend and me. He was about 800 meters away and could not see the cave. (I hadn't been able to see it from closer.) He could not have heard us either, because we all sat in silence. We realized that he somehow sensed us and, after a short pause, he kept on walking.

Shortly the atmosphere in the cave became unbearable; we left, and walked to the entrance of a huge rock formation. Within a couple of minutes, I turned my head back in an attempt to remember the way we had come in. I've always had a good visual memory, and easily get oriented on the streets of an unfamiliar city and in other places that are not known to me. But when I looked back, after just a hundred meters, I realized that I would not be able to find my way out of there alone. Solid shapes of rocks were all around us. Some had images of animals and others, human. I had the feeling that as soon as we entered, an invisible door had closed behind us.

We moved slowly between the stone monuments. Along the way, don Victor showed us the important places: the face of a shaman painted on a mushroom- like rock formation emerging from the ground and places for the offering of sacred tobacco and coca leaves. Later, we went to an area that offered beautiful views of the Forest of Rocks. Here, everyone found a comfortable spot and immersed themselves into this unusual experience. The energy there was so strong and pure that crys-

tals were forming everywhere on the ground and could be collected with a teaspoon.

Looking at my life from there was very different. Here the sense of time was suspended. It seemed like this entire, gigantic, rocky place was a portal to another dimension. I began to feel that the forest was a giant stone socket of the planet, connecting to any person who could go be-

yond the usual perception of space and time. Surfing the waves of this energy, I pondered upon the words that had been given to me by Eldon, who was told by his Huichol friend from another village, that what had happened to me in Mexico was my payment for a change in my fate.

These words now held a deeper meaning among the rocks. It was here that I truly understood them.

I lay on the ground and let myself drift into the soul flight, calling for the future to become my present. I wanted to live in Peru, work with Huachuma, and build my life around it. A herding dog brought me back from my flight, licking my face until I came to my senses. It was a brief moment with this animal, but long enough to make a bond with him. I never saw this dog again, but I do remember him often.

On the way back out of this place, we passed small houses built of stones about 3-4 feet high and possibly 5 feet in width. They had thatched roofs attached directly to the stones. In front of one of them, I saw the man in the bluish sweater, the same one we had seen in the field. He sat at the entrance, but turned his back to us, so we went in silence without disturbing him. Don Victor said that he was a shepherd, and that there were few of them living here, adding that, on the other side of the cave, there were a few more of those same houses.

They probably really were shepherds, judging by the flock of sheep and dogs around, but why did they live so far from populated areas? The nearest town was several hours drive away. And why so high in the mountains? This place was freezing by sunset with blowing, icy winds, not to mention the nights. How could one live in such conditions?

And cold was not the only problem. This place was the most powerful place I have ever been to, and with the darkness, its power was becoming even stronger. Staying there at night would be like staying in a power plant between high voltage cables. Who those shepherds really were, and why they lived that way, remains to me still a mystery. Indeed, one could build similar houses at lower altitudes, where the fields are just the same. They would be warmer at night and closer to the highway. In such an altitude, 500-700 meters is significant.

After returning home from this journey, I stayed three and a half months more in the states and then I moved to Peru. But, my moving to Peru was preceded by certain signs that I will describe in the next chapters.

Path

My Meeting with Hawk

We came back from Peru on December 26, 2008. About a week later, I had an interesting encounter with a new flying friend. I lived half an hour from Sacramento, California, on a small island twelve miles long and two miles wide, and could only be entered through bridges. The whole island was mostly farmer's fields, with some houses around which were hidden from one another in wilderness.

This was the last place I lived in America and the best one. I loved it. It had an open view of the fields where I watched sunsets daily. I loved to

sit by the river, enjoying the silence of the wildness which I was slowly getting to know. Years of living in the city prior to that, felt far away, even though the driving distance to Sacramento was only about 40 minutes to an hour.

This was the place where I felt at peace, surrounded by nature. The only gaping hole was Alfa, whom I was missing greatly. Walking through the fields, I imagined how much she would have enjoyed running there without me worrying about the passing cars.

Anyway, it was just one of those usual days when I had to do something boring in the city. Getting done with things as quickly as I could, I headed back home to the island. Leaving the highway behind, a sense of easiness was wrapping me as it always did. Getting to the T cross, I took a left towards the ranch. I loved this country road; it was such a pleasant ride. I was within a few miles from my house, and while driving behind another car, I saw that two big birds had landed on the road ahead, but the car in front of me did not slow down. As it approached, the birds started to fly up, trying to escape, but they were slow to take off, and one of them was hit by the car and fell, while the other flew away.

I thought the bird might have only been injured, and I wanted to remove it from the road so that it could heal. I made a U-turn and headed back. As I approached, I prayed that the car in front of me would not run it over and, luckily, it didn't. The bird was sitting still. I went a little past it and stopped where I could. I stepped out of the car and walked back toward the bird. There were a few cars coming fast toward us. I moved faster toward the bird, and the cars slowed down as they passed us by.

As I came closer, it flew up with an effort, and I was glad he was away from the road. He landed in a pear tree nearby. I felt better and returned to my car. A few minutes later, while slowly driving again past the spot where the accident had happened, I looked to see if I could spot him.

He was in the same tree, stuck in the branches upside down, lying on his back. His wings were spread and he was crying out helplessly. I parked the car and then ran back to the tree.

I began climbing the tree, thinking that if he bit me, I could get an infection since he probably ate mice. Slowly, I made my way toward him, and told him that I was a friend who had come to help. I reached out and touched him lightly on his head. He looked at me quietly—he wasn't scared. I gently grabbed his back and tried to pull him from the branch he was grasping, but he would not let go. I kept trying, but realized that he was not going to let go of the branch. He was really stubborn.

I saw some blood on his leg near his talons, but couldn't make out any other damage. His wings seemed fine and his wide tail looked good too. I thought that if I could push him up so that he was standing on his own, he might be able to fly. I gently pushed him until he stood up straight. As he felt himself standing, he leaned somewhat forward, spread his wings a bit and looked at me as if he was trying to remember me. For just that moment we were looking at one another from about two feet apart. This was first time in my life that I had seen a wild bird of prey from a distance of an outstretched hand. I thought that for him, this also was probably the first encounter with a human.

His look was fearless, determined, but also friendly and seemed full of gratitude. He looked me straight in my eyes as if trying to remember me and then flew to a tree farther away. Overcome with emotion, I climbed down, and wanting to make sure he was still fine, I headed in the direction that he had flown, but I never saw him again.

I returned home with a mixture of compassion for his pain, and joy for having been able to help him out I will never forget the way he looked at me, and the way I felt looking back at him in that tree.

It was an interesting synchronicity that on that very day, as I was meeting a wild hawk, my friend, who was going with me to Arizona, was meeting another Hawk, a man who called himself by that name. He was a Soma shaman living a few hours' drive from us up North. My friend went to have a Soma (fly agaric mushroom) ceremony with him and was already in the forest when I called him. He said he would call me later that night.

At one time, I thought about going to Siberia to search for our Russian shamans with whom I could ritually work with fly agaric mushrooms, or Soma, as some people call them. But, after studying the subject, I found out that during the time of Stalin, shamanism was persecuted and medicine men were killed, taking their knowledge of ancient tradition with them to the grave. Based on that historical fact, it was reasonable to assume that the old shamanic traditions were either partially or completely lost in this region, and folklore without its kernel was not of interest to me. So, to find out that this Soma shaman, Hawk, was actually my neighbor, relatively speaking, was quite a surprise. But, at that time I had already bonded a deep friendship with both Peyote and Huachuma and was not much interested in other sacred plants. Nevertheless, I was glad that my friend went to see him, which turned out to be quite beneficial for him.

Hawk and his wife have written a book called *Sacred Soma Shamans*, in which they share a lifelong experience working with fly agaric mushrooms, or Soma. In this book, they disperse the myth of the deadly danger with which we have been threatened since early childhood regarding the use of Soma. They explain that it is safe if taken wisely and in moderation.

I do not recommend experimenting with fly agaric mushrooms or with any other sacred plants without proper knowledge and necessary guidance.

Meeting the Owl

Exactly two weeks after meeting the Hawk, another friend was just about to appear and change the course of my whole life. It was January of 2009, two weeks after meeting the hawk on the road and two months after bonding a new friendship with Mexican scorpions.

If I had learned anything so far from meeting the hawk, it was to carry my camera with me. I could hardly forgive myself because on that day I didn't have it to take pictures of the hawk in that tree. After that, I carried my camera with me and took pictures nearly every day of a hawk, similar to the one I met, who was waiting for me close to that same spot. I would see him sitting on the street lights, on the electrical wires, and in trees, or just flying along the road. I did not know whether it was the same one, but I had

the feeling it was him.

It was an ordinary day when I went out to the field to watch the sunset. Walking along, my eye suddenly caught something jumping out of the little bushes ahead of me. It was an owl! It was not just any owl, but the most beautiful owl I had ever seen—in documentaries about wild life or in pictures. She sprang toward me and just looked at me. I immediately grabbed the camera and started shooting pictures. I started to approach her, moving slowly, trying not to scare her. After a while I came close enough to grab her with my hands. She grabbed my hand with her talons, leaving three red dots on it. It hurt enough to make me realize how hopeless were the mammals that were subject to its grasp. Fortunately, I thought, the hawk I had met two weeks earlier was too busy in the branches to grab me with his talons—which would have hurt much more.

Holding the owl in my hands, I looked into her eyes. She had a look that I had been searching for in people all my life. We stared at each other for several minutes. I made a couple of shots right there, holding her in one hand – using the other hand for the camera.

It was apparent that she had a broken wing, so to leave her in the field would mean leaving her for the Coyotes whose creepy howling I often heard at nights, but had never been able to see. I had lived in a house on the island for almost a year. Thinking about the coyotes, I remembered my two cats, who often brought me "gifts." The remains were mixed with feathers I had to clean up in the mornings. Certainly, I was not eager to leave the owl in the field alone. Before returning home, I decided to spend a little time at the spot where I normally watched the sunset. I walked with the owl in the field. I held her with two hands, convincing myself that I was not dreaming.

We came to my spot and sat on the ground. Her eyes were amazing. I was struck by one detail. When I gently blew into her eyes, they closed down; not with the external eyelid, but with another one, internal, through which she could continue to see. I thought it was some kind of a protective mechanism, allowing her to see and hunt during the day

while flying against wind or sun.

While I was playing with her eyelid, gently blowing air into her eyes, the owl jerked sharply, almost dropping out of my hands. I turned around and saw, about thirty meters away, a large coyote, slowly walking parallel to us. This was unbelievable! A wild owl in my hands with a coyote passing by! He stopped right in front of us, turned his head a little to the right, toward us, sniffed the air and calmly continued to walk. I was shocked. It was the first time I had seen a coyote. What struck me most was not the fact that I saw him, but how calmly was he walking. Coyotes are prairie wolves, wild animals who avoid people in general, sensing them from afar. But this one had no fear of me at all; in fact, it felt to me like he was friendly. I kept watching him walk until he became a dot in the field; then I took my owl home.

My cats greeted us with excitement. I took the owl straight to my bedroom, closed the door and let her free. She walked on the carpet, then jumped on a box, which had been there for almost a year since moving in, and then to my bed, looking me in the eyes.

We were sitting quietly for a while when I thought to call my friend who had gone with me to Arizona. I told him that he must drop everything he was doing and come to me right now. I did not want to say anything more on the phone. He probably felt a certain urgency in my voice and within an hour was at my house.

We went into my bedroom, he sat on my bed and I sat on the floor. In silence we were staring at the owl, and she was staring back at us. A few minutes passed, and I noticed my friend had tears coming out of his eyes. He said that for the first time in his life, he heard the voice of his conscience. His words made me shiver. As it turned out, the conscience can not only be felt, but also heard, and the phrase "voice of conscience" was no longer a metaphor. Could it be that my friend may have heard that very same voice, which is known as the inner voice, and mentioned widely in esoteric circles?

We talked about clairaudience and what that now meant.

I believed him, not only because I knew him well, but also because of what had happened the day that I brought owl home. Alone with her in my room, I heard a strange melody in the middle of my head, reminiscent of an owl howling at night. But it was not exactly the same sound, more like Morse code with a certain rhythm or melody. It took me about half a minute before I realized that I was hearing this tone in my head and not thru my ears. I was completely alert and felt the sounds physically. Then it ceased. I had the feeling that the owl had told me something I could not understand at that moment. The words of my friend about hearing the voice of his conscience were so impressive, since they confirmed my recent telepathic contact with an owl.

I asked him to take some pictures with the bird in my hands, since no one else might believe my story. We sat for a while longer, talking, and then he left. Evening came. The owl did not eat or drink. I had frozen mice in my refrigerator, a menu I was feeding my little python which I recently acquired. I gave these mice to the owl, but she did not eat them. I began to think about its future. It was obvious that she needed an operation, otherwise she would not be able to fly, and I didn't want to let her leave like that. But it was a Sunday so the clinic was not open. I thought that I would take her first thing in the morning to a medical care facility.

I lit a candle in the bedroom, sat on my bed and watched the owl who watched me back. What happened next is difficult to put into words. I can only say that in candle-light, I saw in her eyes the world I always sensed but had never seen. This world was calling me, and the owl was his messenger. With a heavy heart I began to pray for the bird; I really wanted her to not die, but to live. Toward the morning I fell asleep. And in that time, I realized I had to move to Peru.

The next morning, I immediately went online to find wild animal clinics in Sacramento, and immediately called several places. Everywhere was an answering machine, with the asking to leave detailed information including a specific reminder that hawks and owls are illegal to keep at home and they should not be fed or given water, but brought immediately to a medical facility. That particular part gave me an uncomfortable feeling, but regardless, I found the best rehabilitation center in the city specializing in hawk and owl care.

At about five that evening my friend came to pick me up and together

we went to the clinic. I sat in the back holding a box with the owl. On the way to the clinic, I had a feeling that I would never see her again, but still I had to help her. At the clinic, I came and signed my name on the form at the counter. A receptionist asked me what I brought and I replied that I brought an owl with a broken wing, which I had found yesterday in a field.

I asked the girl whether they released the birds after their recovery. She said yes. Then I asked what would happen to the owl if it still could not fly after the operation. The girl explained that in this case, it would be transferred to another location for training, and then said that the owl would be taken care of and that I could go. I asked if I could see a vet and was told no. I said that I would not leave the owl without seeing the vet. It seemed that my words somewhat confused the receptionist, but she said to wait a moment and passed into another room. A few minutes later, she came back and showed me a little room to enter, saying that the vet would join me shortly. I waited. Suddenly, the door opened and the vet appeared, shouting "You do not understand! You do not understand!" I was shocked by such a greeting.

Without letting me say a word, she continued to scream at me that owls cannot be kept at home, and must be brought immediately to the clinic. Her oxygen-depleting yelling stopped for an instant giving me a chance to respond as she inhaled to get ready for the next blast at me.

I explained that I had tried to come earlier but that on Sunday the clinic was closed. The vet looked at the owl and announced that I had had the bird for five days. I told her it was absurd; the owl had been with me 27 hours, and how could it be a crime to bring it into the clinic for treatment and asking to be informed of the owl's recovery and to be present for the release. She reluctantly agreed to call me. I learned from the receptionist, this vet was the chief of staff and owner of the clinic.

I gave them both my phones, an e-mail address, and the physical address, an left with a strong feeling of discomfort, feeling spiritually robbed and wondering to myself how such a cold-hearted person could be a healer. Why for example, could she not believe that a person can bond with a wild animal in just few hours?

The next day I phoned the clinic and asked how things were going. I was told that surgery was scheduled for Friday at about noon; I politely thanked them and decided to go on Friday and support the owl during the operation.

Arriving early, I parked my car, but didn't enter in order not to cause unnecessary emotion. Instead, I walked around the building figuring out about where the operation might be taking place. As I walked, I was talking with the owl, hoping she would hear my voice and feel more at peace knowing that I had not abandoned her. I lit mapacho and mentally began to ask about the success of the operation, visualizing her eventual release. I wanted to be by her side. I had thought about her life during the day and felt her pain as she sat in a cage with the broken wing. Finishing with my prayers, I continued to sit on the curb.

Suddenly the back door of the building opened loudly and a whole crew of people came out to the parking lot, headed by the chief vet, with whom I had a conflict earlier. She seemed hysterical as she yelled the words, "What are you doing here and how dare you come here?"

I calmly explained that I wanted to support my owl during the operation, but my words caused her to explode, shouting that the bird belonged to the state and I had no business in it. To which my immediate answer was: "The bird belongs to God."

My response made her pause, giving me sudden hope that she was about to come to her senses, but instead, after a short silence, she said that if I did not leave right now, she would call the police. Dealing with the cops was something that I wanted least that day. I'd already learned that conversations with people in uniform are useless at best and dangerous at worst. So I told her that I would leave, but would call tomorrow.

The next day I called the clinic to find out how the operation went. I was told that someone would return my call. Sometime later the phone rang and a male voice said that the operation was successful and that the owl was recovering. I thought I recognized that it was one of the quieter guys from the team in the hospital parking lot the day before, and I remembered sensing at the time that he was uncomfortable. I sensed that he was a decent person, but having a lower position, could not interfere in our confrontation .I thanked him and asked if I could call him in a couple of days to see how the owl was doing. He said that would be fine.

But the next day my phone rang again and the cold voice of the owner of the clinic announced that the owl had died and I was not to call the clinic anymore. I asked her how that was possible if only yesterday I was informed that the operation went just fine and the owl was recovering. To which, with the same lack of emotion in her voice, she added that things like that happen and I should not call them anymore.

I was overwhelmed. I remembered so clearly the single night I had together with the bird, and I felt heart ache. I went to that same spot in the field where I first met her.

For some reason, I didn't believe the vet. But I could not go there again and could not call. The only thing left was writing, so I typed a letter and sent it by fax, requesting evidence to support the death with documents within the next five days. Otherwise, I said, I would attract media attention and get legal help.

Apparently, my letter was convincing and three days later, I received an envelope with papers, which confirmed the death of an owl. Additional information was attached written in medical terms that I could not understand. I realized that even this official letter did not disperse my doubts. I didn't feel like they were telling the truth, but if they were, I finally decided, it was sad but good news at the same time; I thought that for a free spirit, death was better than slavery. That same day, I bought a ticket to Peru. Three months later, I moved there with my two Californian cats.

Cutting off the Roots of Confusion

Life in Peru became my dream after my first visit there at the end of 2005, but it would mean my third immigration, third culture, and third foreign language to study—there would be a few years as a "handicapped person" until learning Spanish, not a pleasant prospect.

I had lived eight years in California, dreaming the American dream. During that time I had married, divorced, and had financial ups and downs. I had friends, places in nature that I loved, and a business, which for the last few years was in decline due to the nationwide economic crises. Still, deliberately cutting off roots and starting all over again for the third time on another continent without money or knowledge of the language in a "third-world" country where chaos seemed a norm, was not an easy decision to make.

Leaving my comfortable life virtually with nothing, only following my heart, was bordering on the verge of insanity. Once, I had made such a "jump to nowhere," when I moved to the US. Back then, I had no money and spoke not a word of English. But, at least, I had a vague idea of the places I was headed to. But in Peru, there was none of that. Making this move was like jumping off a cliff—hoping to spread wings that would fly or crash on the rocks below.

These thoughts had swirled constantly in my head before the appearance of the owl. The bird was not only a herald of the coming change, but also brought hope and faith in my destiny.

A few months before leaving for Peru, after my meeting with the owl and the coyote, I slowly began to lure coyotes, each time leaving food for them closer and closer to my house. It all started with seeing these "prairie wolfs" at the same spot where I had seen the one when I had the owl in my hands. A day after first seeing him, I left him a piece of meat. When I returned the following day, I found numerous paw tracks and a few pieces of excrement. Ironically, I thought, my friendship had been accepted. Then, every day I began to bring fresh meat for the coyotes, until one night I heard their howling under my window. It was a sound that made my skin crawl. Later on, I returned to where I had met the first one and saw two and sometimes three or four of them roaming through the field. They always saw me because I never hid. I just sat quietly and watched them enjoy the wildness.

One day I decided to follow them through a field with the hope of finding their puppies. After a while, I lost sight of them, but stumbled upon a river bank I had not been to before. There were trees and bushes, and on one tree I spotted the nest of an owl with little chicks. I took footage of that beautiful scene and posted it on my website here: www.shamansworld.org/owl.html.

I thought about how the owls had led me to the coyotes and then the coyotes brought me back to the owls. But most interesting is that, where I found the nest of owls, I also saw hawks enjoying their flights. These hawks were beautiful, but different in color, with gray and white, and they seemed a little smaller. I came there every day in order to shoot more footage for better memories. It was usually quiet when I came, and I did not see any one. But, soon after finding my observation spot, the hawks appeared, and I felt they were playing with me, flying right towards me and turning immediately above my head, sometimes within a few feet. At other times, I could see them hunt. Before moving to Peru, I spent days there, shooting footage to remember. Some of this footage can be seen here: www.shamansworld.org/hawk.html.

I thought about taking my python to Peru with me. I actually considered hiding him in my underpants. But, after realizing how dangerous it was to try to smuggle a snake on the plane, I thought that it would be better to leave it in good hands and a good home. I didn't want to make the news with my arrest on charges of python smuggling—for one thing, that would put my cats in jeopardy. I thought about setting it free, releasing the snake in a river, but since it had been born in captivity, it wouldn't make it in the wild world. It would either freeze to death or get eaten. I talked to a friend of mine who I trusted to see if she would agree to take care of it. She did, and I found peace in my heart in regards to the python. She often sent me photos of him by email.

Well, after saying goodbye to people and places I loved, I moved to Peru. Martin, a friend, was supposed to meet me at the Cusco airport. I had met him in the jungle at the end of 2005 where we had bonded our friendship while sharing our common sectarian past. For 25 years he had been a follower of one Indian guru while living in US, so he well understood the feelings I shared with him about my years spent in the cult. I've already talked about how he ended up in Peru when it became a reality during a Huachuma vision. As foreseen, a few months after moving to Peru, he met a Peruvian woman and developed a relationship that grew into marriage. And, as he had also seen in his prophetic dream, she had seven children and many grandchildren. He greeted me at the airport as agreed and took me to the Sacred Valley, where he was living after moving to Peru. He found me a little place in a nearby village, dropped me off there and wished me a good luck. That's how I started my new life.

But, my long wished-for dream to live in Peru had not started as I had imagined. The drastic change in the level of comfort I was used to while living in the States, was not easy to handle. During the first month of my life in Peru, I had to spend 10 days in a row without electricity in the house. I didn't have any books to read, and my laptop didn't work. I shared silence with my cats by candle light. Then, when I got the electricity back and wanted to finally take a hot shower, there was a disruption in the water flow which continued for four more days.

And my first night in Peru was not peaceful either. I lived right next to the church, which was built by the Spanish conquistadors in 16th century and had a lot of art work in it. This church got robbed when I couldn't sleep because I was still adjusting to the altitude. It was about 1am when I've heard a lot of noises outside and realized that something was happening there. Getting out I saw people running around the church with sticks and machetes, screaming and yelling. It reminded me of a movie about the middle ages, only now I wasn't watching it on the screen.

Besides the comfort level, or more correctly, the lack of it, I began to feel lonely. Martin had his family and work, so I didn't want to bother him even though he was the only person I knew in the valley and could talk to on a certain level. He was well informed on the global affairs and deeply understood the level of corruption and conspiracy worldwide.

I didn't speak enough Spanish to make new friends with the local people. What was left was socializing with gringos like myself who were visiting or temporarily living in Peru. Most of them were easy going, laid-back hippies, while others were quite outlandish in appearance and manners, to say the least.

Nevertheless, their appearances, according to them, symbolized detachment from the system and contributed to their spiritual life. I didn't mind this so much but I wasn't attracted to their mentality or pseudo-esoteric verbiage of the new age movement—of which I was already quite tired in the US.

I will refer to this new-age movement by its more well-known term— new-age thinking.

In fact, new age mentality is nothing else but a superficialization of age-old deep spiritual ideas and a lack of willingness to engage with source material, which is a discipline, requiring dedication. We can trace this phenomenon back to the Theosophical Society of early 20th century, when Madam Blavatsky and other thinkers like her, made an attempt to bring the spiritual tradition of the East to the West, in order to shake the West from its materialistic quagmire. This stage was necessary, not just for the West, but also for the East, who knew about the basic nature of consciousness. Yet it would take a process of engagement with the western analytical mind in order to learn that consciousness itself evolves, as a radically modern view and a base for the future spirituality, allowing for a mutually beneficent evolution of us both.

Unfortunately, this attempt of bringing Easter wisdom and philosophy to West, was taken as the teaching itself rather than as reference to the real teaching. Being taken away from its land, the teaching went through another transformation whereby it became displaced from its original ethnic roots, in which spirituality was deeply embedded in the culture, to a culture practically devoid of any authentic forms, systems, or understandings of spirituality. This separation from its cultural roots, was already a step removed from direct engagement with what is. The moment direct experience is codified in language, it automatically becomes caught in a web of deceit, a litany of lies and a linguistic prison. This can be likened to a basket of flowers, whose bloom and beauty is destined to be short-lived due to their separation from their roots. It is unknown whether Blavatsky and friends understood this themselves, but the fact is, that a language is a tool, a finger pointing the moon and not the moon itself (and certainly not a fingertip as in the Blavatsky case!)

Thus at best, Blavastky's work could only perpetuate a much deeper confusion: the mistaking of the menu for the meal, or the map from the territory. As it is becoming apparent, language collapses possibilities and confines infinite and eternal consciousness to a word. This understanding, if developed, would question the foundation of western religion and line of thought, the very underpinnings of the basis of western civilization, which is a way of conceptualizing reality. Thus any ideas that were taken out of context and deprived of a free, open, explorative, and formless spirituality, have become painstakingly turned into a formed "spiritualism" with a label and a price tag. An ancient teaching of Advaita, which has little in common with neo advaita of today, just as the Fourth Way teaching presented by Gourdjieff ,which was fairly called by P. Ouspensky "fragments of unknown teaching"- both could serve as good examples for my point. Both teachings may do more harm than good to people seeking and receiving "spiritual" knowledge too early in their lives, without preparation, training, and understanding they are sent forth to make their own interpretations of what they read and hear. It's now like a herbarium, which once was living plants. Buddhists are not Buddha, Christians are not Christ. Followers of any kind, rarely transmit true teaching. Only a direct spiritual experience, which is mystical in essence, can bring one to that point of clarity in which all things are seen.

It would be true to say that same has happened with age old shamanic practices which were also co-opted, watered down and sanitized by the new-age movement, to make them fit for ready packaging and consumption. Nowadays, a shamanic experience in the West is, at best, a journey in your imagination—for the taboo against the use of sacred plants has penetrated deep into the western mind since the time of the Inquisition, and the new age has embraced this idea readily. Yet, the truth about sacred medicine remains. Correct use of medicine plants, under the tutelage of trained shamans, provides us with an objective viewpoint in which we are able to see ourselves reflected in a bigger mirror than just our own subjective consciousness. They provide us with the necessary and vital outside perspective, letting us use plant's consciousness to see our own. By denying us the plants' perspective, we deny ourselves the opportunity to know ourselves as we are, while also allowing ourselves to be lied to and deceived about who and what we are, so we can be bought and sold like cattle—for whom we in fact are the shepherds! The plants are our best hope of spiritual survival.

It would be fair to give some credit to the Fourth Way, whose teachers have admitted that outside help is necessary but have not identified what help, leaving a space to more superstition and a vague conception of higher forces, which do exist and yet are elusive and impersonal. In that sense, any kind of taboo on use of ancient shamanic plants is simply nothing more than a malevolent attempt to control human mind.

In a bigger sense both ancient shamanic tradition and eastern tradition are post- linguistic (pre-linguistic is just primitive); both are pointing to the wordless, experience which can be only directly perceived. The relationship between humans and plants is an alchemical symbiosis in which together we contribute to the evolution of universal consciousness, which is awakening to itself.

Teaching of non-duality is a popular doctrine in today's world, especially among those who become exhausted working on themselves by following the Fourth way system or any other way which requires lots of effort while yielding little or no results. These new age methods are easy to adapt and follow since they "ask" for nothing, stating basically that you already know it and this is all there is. Quite a change from working hard to doing nothing.

I had gotten so fed up with this while living in US, that I was forced to isolate myself from the crowd I usually socialized with. And, in the beginning, after moving to Peru, I chose loneliness with sanity over social life with all the frustration that can come with it. But, that was good because it gave me the chance to work alone with sacred Huachuma and contemplate my life surrounded by the stunning beauty of the magnificent Andes, looking for the greater clarity, deeper understanding and inner peace.

Just to give you an idea about what it felt like talking to some people, I will bring up few points which came up frequently during our arguments.

These conversations were very disappointing because they were attempts to discredit my way of thinking and impose instead another mentality which consisted of "ideas" they knew nothing about. But more difficult than the shallowness itself was the way it was conveyed – thru regurgitation of what had already been said.

This scene was painful because I saw well-meaning people get trapped once again without knowing.

To mention just a few of those often repeated ideas: We are all One, be positive, there is no duality, all is GOD and all is Love, no sides, no good, no evil, no right no wrong, no true no false. Freedom is effortless, we have arrived, there are no mistakes, and truth is relative (among many others).

It was only later when I thought about the possibility that the ancient spiritual teaching of Advaita was not only misunderstood by the people but was also hijacked by the powers that be with the intent to control the human mind through ideological warfare, mixing deep, liberating ideas with new-age pseudo esoteric thinking and then injecting it like a virus into collective subconscious, which now is spreading via regurgitation, consequently destroying the human spirit by demoralization and disorientation, thus confusing the people so that they cannot fathom the real intent. But what is the human spirit?" Well, I was thinking, our spirit was not our body. And it wasn't our soul either, which animates the body into life, but rather something in between them, a link which was connecting both. I thought it was a certain qualities or set of principles of guiding nature. Morality and ethics came to mind.

Ethics 'ethos' (from Greek 'character') is the system of moral principles of a human being which sets him apart from animals and barbarians and form the base for human action. The conscience—an inheritance of pure heart, is the ability to make the judgment between ethical and unethical, moral and immoral, right and wrong actions. That is the main spiritual organ just as significant and important to the well-being of the spiritual harmony as the physical heart is to a body. Without conscience man would be lost. He would not know how to distinguish truth from falsehood, or right from wrong, and would be merely a puppet, psychologically open to other people's influences and manipulations.

But how could conscience function without the morals? How would it distinguish between right or wrong if there were not a moral code of ethics? So could it be that ethics, morals, and conscience were interconnected qualities of our inner being, our character or our spirit? What would be a better way to control the population if not to mislead them into confusion by teaching them that right was actually left and up was down? Such confusion would lead directly to relinquishment of the power of reason and critical thinking, thus creating a vacuum to be filled with submission.

In numerous conversations with people, I tried to draw their attention to contradictions and holes in their ideology which could be only sealed with blind faith.

For example, I mentioned that if we all are One, would that not mean that there was no difference between a liar and an honest person, a prudent, moral man and a criminal? And if there is no difference between these opposites, would that not mean that it doesn't matter how you live your life and how you should treat other people? After all, if we all one and nothing matters, then it's all the same—which brings us once again to the subject of integrity, ethics and morals—which all would be void following this logic.

Would ancient Greek philosophers like Socrates have agreed and accepted the idea of Oneness, which if misused, would nullify all ethics and moral principles? Of course not. He would die standing up against it, challenging and questioning its very core. After all, this is why he was poisoned to death, choosing to follow his ethic, morals and conscience rather submitting to the status quo which he perceived was nothing else than immorality.

In numerous conversations with people I kept on asking whether they considered themselves one with thieves, rapists, pedophiles, murderers and other depraved individuals? Their answers were "of course not," contradicting the idea of unity and oneness among people. After all, if they do not consider themselves to be ONE with everyone, then division is apparent and so is contradiction.

More sophisticated answers like "we are ONE on another level" didn't seem to make sense either. If we supposedly are one on some other, invisible level, of which we are not aware in daily life, then what philosophy should be applied for living on this level where we aware of daily life? Or did it even matter?

It is an absolute truth that on a larger scale everything is One because no one can ever see the Universe from outside of it or be separate from it. The Universe is all there is, and all of us are "microcosmic" matter of Universal consciousness, regardless of who we are and in what pixel of this gigantic matrix we reside. However, this philosophy wouldn't be so practical if you were attempting to apply it to your neighbor who is trying to steal your sheep!

Usual responses I heard were that I was engaged in thinking too much, which was another way to say "let's not examine anything, instead, let's just believe it."

There is nothing wrong with thinking, in fact, real thinking is the path to understanding. We think, we realize, we act. This is how we make a difference in our lives and our world, step by step, human by human.

But, how can good decisions be made without thinking anyway? Usually, decisions without proper thinking do not bring good results, in fact, in many cases they lead to suffering and pain of the person who makes them and those who are affected by them. So yes, I think and I try to do it often.

But, at the same time, I know how and when to switch off my mind and simply be in the moment, perceiving the world through my heart. There is no conflict here at all, but simply a time for different things. Playing chess takes concentration, memory and a deductive logic, not feelings… and love—is not created or flourished through intellect.

Besides, through thinking and processing knowledge, we are expanding our awareness and thus spiritually we grow and evolve. To disrupt this process could result in fixation on a certain points of view which without critical thinking could easily turn to dogma. In straight terms, I am saying that enlightenment doesn't 'just manifest.' And this is so much the new-age view, or come right out and say wishful thinking.

This I will say: to possibly find enlightenment, you must be willing to work to perfect your morals first.

And then there is the idea of always being positive, regardless of the circumstances. Well, I've been through that already in the cult, where for 6 years I watched how people were psychologically raped, going against their common sense and their conscience, trying to remain always positive regardless of abuse they were subjected too. This idea of being always positive, was designed to disarm the students by suppressing their critical thinking, crippling their will and thus making it easier to keep them under control of a little tyrant who though he was a second coming of Christ.

I felt that instead of trying to be falsely positive, one had to be always adequate, reacting naturally to injustice and abuse. Acting otherwise would be another way of lying to yourself and allowing the actions of others to suppress your own conscience in the process. There is nothing spiritual in submission to abuse, injustice and tyranny. It only points to the weakness of the person's spirit and lack of one's character. I say strive for peace but stand for truth and justice and always be prepared to fiercely defend yourself and your family.

In the cult, we were bombarded with the idea of acceptance, which implied acceptance of anything, including mistreatment and abuse. Those who rebelled against it were considered to be bad students, and I was one of them.

But, let us suppose for a moment that we truly are One on the level of energy, do we live in this molecular reality in our daily life? Do we raise our families on that level? Do we make our living there? Do we interact with people there? Or, is our daily dwelling in physical reality, which has its density in which we sharing common sense?

And what about the "all is God" idea? If all is God and all is perfect and all is love then what about the 9/11 tragedy? What about wars that kills millions of innocent people, woman and children included? Are these are acts of Goodness and deeds of God? I've heard that in the cult as well and deeply disagreed with that. It feels to me that behind this idea there is an intention to undermine the search for truth and justice. After all, all is God and all is good!

Well, I never got a reasonable answer to my question. And how would I? Can anyone in his right mind argue that there is no evil in the world or there are no bad people around? Whoever thinks that way had better think again before harsh reality sends him a personal awakening one day without notice.

Living in denial isn't safe and masquerading fear with certain ideas, teachings or worldviews is not effective. It reminds me of an ostrich who sticks his head in the sand when seeing a lion in the field, thinking that the lion cannot see him because he cannot see the lion.

Evil does exist and it is as real as a heart attack, but good exists as well and is equally as real—and both are open paths for anyone to follow. Regardless of which path you choose to walk, good and evil are obvious forces and are in confrontation in today's world like never before, a fact which makes non-duality a fiction. And would not a prudent, moral person vs. a psychopath and pervert invalidate the idea of "we are all one?"

In addition to the contradictions of this idea, I also felt some criminality behind that. After all, if we are all ONE, then it implies that all belongs to all. But, does it not open the door for invasion of privacy by erasing the boundaries between people? Does it not invade their personal lives, potentially claiming rights to their privacy and possessions? Following that logic, all is shared and all is common... including your property, your money and your spouse. On a bigger scale it could be used to target sovereign nation states, removing boundaries between countries, turning it all to one global community with all resources "shared" and controlled by the power elite on the top which make this all ideology nothing more than a means to a mind control and a power grab.

There were numerous platitudes thrown out in these conversations that I had heard before and was still hearing:

"*You create your own reality.*" This idea is the most insidious example of an inflated ego, which confuses itself with God, when in fact, the only way this idea can be more practically seen, is as living through the consequences of our own decisions, rather shaping our world with our thoughts. Well, if that would be the case, we wouldn't have a world to live in, if everyone would have the power to shape it as he wants.

"There is no right no wrong." I'm sure that psychopaths and criminals would like to see this idea to be included in the penal code.

"You cannot know what's good and what's evil." Well, knowledge of that kind is fundamental and among the first things kids learn in children stories while still in the kindergarten.

"Don't look for the meaning of life, if it exists, it lies beyond life." Then what is the point of living a meaningless life?

"Don't worry about your mistakes, the Universe might need them." Okay, then, let's make more of them, to help the Universe out!

"We have arrived!" Well, I certainly feel that way when I see my bus station but speaking otherwise, I think we learn as long as we alive and thinking that we have arrived would mean to stop the learning process and turn into stagnation.

"There are no mistakes and what has happened, happened for a reason and couldn't have happened any other way." So there is no freedom of choice, no sense of responsibility or accountability? It's all just happens because it had to happen, because all is perfect and there are no mistakes.?

"You not guilty of your mistakes; they were meant to happen because all happens for a reason." That's a particularly interesting one; if you rob or rape someone, it's all right, because for them it was meant to happen! I thought instead that by admitting the mistake we learn from it, thus becoming wiser. It is a process of learning and striving for self-improvement which is a natural process of evolution of consciousness that our species capable of doing.

"Truth is relative." One of the most-often quoted and possibly one of the most dangerous. If truth is relative than it is not possible to find it, simply because it does not exist. Whatever someone believes to be true makes it so then search for any other possibility or perspective becomes meaningless. It's just enough to have a set of beliefs and think you know the truth.

It becomes easy to imagine a rapist who will say that this is not his truth; in his mind he had consensual sex with the victim, and victim's truth is not objective but only relative to her.

What does this idea would do to the justice system? How can the truth could be found and established if it's always relative?

And what about the idea that freedom is effortless? Does it not imply that if you have to make any efforts it means that you not free? Well, making a living is certainly an effort one must to make in order to survive, unless one turns into a thief—who would certainly feel more freedom in this regard.

Besides, I never saw a bird fly without having to flap its wings.

For me, the idea of unity is more specific and relates to the consciousness of a human being, his wholeness, integrity and action, united in him without contradictions. Another unity I see is with family, and, after that, a unity with nature.

One must understand what he unites himself with. Without such clear judgments and distinctions, the idea of unity can be widely open for interpretation and can be used in a different ways by different people with differing agendas. For example, a totalitarian regime with a communistic mantra calling for collectivism which has proven historically to be disastrous, can also use the idea of Oneness to serve its purpose. After all, we saw that happened in the early 20th century in Russia when the Proletariat was called upon to unite, sending shockwaves through many generations. Not to mention that Nazis who were also obsessed with the new age thinking, just as an example, with the idea of the Aryan master race—which is right out of the Blavatsky's secret doctrine. Hitler even went as far as adapting a Swastika, an ancient esoteric Hindu symbol associated with the sacred force, and turned it to a symbol of Fascism! This historical fact alone should be making the point. And the point is that this thinking can be adapted by both right and left extremes, which makes it more dangerous. Clearly, this kind of shallow philosophy is highly open to abuse and makes it likely that this phenomena are being exploitatively controlled now. See the 2012 hysteria or the Heaven's Gate tragedy for examples.

Due to the smorgasbord of new age "spirituality" all authentic or traditional forms of genuine spirituality get tarred with the same brush with ridicule as reserved for such phenomena as the Lochness monster, which has nothing to do with spirituality (whether it's there or not), or a mysterious planet X, which still is hiding behind the sun, missing its "scheduled" arrival. This can be easily used as the form of societal control in order to limit the people's expression or inquiry into authentic forms of spirituality, true mysteries, unexplained phenomena or conspiracy—and last but not least—the modern view toward the alternative medicine and natural ways of healing which are constantly ridiculed by the media.

Over time, I had come to understand these things on my own. Yet, through Huachuma dialogues with a friend who came to visit me, we found deeper understanding and the words to express it.

What was really disappointing, when I came to live in Peru was to see a lot of people working with the sacred plants while still holding on to those ideas, repeating them like mantras, believing in them like they were spoken to them by God himself. Well, working with the Sacred Huachuma, for example, is like staring at God's face, staring back at you, and in this divine union you have an opportunity to directly perceive reality as it is, easily bypassing all verbal and conceptual means, while apprehending the inapprehensible in a mysterious way. Holding to those new age ideas in the light of sacred plants would be like trying to fit a child's sandals to an adult However, these ideas are maintained even when working with shamans in the jungle. These shamans aren't intellectuals as many westerns expect them to be, but nevertheless, to them duality of the world is as apparent as the morning sun. And if some of these people doubt that for a moment, they will be quickly reminded of the world of duality by their neighbors, whose hostility would leave no room for ideas of oneness and positive thinking. I always felt that the idea of positive thinking, regardless of the truth or circumstances, in fact, was a disarming idea which leads to obedience and submission. I say be adequate instead, and act according to what the moment brings. Actually, life in jungle is not very different from life in the modern world in a certain sense, and if a person does not realize that, it means he or she has not yet learned the lessons that life has to offer.

I felt that this new age mentality is not intended to empower the individual; rather it targets us with demoralization and with intention to transform us to powerless, mindless zombies, bio cells which are only a part of a bigger organism of collectivism, which is in essence a form of communism—nothing else but an oppressive and dangerous political regime which has no place for human freedom… something right out of the communist manifesto.

I am all for striving for a better world, but I know that there will not be a chance for real change unless reality is accepted as it truly is and dealt with instead of resisted. Until then, non-duality will be self-delusion and wishful thinking projected in your own mind.

Timothy Leary said that two people can be as distant from each other as the distance between two stars.

I agree with him completely. A distance in world perception, in understanding, ethics, and morals among people can really be of astronomical proportions, and putting all of us together in the same line would be very wrong.

Thinking about this subject farther, I came to a conclusion that this mentality was bearing in itself a strong sense of nihilism, which is a destructive philosophy of negation of meaningful aspect of life. It was best described by a Russian classic Ivan Turgenev in 19th century, in his novel *Father and Sons*. Bazarov, a main character, was a proud nihilist who among other things was arguing that all people are the same like trees – "you don't need to study every tree to learn about the forest," meaning that it was enough to have one human exemplar to learn about humanity. What could be a better idea to nullify individuality? Bazarov was negating moral, ethical, and all principles—just as he was negating and dismissing art, beauty of nature (which he said was not a shrine but a workshop in which a man was a worker) and inscrutability of the human soul by referring to a man's physiology, seeing him as anatomic assemblage and a collection of organs.

This materialistically driven ideology was strongly echoing of that of the 19th century European scientific elite, who in my opinion never rose beyond arrogance, leading the science in spiritual ignorance. In a spiritual sense, this "progressive" mentality was in fact a regression, a step back rather forward, destruction of order of things and a road to chaos. Could that twisted mentality can become a foundation for new world religion—intended to replace all religions in order to "unite" humanity into one world of slavery run by scientific eugenics elite? After all, it might be the last piece of the puzzle after which an ugly picture of global dictatorship will be forever imprinted on the human mind.

The bottom line is that the divine is moral, and without Love, awareness, and moral principles, everything we know would be nothing more than a vibrating cosmic mass of quantum physics.

Path

Magic Arrows

Back to my story and life in Peru. Soon after arriving to the Sacred Valley of the Incas I began to do ceremonies with different shamans with the purpose of seeing what the local level was. Prior to that, my work was in the Central Andes and I knew nothing of the shamans of the Sacred Valley and Cusco region.

One day we had a Huachuma ceremony in the ancient ruins of Pikil-lacta, which is near Cusco and possibly related to the Wari Pre-Inca culture. This place has not lost its mystical aura for thousands of years. There were only a few of us present. Shortly after drinking I decided to leave the group and wonder through the ruins. After a while I found my place and sat comfortably on one of the ancient walls. It offered a beautiful view. I was simply reflecting on some things in my life when, suddenly, literally in a flash, something hit my chest and blew into pieces the Jaguar tooth, my protective amulet which I had always worn on my neck. My first thought was that someone had thrown a rock, but there was no one around. Shocked, I watched my mind try to tell me that this was just a hallucination, but the shattered pieces of the Jaguar tooth were undeniable proof of its reality.

I remembered Howard telling about the witchcraft which is widely practice in the Amazonian jungle and the magic arrows used by brujos (sorcerers) to attack the curanderos. I had heard many stories about these magic arrows but always remained stubborn in my skepticism about a possibility of psychic power influencing physical matter.

As I understood the nature of these arrows, they were clots of concentrated negative energy, rolled by a power of the shamans like a snowball, then mentally released or "shot" into an image of another shaman they were trying to target. The distance in this case did not matter.

It is quite common in Peru to hear about brujos and their malevolence harming people simply out of jealousy. To find an honest curandero who is dedicated to healing is not so easy now days; many "shamans" are corrupt and motivated by their greed. These are properties of brujos, a dirty shaman who puts his personal gain at the top of the line. For the money, a brujo would cure or harm, heal or kill. Of course, his curing will not penetrate as deep, but still he capable of doing something.

I was lucky to work with curanderos like Howard, don Rober, don Victor and others, both in Peru and Mexico. Their dedication for healing and spiritual awakening has become an example for me to follow. A true curandero will never abuse the powers of sacred plants and will not cause the person harm. Exceptions would be only in case of self-defense. True curanderos will not be bribed and use their knowledge to impose the will of one person on another.

At first I was tormented by the question why sacred plants allow people to abuse them? The only conclusion I came to, was that sacred plants don't have free will, like humans do; they only have a certain type of intelligence with special qualities and properties, which can be used or abused like any other form of energy on Earth. Without the will they simply cannot resist being misused. From that prospective, abusing sacred plants by using them for evil, it is disrespect. Sacred plants are mirrors in which a person can see him or herself. As long as the shaman is willing to see himself in this mirror and learn, he will remain on the path of healing and light. But as soon as he turns himself away from it, he crosses the line and leaves his conscience behind, following the path of darkness. After that the sacred medicine, instead of being his teacher, becomes his servant. That leads directly to self-serving, rather serving others.

If a shaman has fallen into the trap of power, his ego gets inflated with his arrogance and pride, fed on admiration by other people. He becomes another guru figure, with false authority to teach, but lacking real knowledge because real knowledge is not in words, rather its pure content, content of the heart, directed towards healing and spiritual enlightenment.

So I sat there and thought, who had this malicious intention toward me? Obviously it was someone who knew my heart. But who exactly? Several candidates came to mind.

Upon arrival in Peru, I had a quite unpleasant conversation with a local shaman, who could speak English, learnt from his American wife .He was a known shaman in the area and had often big gatherings in his place to which he was inviting many people—many other shamans to celebrate the winter solstice (21 June) and summer solstice (21 December), equinox (March 21) and the autumnal equinox (September 21). I wanted to take part in these big ceremonies and meet new shamans.

When we got talking with this guy, he asked me why I came to Peru and what I wanted to do here. I told him honestly that my heart had lead me here to work with Huachuma. He did not like my answer, and began a long tirade telling me how wrong that was, and that should be the role of native people. We talked for about an hour, after which with a hostile attitude toward each other we parted forever. This encounter left such an unpleasant trace in my heart.

I remembered another conversation, with another shaman, a Chavin maestro Huachumero in the Central Andes, who later became my friend and a teacher, with whom we have repeatedly traveled to the ancient sacred places in Peru doing Huachuma ceremonies there. I asked him once how he was looking at the fact that western people were coming to Peru to walk the medicine path. His reply was straight and simple: "Bienvenido" (welcome). And he added that my interest reminded him of the value of his ancient culture. His words truly touched me.

Then I thought of Immanuel, a North American Apache and a founder

of a Peyote Way Church of God in Arizona, who went even farther by fighting through a federal court the legal right to use Peyote for non-Indians, stating that Peyote is a sacrament for all, and no race, no church nor government can own it.

Thinking some more, I outlined my circle of potential enemies; some of them were quite secretive, but their looks at me were telling. Perhaps they had already seen a competitor in me and wanted to remove me so I would not interfere with their business.

Yes, unfortunately in Peru, shamanism has become commercialized in many areas.

When I returned to the group in Pikillacta, and shared with them what happened, they only looked at my jaguar tooth hanging around my neck, which now was torn to pieces by a mysterious force, shaking their heads in amazement.

Leaving the place that day I expressed intent to mirror this attack to whoever it was and let Justice be the judge. As time has passed, I thought to dig into it further and find out exactly who the culprit was, but felt already too strong in myself to waste time on that. This accident inspired me to look deeper into this subject as a whole. It triggered my interest in learning about shamanic ways of self-defense. It is only later when I realized that I came to Peru already 'sealed,' which was granted to me by the forces of death during my Initiation in Mexico.

Toward my Destiny

A month later, I was getting ready to celebrate my 33rd Birthday, which I felt was very important. I had prepared a special medicine and invited my friend Martin and a few other people with whom I had made connections so far. I decided to go back to Pikillacta, the place where I was attacked by the psychic arrow, for the purpose of purifying the place from a negative charge and removing the trace it had left in my heart. Also, I liked the panoramic view from the ruins.

After all sharing the medicine, we spread out to find our own places. A few hours later, as the medicine unfolded fully, Martin and I had a deep and sincere conversation about different things. Among them, I told him that once in Mexico I was told that I would find the woman of my heart along my path. This path had now has brought me to Peru where it felt like my final destination. Therefore, I thought that my woman must be here. But, where to look for her and how would I recognize her among others? Listening to me, Martin looked into the distance and said that he could see her, our family, and our house somewhere very near.

We talked for a while, and then parted. It was a warm and sunny day. I lay on the ground to watch the drifting clouds. At one point I felt like asking the medicine to show her to me. An unclear image of a woman appeared in the sky above. I tried to take a better look to see her face, so I could recognize her upon our meeting, but my mind could only grasp a blurry image in the shapes of the clouds.

It was only later that I realized that her face was not shown to me that day, in order that I recognize her with my heart and not my eyes when meeting her in person.

Exactly three months after my birthday ceremony, on October 3rd, I went to Cusco without any specific reason. In Cusco I walked around, ate something, then went to an internet café where I spent a few hours. Later, I felt like going home and took a taxi to a bus station from where the minivans and taxis were going to the Sacred Valley. At the station, I stood in line with others who were waiting for the ride to the valley. Suddenly, my eye was caught by a girl who stood at the front of the same line. I had an impulse to introduce myself to her. I came close and started to speak in broken Spanish. She looked at me with a kind smile. Fortunately, she spoke English, which definitely speeded up the introduction. We had about 5 minutes to talk before the minivan arrived. I asked her if we could exchange phone numbers to which she agreed. I sat in front and she sat somewhere in the back. During the half hour ride, I thought about her and felt her presence. I lived near Pisac at that time, and I thought that when I got out at the bus stop, I would look at her and if she looked back at me, then I would call her tomorrow, if not, then no.

Getting out in Pisac, I paid the driver and looked at her. She was looking back at me with a smile.

I could hardly wait until the next morning. I woke up at 6 and thought about calling, but decided to wait a little longer. I called her at about 8; she answered and said she was happy to hear me. I asked if I could come immediately to which she responded that lunch time would be better.

She lived in another town in the Sacred Valley about half an hour beyond Pisac. Right after we talked, I rode my motorcycle to her town. I just hung out, waiting. About lunch time, I called her again and we agreed to meet in the central plaza. I cut a few lovely flowers right from the ground of the plaza while I was waiting her.

When she came, I offered her some ice cream. While we ate, she asked me if I would like to see an archeological site, which was within a few minutes' ride from the town. I said, of course, and we went to visit Urco, an ancient ceremonial fertility site with a lovely, peaceful energy surrounding it.

Sitting there, listening to her tell me about the place, I was busy thinking that this was the first date in my life on an ancient power place. I saw in it a certain sign. She asked me if I would like to join her for lunch with her parents to which I said yes. When we arrived and as we ate, I felt easy even though I could not speak with her parents because of the language barrier.

We spent a lovely day together and started meeting every day after that. It was amazing to find out on that first day when we met in Cusco, I was not the only one who had followed intuition; she was doing the same. She was usually working in a hotel during the evenings, but the day before our first meeting, she was asked to come to work the next morning to replace another person. She was obviously exhausted so she decided to rest a little before going to see her parents. But, after lying down in her bed, she felt anxious and couldn't rest. She then decided to go to the bus station for the Sacred Valley. What happened next? Well, you already know.

From day one, our relationship was light and easy. From the start I wanted to be straight up with her. During one of our earlier talks, I told her honestly that I had nothing and expecting nothing from anyone—adding that all I had were my two cats and a used laptop, both of which I had brought with me from the States. Also, I mentioned my Chinese motorcycle and just enough money to make it through the next six months.

She said that money didn't matter and that we could always work to make a living, adding that she loved me for who I was rather than for what I owned. Then, I told her that the reason I came to Peru was to work with Huachuma and if she ever tried to block me from doing that, I would need to leave her behind—as I had done more than once in my life where the choice was between following my path and staying with a woman. She said that it was as silly to be jealous about my love for the plant as to be jealous about my love for my cats, adding that we could respect each other's ways without trying to change one another.

Two weeks later I asked her what she thought about the two of us getting married. She thought a minute and said, "why not?" We made the decision to tell her parents.

The next weekend, we made the announcement during lunch, shocking her parents quite a bit.

Her father choked swallowing the food and asked if it was not too early, to which we both responded, "no."

Thus, a beautiful, kind, intelligent and educated woman from a conservative Catholic family, suddenly became the wife of a high school

dropout, gringo, triple immigrant, poor Jew who worships God in the cactus. We got married a few months later in December, which was a big event for both of us.

In January, a month after we got married, my phone rang. The man was speaking good English, but it sounded as if he had some kind European accent. He said he wanted to learn about the Huachuma ceremonies I was offering. I invited him to come for a talk first. He came to see me the next day.

The man turned out to be a psychotherapist from Germany, who had been in Peru eight years before and had drunk Ayahuasca in the jungle. He said that his new journey was not planned, but after waking up one morning, he felt that he needed to go to Peru again. He first arrived in Cuzco, and then immediately went to the Sacred Valley. On the third day of his stay in Peru, he found the only flyer I had out there and immediately called me. During the conversation, I got the impression that he was a mature and sincere person to work with, so I asked when he would like to start. He replied that he would like to start the next day. He arrived promptly at 9 am. We drank the medicine and went to Urco, the same ancient ruins that my wife had shown me on our first date.

My new German friend was deeply touched by the medicine and later said that we had a long way to go together. His words confused me at first, since I was just walking my path and doing what I love and did not look for either partners or apprentices. After the first ceremony, we spent 7 weeks drinking every other day. Somewhere at the end of our work, in one of the conversations on the way home, he asked whether my wife and I had thought of having children. I said that we would like to very much , but that the finances were difficult right now, neither did we have a place to live. He asked how much it costs to build a house in Peru, I said that I did not know, but I thought it would be cheaper than in Germany. He said that he himself had no money for such a project, but he promised upon his arrival home, to talk to his friends in Switzerland, who possessed the necessary means. I asked him how we would pay him back to which he answered that I would do ceremonies for groups with whom he would be coming to Peru over the next few years. Well, paying him back by doing what I love was a wonderful idea to which I gladly agreed, especially since there was no pressure or a timeline. I appreciated his intention and I did believe his words.

Three weeks after he left Peru, I received from him the good news that he had talked to his friends and they had agreed to lend us the money interest free. I could not believe my eyes as I read his email. They were ready to send us money, knowing that it may take years to get it back, if ever. That was incredible.

A month later we received the first sum of money which we naively thought would be enough. My father- in- law found builders and we signed the contract after which construction started. And while my wife was pregnant with our baby, I was pregnant with our house. But the building progressed quite actively and required more money. I was forced to ask my German friend for money three times before we got it done. I appreciated his confidence and trust in me, because all the money had been given only on the honor of my word. There were no papers saying anything about our debt. In fact, he was indebted to his friends who did not even know me. A year later, he brought his first group from Germany and Switzerland, and I was very happy to work and pay back the first sum.

As time passed by, our nest was getting stronger and warmer, giving care and love for our daughter. I began to feel that now I had the time and energy to finally write my book which I had wanted to write for so long, but never knew where to start. As my friend Martin had once told me, I couldn't write before because I had not lived it yet. Now, having lived through it, I was ready to write about it. He was right. I needed to come to a certain point in my life, from which I could see, evaluate and understand my path, where it began and where it went.

I remembered, during my last visit to Mexico, before going back to California, Eldon had told me of a sign he saw the next morning after that Peyote night, when I was lying down paralyzed by the scorpion venom. He looked at the semicircle mound of dirt in the shape of a horse shoe, which he told me to build before the ceremony around the fire, facing the East with it inner side. I tried to make it as level as possible, but regardless of my efforts, it was full of bumps, built had leveled out into a long flat surface smoothly merging with the ground at the end. And that was true. All my life had been like rolling on a bumpy road up until that point in Mexico. But a few months later, I moved to Peru where I finally felt at home.

Huachuma Message

I choose to end this story of my path with relating an occurrence that relates to an earlier chapter, "Huachuma Call," which happened when we returned to a retreat center after spending a beautiful day on the Amazon river observing and absorbing the freshness and beauty of the rainforest.

We entered the Maloca, and sat around Howard's mesa lit up with candles.We all sat in silence, listening to a pouring heavy rain outside. The wind blew out some of the candles on the altar. That was when people were invited to come to the mesa for a singado, to experience an infusion of sacred tobacco into the nose, especially prepared for this ceremony. Infusion of this tobacco is taken at the peak of Huachuma ceremony to enhance the vision, a ritual still practiced in some areas of Central Andes.

When my friend Martin approached the altar and took the tobacco extract into his nose, he fell on the floor having a catharsis. Lying there in tears, he suddenly started shouting my name. Everyone was sitting quietly, rain and wind were wild. I didn't feel like responding. He repeated my name three times before I have responded him by saying "I am here, Martin." Hearing my voice he said: "Follow your heart, Sergey."

A strong wind blew out more candles on the altar. The silence was deadly. Martin remained on the floor. I looked at the altar, which had a Huachuma cactus in the middle of it, feeling that the words coming through Martin were actually the message for me from the spirit of the plant.

He and I had only one conversation prior to that, where we shared our sectarian past. Back then, I appreciated his sincerity and was pleased to talk to him. But he usually avoided talking, because he was busy writing. When we went to the Andes, I met him again in Cusco. He surprised me with his decision to stay in Peru. Our next meeting took place few years later when me and my friend from Russia came to Peru for a pilgrimage to Chavin.

I placed this brief story here at the end of the book to remind myself, as well as my readers, that there always threads of light and truth along the way, if we look for them. This brief tale has been my companion for seven years, and I wanted to bring it out in the open once again. The message is not new for me; I have always heard it and sometimes followed its directions. It has long been a trustworthy guide, but this time, it was so loud, that my heart had no choice but to answer. Thus, I find myself happily here in my home in Peru, and offering to you the story of my Path.

Epilogue

My book is a condensed version of my Path which was and still is an adventure that I call Life.

During the writing, I was reminded a number of times by my editors that this book has to end somewhere, and I should reserve material for forthcoming books. Throughout the book, I was tempted to engage deeper in some areas to which I have only made references, and I forced myself to harness the flow of thoughts that were coming thru me like the waves to a shore, forced by the hurricane. While mentally "surfing," I felt a desire to expand on different subjects, but at the same time I trusted the feeling that what I had written was enough for the time being.

But moving between the two, I felt like there was one final area I had to address in this book, and that is Carlos Castaneda's writings, which have been sold in millions of copies worldwide and are still selling. I felt it was a duty to bring clarity to the subject by sharing my thoughts, my findings, and personal experiences, some of which, as you know from previous chapters, were certainly unique if not extraordinary. I touched upon new-age thinking earlier, where I made a mention of Neo-shamanism being a part of that new age model that appeared in the West with its "ambassadors" aka the new-age "shamans" who I regard as only pretending to be a shamans rather than truly being them. I pointed out that they appear to others as the source of the knowledge itself, while playing on the naive views held by people who are discouraged from engaging with a core shamanic practice—using ancient sacred plants—thus contributing to a greater confusion and misunderstanding of what true shamanism is about. It would require another entire book to go deeper into this subject, but I will say some things by way of forming a background for my thoughts on Castaneda.

Shamanism is the oldest spiritual practice on Earth and predates all religions, a practice of direct engagement with the spiritual world. In fact, religion itself is already a step removed from the wordless spiritual experience which leaves no place for a blind faith.

Shamanism goes back to prehistoric time when hunter-gatherers, out of necessity to survive while searching for food, consumed different plants in order to find the edible ones. This relationship with the plant kingdom not only allowed them to survive by also to evolve. These experiences with different plants were more than just entertainment to early humans, but an educating process as well. A probable cause for the linguistic capabilities that developed in early humanity, was a psilocybin mushroom, which along with other psychoactive plants, contributed to the general process of human evolution, bringing humans to another stage of consciousness as the result.

The word "shaman" which is a broad term (one could even say "overused") now days, originated in Siberia, where up until the early 20th century, as part of shamanistic tradition a fly agaric mushroom had been regularly used before a brutal attempt to eradicate shamanism was made by Stalinist regime. Even though the word itself seems a relatively modern term, the symbiotic relation between humans and plants actually goes back to antiquity. In this sense what we call a shamanism today, in reality, is an ancient way of interacting with the spiritual world—a relationship that was sacred and held in the highest respect as being the source of healing and inspiration. Thus a spiritual bond was formed and became a constant dialogue between Humans and Nature—thus giving birth to what today we call shamanism.

It should be quite apparent that shamanism without direct interaction with plants would be incomplete and thus impractical—since practice itself is what it is. Unfortunately, this sacred relationship with the natural world has been unfairly wrapped in negativity by the western imperialism which really got going during the Judeo-Christian Era 2000 years ago. Out of desire to control the people through religion, the powers that be developed extravagant names for it like the paganism and even a devil worshiping, while referring to the age-old practices—which are much older than the Devil himself—since Devil is a Christian concept, not even present there before Christianity. So, again, shamanism, sometimes referred to as "paganism" was simply a communion between humans and spiritual world, and until now was totally negated by the western thought—which is finally beginning to change as the spiritualization of the West evolves. This in fact may become for future generations the very important paradigm shift long awaited by civilization. The counterfeiting force to this great phenomenon of human awakening is trans-humanism, which is now promoted by the same powers that be in order to dehumanize and degrade us to a point of machines.

Of course it would be impossible to replace human spirit and consciousness with artificial, soulless intelligence just as it would be to breathe life into a scarecrow. But out of desperation and fear of losing control over humanity, these efforts are being made and will continue until the intellectual revolution and spiritual awakening of 21st century comes into full bloom. I think it will not be a matter of decades but rather only a matter of years before Quantum physics—which is a Western Yoga in a way—through mathematical equations and attempts to further break down the atom essentially to nothing, will stumble upon a stubborn fact that consciousness is all there is.

Consciousness arises from the emptiness and nothingness, and yet it is a phenomenon of the highest order, which IS and WILL REMAIN a mystery. This understanding, long held by mystics of all kinds, going back to Buddha (and even earlier) who figured that out early on (and here I am paraphrasing for purposes of clarity) that emptiness IS the form and form IS the emptiness. History is full of points when knowledge and a free way of thinking were suppressed. This unfortunately reached a point of absolute madness during the time of Inquisition and brutal conquest of New World. Nevertheless, a true shamanic tradition has survived all repressions in its original form. When I made this discovery I realized that as long as the human race is alive, the symbiosis with the plants will thrive.

The Inquisition of the middle ages was not the only suppression in our history. In fact suppression has reappeared many times in different shapes and forms: such as the Native American Indian genocide, for example, which managed to a certain degree to deprive the Native Americans of their spiritual tradition by cutting them off their ancestral roots. Even more serious, because it is happening at this very critical time in our human history, the "pharmacological inquisition" of today is the latest form of the centuries- old attempt to control the human mind.

Yet, there is hope. Even all those forms of evil were unable to completely eradicate or break the link between humans and nature, which is just as strong today as it was before (in fact, it may be having a rebirth of sorts.). This intimate and special ancient relationship with the plants is especially alive in certain places such as Mexico and Peru—where in some areas it still practiced as it was in the ancient times. Unfortunately, these ways are often repackaged and sold to the West in the form of superstition, which fairly can justifiably be called Neo-shamanism, or new-age shamanism. It offers drumming and imagining shamanic journeys in your head. This is so far afield from the age-old shamanism, which offers among other things, a direct interaction with the spiritual realm whose validity is undeniable when experienced.

Here I would like to discuss the work of Carlos Castaneda who for so long has been an icon for New age shamanism which is only a vague reflection of ancient shamanic practices which still are alive in places like Mexico and Peru. I must add that this book would go on far too long if I were to address all of his writings from an ideological and shamanic point of view, so I will try to confine myself to historical facts and use some logic to highlight a few important concepts that may well help you on your Path.

The long asked question by many, including me, has been whether don Juan Matus, Castaneda's teacher was a real person or a collective image of different people who Carlos met on his path. Well, traveling to Mexico myself and working with Mexican Indians and Peyote many times, I can tell you with great certainty that Peyote is real—as are the Mexican

Indians who are working with this sacred Teacher Healer plant. So personally speaking, this question is no longer relevant to me after meeting Peyote people in Mexico. But for the sake of argument, I will share with you some of my findings and thoughts, thus letting you draw your own conclusion.

Before I begin, I would like to say that to challenge Castaneda's writings, one must know Mexican shamans and work with the sacred Peyote; otherwise, it would be impossible, similar to trying to interpret the Bible from the perspective of the Upanishads or vice versa. Only by an immersion in ancient Peyote tradition of Mexico can one offer validity and objectivity on the subject. My commentaries on Castaneda's writings are based on my research and personal work with Mexican Indians, proof of which I humbly offer to you in my book.

Among the things I learned from coming face to face with meeting my own Death in Mexico, was an understanding that Life itself matters and living it consciously, with courage and dignity before one's actual death, is infinitely more important than being preoccupied with the afterlife—which seems to me to be a mental projection of the "ego" that fears Death.

Peyote's lessons are the same and all about life and living it the right way. It teaches us to go through our lives like a warrior who does not look for war, but instead, looks for peace—and yet is always ready to fight the good fight, fearlessly facing the challenge. It teaches us to walk on Earth without harming others and makes us want to ease the suffering of others. It teaches us that inner peace is found through good conscience, and it shows us that the path to our soul is through the heart.

In this same context, having a family is our best chance to learn to live our lives for others, and this is what true living means to me, which is giving and loving without any expectation for a reward, understanding that the Love itself is the highest reward. This is something I was missing all alone and only later, when I met the sacred Teacher-Healer plants, I understood that Love is the Fifth element, a unifying link, or string which holds together the other four elements of nature like jewels on a necklace. Thus, the missing concepts of Love, Compassion and morality in Castaneda's writing, the virtues to which Peyote leads, point to a lack of depth in his work, if not to a fiction.

On my journeys, I met people who left their families with little children in order to erase their personal history—as they understood from Castaneda's writings was a necessary step for a man on his path to knowledge. I was thinking about that a number of times, while observing the personal lives of the shamans I was fortunate to work with in Mexico and Peru. All are family centered, loving and caring husbands and fathers.

All ways lead to Huichol

In Castaneda's book, *The Teaching of don Juan: A Yaqui Way of Knowledge* in the 30th Anniversary edition, in his author commentaries, Castaneda begins with an acknowledgment to Clement Meighan for inspiring him for the field work, thus introducing him into shamanism as the subject. Meighan was a notable archeologist, anthropologist, and a professor in University of California at Los Angeles, in whose classes Castaneda was enrolled as undergraduate student. During the spring of 1959, a University of California at Los Angeles undertook an extensive archeological excavation at Amapa archeological site related to the Atzec culture, in the state of Nayarit, Mexico. During this field work Dr. Meighan realized the importance of immersion with the indigenous culture, which in his opinion was in decline due to the expansion of modern civilization. One would think this inspiration alone would be enough for Castaneda, who was fluent in Spanish due to his South American roots, which he admits in his first book, to travel to Mexico, following the footsteps of his professor in order to establish connection with an indigenous population of this area.

In support of his professor's inspiration, Castaneda could have spent time in the UCLA library and researched the ethno-history of the region Clement was referring to. He would quickly find that the ancient Atzec's land, for centuries, was populated by the Huichol Indians. Learning that, the next logical step would be to research the Huichol culture from an ethnographic point of view. Doing that, Castaneda would have found that an extensive research in that field was already done by the people such as Carl Lumholtz, a Norwegian explorer who spent five years traveling in Mexico documenting his field work in different areas—not least in the region of Tepic; visiting Huichol communities in Tuxpan, a place within ten miles from Amapa where Meighan was doing his archeological excavation. After that, Castaneda would find the work of Robert Zingg, who also among other places, visited Tuxpan in 1934 documenting Huichol life and its mythology with over 200 photographs.

He would also have found others, like Peter T. Furst, a Ph.D in Anthropology who had done immense fieldwork among Huichol Indians in Mexico and wrote extensively about it. In 1968 he had the first exhibition of Huichol art at the Los Angeles County Museum of Natural History.

Besides, in 1966 and 1968, P. Furst had the good fortune to participate in the Peyote pilgrimage to sacred Wirikuta lead by a prominent Huichol shaman, José Benítez Sánchez, during which he was able to make a film entitled "To find Our Life: The Peyote Hunt of the Huichols of Mexico," which immediately became an hour-long educational film distributed by UCLA.

And last but not least, he would have become familiar with works of already-seasoned anthropologist Weston La Barr who received his doctorate from Yale in 1937 with his dissertation on peyote religion. In his works La Barr also spoke about Huichols as the only pre-Colombian tradition that survived best and remained at its fullest.

So from 1960, when Castaneda enrolled in the Clemente Meighan classes on Field Archeology, until 1968, when his first book was published, he had eight years to do his library and field work, which would have yielded tremendous knowledge of indigenous cultures of Mexico and Peyote. This work would both add an immense value to his academic study and personal spiritual growth. Instead, it appears to me that we got a story about the mysterious don Juan Matus, allegedly a Yaqui Indian whose face no one ever saw.

If we take seriously the work of the scholars mentioned above, Huichol culture is the only indigenous culture in Mexico that has survived repression, conversion and prosecution in its original form even today, actively practicing its Peyote religion, which was long forgotten among other ethnic groups of Mexico, such as the Yaqui, for example, whose history consists of constant wars against Spanish and later Mexican armies. Historically speaking, Yaqui are known as great warriors who had defeated Conquistadors over and over again. But their physical strength was apparently greater than their faith, which led to their later conversion to Christianity by the Franciscan clergy, and consequently to the loss of their culture. It is a classic case of conquest by ideas rather by force; ripping the Indians of their faith led to their final submission.

The Yaqui tribes are historically known for the warfare, migration and prosecution beginning with a confrontation with Spanish conquistadors in 1533. Yet, being brave warriors who could not be conquered by force, Yaqui got converted to Christianity by the Jesuit order, which had a profound influence on the Yaqui culture. By Jesuit request Yaqui abandoned their widely dispersed settlements and settled in eight new towns controlled by Jesuits, where they lived for 200 years under the colonial regime, which became more oppressive in eighteenth century and led to the Indian uprising in 1740 and 1742. In 1821, Mexico had become an independent republic. During that time Yaqui Indians saw an opportunity to create an Indian federation in Sonora under the leadership of Juan Banderas, which was not well received by the Mexican government, leading to more bloodshed during the next decade until Banderas was defeated in 1832. Military confrontation between the Yaquis and Mexican government forces continued resulting in bloody massacres. In 1868 the Mexican army set a church on fire in which hundreds of Yaquis had been locked up as prisoners; many of them were burn alive.

In 1872, Mexico became a dictatorship under Porfirio Diaz. Shortly after that, new Yaqui leaders emerged who tried to unite the Yaqui nation by establishing a republic in the Yaqui Valley, situated on the west coast of mainland Mexico. In 1886 a Yaqui leader called Cajeme along with 4000 warriors and was defeated by Mexican army, but that too, didn't break the Yaqui's spirit. New leaders appeared and more resistances continued. In January 1900 over a thousand Yaqui Indians were killed in a massacre at Mazocoba, a rocky plateau in the Bacatete Mountains, marking a new clampdown on Yaqui resistance.

A further attack on Yaqui was of a different nature. Porfirio Diaz, a Mexican dictator began to encourage white colonists from Europe and U.S. to invest and settle in northern states leading to further dissolving of Yaqui culture.

A final desire to remove Yaqui Indians from Sonora resulted in deportation of all Yaquis rebels to central and south Mexico. Regular manhunts were organized by the state and grew into a war on the indigenous tribe between 1904-1909, resulting in thousands of Yaqui prisoners of war being sold into slavery. This" ethnic cleansing" forced many to hide, and they migrated to Arizona, establishing settlements near Tucson and Phoenix. Those who made it across the border into the U.S. were granted asylum by the federal government of North America, and today remain the only indigenous tribe in the U.S. who are not considered to be reservation residents.

In 1911, following the successful Mexican revolution, slavery came to an end, and Profirio Diaz was forced to flee the country.

Fransicsco Madero, the first new president of Mexico, promised the group of Mexican Yaqui survivors compensation for their losses and restoration of their land. These Yaqui warriors had joined the Madero army, attracting Yaqui refugees from all over the place. After the victory, however, the promised land to the Yaquis was forgotten, resulting in another war against them in 1917.

The last military assault against the Yaqui occurred in 1926, which was a total devastation for the Indians. A year later, the Yaquis were finally defeated by the Mexican government.

In the 1970s, internal clashes followed between Yaqui Indians and mestizo peasants for the water resources needed to farm the land. So from 1533 up until 1970, Yaqui Indians have had no peace and no religious freedom. Instead a history of tragic survival of the Yaqui culture under constant suppression and wars. The intent behind the assault on their native religion was to disconnect them from their ancestral roots, which over time has created an inner vacuum and a cause of suffering. It is reasonable to assume that this very vacuum was the reason for their conversion into Christianity, possibly seeking a spiritual belonging. Thus the fragments of their native beliefs together with newly adapted Christian dogma, has become a syncretic religion bringing the Yaquis of both Sonora and Arizona into the 20th century as a political entity rather than an ancient spiritual tradition.

Huichols, on the other hand, were men of knowledge, unlike the Yaqui warriors, and were conquered by the Spanish in 1722. Franciscan missionaries built on their land numerous Churches for purpose of converting the Huichols into Christianity. But having such a rich spiritual tradition and strong spiritual context, the Huichols strongly rejected persistent attempts of conversion to Christianity, sticking to their ancient beliefs and ways of life. From the ethnographers of the early 20th century, we can see that other ethnic groups of Mexico have too used Peyote but to the much lesser extent.

As we know today, the only indigenous culture in Mexico that has survived to this day in its original form, carrying tradition and knowledge without distortions, are the Huichol Indians in the central western states of Mexico. Huichol tradition is deeply intertwined with Peyote use, which goes back to antiquity and still actively practiced today. The use of Peyote among Huichol Indians is central to their life, giving them healing, meaning and strength to survive. Peyote for them is a sacred Teacher Healer spirit, whom they worship in prayers, rituals and art. The Huichol way of Peyote has survived conquests, repressions, oppressions, conversions and prosecution. It has been carried out by Huichol people for millennia until this day. Other ethnic groups in Mexico, such as Cora and Tarahumara Indians, were also heavily influenced by the Spanish, and they too, were significantly cut off from their roots, consequently resulting in the loss of their original culture.

It is not my intention to spark a historical debate regarding the Huichol ancestry, whether they were Aztec descendants, were not related to the Aztecs, but a different ethnic group and had maintained a separate tribal life during the Aztec empire, or were one of the Chichimeca tribes, who were forced to migrate from east to west by warring tribes centuries ago. This debate would be similar to the one about the Toltecs, who by some scholars are thought to be a polysemic and referring to the Nahua people, who were urban craftsman and artists rather than a specific ethnic group—which is still an open question.

However, there is no debate among the scholars on whether Huichol tradition survived best among all other ethnic groups of Mexico, and its religious customs and practices are considered to be of great value for academic study. All things considered, it would be logical for Castaneda to get in touch with Huichols if he wanted to learn about the sacred Peyote.

Following the historical facts I have summarized above and using one's logic, Castaneda would have been able to come in touch with a living

Peyote tradition, which has survived to this day. What perfect circumstances he found himself in, having been inspired by his professor to do the field research both building his credential for academic study and satisfying his spiritual thirst (if he had indeed had one)

Ironically enough, the archeological site of Amapa, where Clement Meighan was carrying out his excavation work, is located within thirty miles west from the Huichol village

where I had my Peyote apprenticeship during all of 2008. I was not drawn there because I knew anything about it, in fact the first time I ever heard about Huichols was from my contact in Mexico. My circumstances were different and were fueled by a burning desire and thirst for knowledge, rather than motivated by academic research. Regardless, I am certain that I would have gone to the same region and places that were discovered and mentioned earlier with the intention to establish a personal connection with Huichol Indians, if I had known back then the historical importance of the people and places mentioned in academic studies.

So my logical question would be why Castaneda decided to ignore the leads to Huichol Indians and chose another road that would not lead nearly as far? Or perhaps Yaquis was a deliberate misleading by him and he did establish contacts with Huichols. But if this were the case, wouldn't there be in his books at least some resemblance (recognizable to any alert reader) of the Huichol culture instead a total absence of it? It occurred to me more than once that maybe he never even went to Mexico and had an informant from one or more Native American tribes in Southwest who still knew something about the power plants like Datura used in the region. After all, this is how Castaneda begins his book, describing the events before meeting don Juan in Nogales,

Arizona. In any case, it cannot go unnoticed by readers that there is a complete absence of field notes to back up his field work—thus raising more questions.

Where is the proof?

One question that arises is why in 10 volumes of Castaneda books, he did not offer any pictures of people about whom he was writing, or even one of himself? Could that be that he managed to erase the image of his face along with erasing his personal history? I cannot help but wonder if one reason he didn't present any photos, that would be visible proof of his work with Mexican Indians, could simply be that he did not have any. Doesn't this raise doubts about the veracity of his work with don Juan, whose image could then easily be considered invented? Thought and feelings in accordance with the imagination of any good author can be ascribed to invented characters. (Sometimes, it even makes for the most compelling literature!)

Castaneda wrote that don Juan did not allow him to take photos or record conversations on tape. But why such secrecy? My personal interaction with Mexican Indians was way more open. During my travels in Mexico, I freely photographed Huichol shamans and always with their permission. When I was asking them if I could photograph them, they smiled back and nodded their heads affirmatively. Moreover, I have pictures that were taken even during the Peyote ceremonies. In Peru, for example, I was recording the ceremonies on tape and even made a short video footage.

Also it must be noted that in the early 20th century, explorers such as Carl Lumholtz (Unknown Mexico 1902) who spent five years traveling among the indigenous tribes of Mexico, brought back with him large collections of photos and other visuals illustrating their lives, tradition, customs, religion and myths. He also has recorded sixty melodies from

Tarahumara and Huichol tribes on the gramophone. Robert Zingg (Huichol Mythology) who traveled to the same Huichol region around Tepic also thoroughly documented his work with Huichol Indians backing up his fieldwork with over 200 pictures. Peter T. Furst, who wrote extensively about Huichol, besides the pictures, provided even a video of his pilgrimage to sacred Wirikuta. And finally, I have made hundreds of picture myself, many of which I am offering in my book.

So how come all of these pilgrims, anthropologists, archeologists and explorers, who visited Huichol tribes, which are even more obscured to outsiders than those I had the good fortune to meet and work with, possibly due to their greater vicinity to Tepic, all had an incredible amount of field notes made public with accurate and complete data supported with pictures, audio and footage, all presented in their works backing up their field research? None of their work was carried out in secrecy.

To me, it appears that it was rather their personal integrity than simply academic tradition or protocol to be straightforward with the people and culture they were studying, participating in their lives and then objectively describing their observation and the way of life of the cultures they studied. It would be difficult for me to imagine them making notes in their pockets without others noticing it—like Castaneda did in the beginning, reporting that he took notes of his conversations with don Juan hidden in his pocket.

In my case, I didn't have an academic format to be followed. I was an independent spiritual seeker who wanted to learn about Peyote. But instead of any kind of formalities I simply followed my intuition and I understood that in order to learn about the culture, its tradition and customs, especially when it comes to the medicinal plants—which are held at the heart and being a center of their lives, it would be better to just observe and listen, preferring a spontaneous conversations to academic interrogations. I felt that fewer words willingly spoken from the heart would be more informative than intense questioning.

In fact, watching dona Maria frying tortillas, brewing coffee or preparing Peyote, watching don Rufino working in his hibiscus and corn plantation, and then resting in his garden, sitting on his white plastic chair was telling me a lot about their life in a satisfactory way.

Did Castaneda write his books with the purpose of helping people to understand themselves and find their path? If yes, how he tried to achieve this goal, leaving no "return address" to the reader whose heart was kindled with his stories? Like the hero of the novel, who causes a woman to fall in love with him, then disappears, but does not let her forget him because he sends periodical "love" letters from afar. This reminds me of what Castaneda was doing with his readers each time he wrote a new book.

Well, let's look at some of the facts.

First of all, I never heard from anyone, either Mexican or North American Indians, the word "Mescalito." North American Indians called the peyote "peyote," and the Huichol Indians of Mexico call it simply peyote or "hikuri," which in their own native language, Wixarika means "divine, sacred." Tarahumara Indians, the second ethnic group who were using Peyote—although to a much lesser extent than the Huichol, were calling the same as the Huichol. This was well documented by K.Lumholtz in his work, Unknown Mexico. We can look farther back into the ancient Aztecs, who call Peyote "peyotl" which in Nahuatl language means "divine" or "sacred." All this is known from the priceless works of the Franciscan monk, Bernardino de Sahagun, who accompanied the conquistadors in Mexico in 1529. Fortunately, he was more an

ethnographer than the missionary, and, recognizing the value of Aztec culture, for fifty years was collecting information on social, religious and medical aspects of this culture, directly communicating with the Atzecs in their own language Nauhuatl.

Bernardino de Sahagun called his study the "General History of the things of New Spain," and later, this work became known as the *Florentine Codex*. This ambitious work consists of twelve volumes, including 2400 pages and over 2,000 illustrations, made by the Aztec artists who captured the images of their era. This documentary, an extensive project about their culture, religion, and the practices is the first authentic anthropological work in North America.

Second, the Mexican Indians do not know anything about the chemical composition of peyote, just as the Amazonian Indians have no idea about the alkaloid content in the plants they've worked with all their lives, and mescaline, a naturally occurring alkaloid in Peyote cactus, is not known by Mexican Indians. Furthermore, Amazonian Indians are not aware of the DMT alkaloids, which are present in Chakruna leafs and harmine and harmaline, compounds found in Banisteriopsis caapi vine, which together with Chacruna leaves decocted into Ayahuasca brew in the Amazonian rainforest for millennia.

Mexican and Peruvian shamans are working with the spirits of the sacred plants, the sacredness of which for them is not measured by the number and diversity of alkaloids. The chemical knowledge, and a break down into the compounds, was a property of research of the western people, who were fortunate enough to get acquainted with it. Therefore, no sacred plant is called after its chemical structure among the indigenous people.

However, Castaneda is referring to Peyote as "Mescalito," which according to him, was the name he heard from don Juan. But if we look at the root of the word mescalito, we will find that the root word is mescal, and the "ito" is a form of playful speech in Spanish-for example, besito (little Kiss), abrasito (little hug), etc. So without the "ito," it would be simply "mescal." Before we go farther, it is important to note that this colloquial, playful way of speaking is Spanish and has nothing to do with any native language of any ethnic group of Mexico, who had their own word and name for Peyote, as I mentioned earlier, long before Spanish conquest. Mescal is a distilled alcoholic beverage made from the agave plant native to Mexico and has nothing to do with either mescaline or with Peyote.

Considering the above, it would be reasonable to assume that seeking to establish a connection with Yaquis Indians or with any other ethnic group who were not known for their Peyote practice as widely known as the Huichol, would be ineffective, yielding little or no results in terms of gathering information on medicinal plants, especially on Peyote—in comparison to working with Huichols, who were known to the western world at his time by anthropologists like La Barre and others who already had well- documented Peyote religion practice by Huichol.

It would be more reasonable to conclude that either Castaneda knew the history and contacted the Huichols, but for some reason did not mention that, confusing the possibility of readers tracing his stories by referring to Yaquis. Perhaps the more generous conclusion is that he really didn't know and simply went down the wrong track.

Subjective perception of Castaneda (which abounds in regards to the teachings) can be debated, but I have spent much time concentrating my efforts to determining the source of don Juan's knowledge by examining facts as much as is possible. For example, he writes in his first book that in 1900, don Juan and his family, along with thousands of other Indians were expelled from Sonora by the Mexican Government to Central Mexico, (which is coherent with the historical fact) where he lived until 1940, in fact, his entire adult life. He also acknowledges that in connection with forced relocation (which can hardly be called traveling), so, in fact, his work could be the product of different influences on him. As we know for a fact, the indigenous population of Central Mexico consists of Huichol and Cora Indians. But from the works of known anthropologists, ethnologists and historians, and as I detailed above, we know that Huichol culture is the only one that survived in its entirety to our days. The continuity is clearly reflected in their arts, and traditional costumes, where Peyote and deer are always present. They also are not ashamed of dressing up and going into the cities to sell herbs and yarn paintings at the local markets.

Also as I wrote earlier, it is known that Peyote was also used among Tarahumara and Cora Indians, but to a much lesser extent, as their traditions as well were increasingly diluted by Catholicism. Again, based on that, it would be reasonable to conclude that in order to search for knowledge about the medicinal plants, especially peyote, Carlos should have been seeking to establish contacts with Huichol Indians rather with Yaqui or any other ethnic groups.

So, I must pose these questions to the reader: Was don Juan a Huichol shaman, created by an author who invented a Yaqui scenario deliberately to mislead his audience? If so, then wouldn't we be able to discern Huichol teachings in his writings? And if, in fact, don Juan was an authentic Yaqui, then a flavor of Catholicism should be present and felt in Castaneda's writings. And if don Juan migrated to Central Mexico, where he says he spent most of his adult life, then shouldn't Castaneda's writings be a mix of a Yaqui's syncretic tradition with strong Christian element and a Huichol tradition with its symbolism, art and Peyote rituals? I found none of these things evident in his books. And I cannot be the only one, of that I am certain. Sadly, after so many years of my own searching, as the reader remembers, began with my first introduction to him nearly twenty years ago, I had to conclude that at most, he spent his life among people where the central use and regard for the true sacred teacher healer plants had long been forgotten.

I would like to take my readers back to Mexico, and reflect on that experience. Mine wasn't simply mysterious encounters with supernatural powers, which I was looking to meet all alone, but was a body of important teachings, which became a solid foundation that I was able to build my spiritual house in which I now live—protected from the rains of illusion, the winds of confusion and the coldness of lies.

On my every visit to Mexico, I felt greater proximity to the Peyote and Huichol Indians, understanding the difficult conditions of their lives,

which to me, who was spoiled by a comfort of a civilization, was shocking. After even a week spent in Huichol village, I was beginning to think about a hot shower and soft bed waiting me home, mentally drifting away from the magical world I was wrapped in.

During the work in Mexico, I had many conversations with Eldon on various topics. Some of them were spiritual in nature and others were

not, and concern aspects of life like a daily survival and life in a place which had no drinking water, forcing the Huichol go to town few times a week to fill up their barrels and bring it back to the whole village. Eldon shared with me how long he had been trying to have the local authorities assist with digging the pit in the village, but all in vain. We talked a lot about the attitudes of Mexican government toward the indigenous Indians—attitudes which have not changed much since the repression begin centuries ago.

The more I observed and learned, the more I became convinced that any attempts to grasp their world with a western analytic mind, and coming from a completely different cultural background, would be similar to trying to measure the humidity of the air in millibars by counting the number of dewdrops on the morning grass. Nevertheless, the inner order of things became more and more apparent, as I immersed myself deeper in their culture. I was observing and communicating with and indigenous population whose perception of the world was not intellectual or systematic, but rather spiritual in the full sense of the word—unconditioned by the verbal limitations. Perceiving and experiencing new ways as they are, seemed to be the only way to understand anything about these people.

I felt that my appearance in their village was a sign of hope, signifying water, which to them meant life. In our ceremonies I was praying for changes to happen so these financially poor but spiritually rich people would have their own water. (Here is how you can support my Mexican friends: http://www.projectclearwater.com) Perhaps in my respect and appreciation for them, they saw another meaning, more spiritual in context in regarding to survival of their traditions. These age-old ways are losing interest among the young people, who are becoming more "mexicanized" and leaving the ancient tradition of their ancestors behind.

This is the current reason why the indigenous culture is in decline, even though it is still actively practiced among the older generation. For example, don Jose Matsua, a legendary Huichol shamans with whose son, don Catarino, I was fortunate to work and share the Sacred Peyote many times, had many children of whom only three went on to continue his shamanic linage. One of the children of don Rufino for example, became a teacher and teaches at a local school of Tepic. A good man but maintains only a distant relation to Huichol tradition.

It is difficult to describe how deep these kinds of talks were penetrating into my soul, but I will try. My friendship with Eldon was very sincere from the beginning, but never easy, and only my genuine interest in Peyote tradition and his authentic service to it, served as a solid bridge between us. Even though he was a true teacher, who one would be lucky to meet on the Path, I could not relate to him as such—due to my previous life experiences. Instead, I saw him as a dear friend who has been on the path much longer. This state of affairs complicated my apprenticeship on one hand, but strengthened my character on the other. And despite the fact that I held Eldon in the highest respect and have regarded him as special friend, I was ready to leave him at any time.

When my dog got killed by the car, Eldon was the one who helped me through despair and sadness. He understood my pain because he had his own. He too had a deep bond with his dog, living with it along in the woods for many years. When they were parted by death of his dog, it was hard from his as well. During one Peyote ceremony, after experiencing deep grief from losing my dog, I asked him if he believed in reincarnation, hoping sometime in the future to recognize the soul of my dog in another puppy. His response was that he looked at reincarnation as a tree that gives life to its fruits, which then through its seeds gives birth to a new tree. To him, reincarnation was more a process of the transmission of genetic memory of a kind to its own, rather than a reincarnation of the soul. We talked about it that night and then remained silent lying around the fire and waiting for the sunrise. I remember reflecting on his words throughout that night, thinking about the fatality of our death and fragility of our lives. To me personally, the idea of reincarnation of the soul or "entering the flesh again," felt rather unlikely. Instead, I thought of this process as transpersonal in the sense of after death, the soul would merge with history of evolution of the human species. I felt like the idea of being born again was somewhat neutralizing the fear of Death. Of course, it would be easier to accept the losses in our lives if we could believe in future reunions with our loved ones. But, in truth, the painful but sobering reality that we don't live forever can help us to actually appreciate and value our lives, the only ones we have in which we are given an opportunity to realize the Universal Consciousness in human form.

About the author:

Sergey Baranov conducts Huachuma ceremonies in the Sacred Valley of the Incas in Peru. Contact him at:

www.shamansworld.org

Printed in Great Britain
by Amazon